D0073581

Benevolence Among Slaveholders

Benevolence Among Slaveholders

Assisting the Poor in Charleston
1670–1860

Barbara L. Bellows

27430830

Louisiana State
University Press

Baton Rouge and London

Copyright © 1993 by Louisiana State University Press
All rights reserved
Manufactured in the United States of America
First printing
02 01 00 99 98 97 96 95 94 93   5 4 3 2 1

Designer: Amanda McDonald Key
Typeface: Sabon
Typesetter: G & S Typesetters, Inc.
Printer and binder: Thomson–Shore, Inc.

Library of Congress Cataloging-in-Publication Data
Bellows, Barbara L.
    Benevolence among slaveholders : assisting the poor in Charleston,
    1670–1860 / Barbara L. Bellows.
      p. cm.
    Includes bibliographical references and index.
    ISBN 0-8071-1833-8 (cloth : alk. paper)
    1. Poor—South Carolina—Charleston—History. 2. Charities—South
    Carolina—Charleston—History. I. Title.
    HV4046.C34B45 1993
    361.7′4′09757915—dc20   93-18057
                                             CIP

The paper in this book meets the guidelines for permanence and durability of the Committee on Production Guidelines for Book Longevity of the Council on Library Resources.♾

For Steven

He who takes note of every sparrow that falls, who will not break the bruised reed, and who tempers the wind to the shorn lamb, has not been forgetful or regardless of wives, children, and slaves. He has extended the broad panoply of domestic affection over them all, that the winds of heaven may not visit them too roughly.

—George Fitzhugh
Sociology for the South

Contents

ILLUSTRATIONS
following page 55

Sarah Russell Dehon

Mrs. John Faucheraud Grimké

Christopher G. Memminger

W. Jefferson Bennett

Bishop John England

Charleston Orphan House

Memminger School

Roper Hospital

St. Stephen's Episcopal Chapel

Cathedral of St. John and St. Finbar

Nathaniel Russell House

Charleston Orphan House indenture

Charleston Almshouse record book

Memorial plaque to Sarah Russell

PREFACE

Few aspects of public life reveal as much about a society as its response to the needs of the poor and powerless. Appropriately, there is now a rich literature examining poverty and poor relief in eighteenth- and nineteenth-century America. Yet the South has been largely ignored. During the last thirty years especially, historians of the region have directed their energies toward unraveling the complexities of the South as a slave culture. Other scholars probing the nature of humanitarianism have for the most part limited their investigations to northeastern urban centers. This book seeks to bridge the gap between research in southern studies and social welfare history by focusing on the evolution of poor relief in Charleston, South Carolina. To support the argument that another social order existed alongside slavery, this study shows how the presence of a white laboring class influenced poor relief and introduced the politics of class into the Lowcountry town.

Before the Revolution, Charleston was one of the five most vital cities in America. In his sweeping study *Cities in the Wilderness*, Carl Bridenbaugh describes how the Carolina port confronted the same urban problems of disease, poverty, and public order that Boston and New York did. Even when Charleston glided into its "golden age" supported by rich harvests of rice, indigo, and cotton, its population of poor whites swelled as destitute newcomers from other colonies and Europe sought a share of the southern bounty. Charleston's traditions of private benevolence and public poor relief coalesced during the high tide of Lowcountry prosperity in the late eighteenth century, and survived into the early nineteenth, when the town, bypassed by new trade routes, slipped into a languishing regional port. Even at the city's lowest point during the 1820s, citizens fell into the "spirit of the age" sweeping the nation and formed myriads of voluntary associations to promote welfare and moral reform among the poor. But at the same time, their renewed commitment to slavery, now so aggressively at odds with the sensibilities of the humanitarian movement, divorced Charlestonians from the mainstream of reform organizations.

Consequently, benevolence and poor relief developed as an intensely local affair. Research into traditional sources, such as the records of national organizations, yields little about the attitudes of Charlestonians.

But the rich, well-preserved local materials upon which this study is based bring to life a community often generous beyond its much diminished means and a municipal government actively engaged, for ill or good, in the life of the poor. Close examination of the extensive records of the Charleston Orphan House, Poor House, and numerous smaller institutions shows that in the decades before the Civil War, Charleston ranked favorably with any city of its size in America for per capita spending and services to the white poor. Although its position as a leading defender of slavery diminished the city in the eyes of the nation and the world, Charleston's people firmly believed they had a social conscience as well developed as any in America. And they were desperate that this fact be known. With national opinion firmly against them, the incentive to do good pressed hard upon Charlestonians.

Urban life forced self-interest to bend to the public good. Philanthropy in Charleston was not just an extension of the highly ritualized paternalistic relationship between master and slave. It was shaped by the same forces that were at work in all American cities—intemperance, foreign immigration, anti-Catholic sentiment, intense poverty among women and children. Confronted with similar necessities, Charlestonians responded in much the same way as New Yorkers or Bostonians. The Sunday school, the temperance fair, the medical dispensary, the sailor's bethel, the foundling home, the almshouse, and the orphanage all developed as important cultural landmarks on the Charleston peninsula.

Social relations between the rich and poor in Charleston were dynamic and changed markedly over time. This account chronicles their evolution from the colonial period to the 1860 debates over the role of nonslaveholders in the South. Tracing the change in the practice of poor relief and benevolence from romantic and paternalistic to systematic and impersonal shows in detail the internal social tensions at work in the city where the Civil War began.

Many years ago, when I first began studying history, the standard description of the antebellum South depicted the region as conservative in politics, homogeneous in population, evangelical in religion, rural in geography, retrograde in education, divorced from the national cultural life, and more concerned with family than civic duty. Conservatism in politics was the only characteristic that jibed with my understanding of "the South," growing up as I did in Charleston, South Carolina, a most southern city. As a child of the city, I lived in the wake of dedicated men and women who cared about the future, and I benefited from institutions they built as they tried to keep pace with the "spirit of the age." I started this project because I wanted to reconcile the past with my own experience and understand better the forces that shaped Charleston and made it, I believe, unique.

In the course of my inquiry, I realize I have accumulated a lifetime of debts. My first vivid memories date from the 1950s among the dusty shelves in the Charleston Public Library, which was then tucked into the faded glory of the town house of the great planter I. Jenkins Mikell. My mother let me skip Miss Jennie Smith's children's "story hour" to help her search through old wills for ancestors lost except to family tradition. We never did verify our fabled Huguenot relatives (we are still looking), but she introduced me to the pleasures of finding personal connections with the past. I entered the first grade in 1956, exactly a century after Charleston began its innovative system of public schools, and attended Christopher G. Memminger Elementary School. Memminger's stern portrait, which hung near the principal's office, belied his apparent love of little children. At the end of my seven years there, competition was keen for the academic awards given to graduates in honor of his adoptive brother W. Jefferson Bennett, who dedicated himself to bringing universal education to all classes of the city. Memminger School drew from the lower peninsula and included children from "south of Broad" and the nearby Robert Mill's Manor, then a segregated white low-income housing development. From my schoolmates who lived in the "project," I understood very early the great economic diversity among the whites of Charleston. The cosmopolitanism of the city was evident from the class rolls, rich with the names of ancestors who were Germans, Irish, Sephardic Jews, French, Scotch-Irish, and English.

The old city, with its museums, parks, libraries, and cemeteries, was a playground for children who lived there. With my friend Sarah Legaré Stuhr, I explored every inch of it. Some of the buildings described in this book, or at least their remnants, are still standing, and we knew them well: South Carolina Society Hall, St. Phillip's Episcopal Church, Hibernian Hall, the county jail, Old Roper Hospital, St. Stephen's Chapel. Although the Charleston Orphan House had been razed in the city's attempt to modernize during the 1950s, the Sears and Roebuck department store that replaced it on Calhoun Street adopted a stylized exterior reminiscent of the institution that expressed so many of Charleston's aspirations for itself. Sarah has maintained a thoughtful interest in this book, always inquiring about its progress and gently suggesting that I wind it up. I am grateful for her friendship and the friendship of her family. Senator T. Allen Legaré, Jr., gentleman-politician and public man, particularly shared with me his love for Charleston and its finer traditions.

My experience at the University of South Carolina taught me to critically assess the southern past. I am grateful to my teachers in the Department of History for their expertise and friendship. Robert M. Weir first suggested to me the importance of benevolence in the political culture of colonial Charleston. John Duffy gave me his sharp insights on Charleston politics. Walter B. Edgar, of the Institute of Southern Studies, and John G. Sproat, former chair of the Department of History at the University of South Carolina, have been the most important forces in shaping my career as a professional historian. George C. Rogers, Jr., now retired from active teaching at the University of South Carolina, has been particularly generous in sharing his acute understanding of Charleston and its past. His personal guidance and historical writings have been an important model for me. I have benefited from the work of trailblazers such as David Goldfield, Blaine Brownell, Randall Miller, and others who have now established southern urban history as a legitimate and fruitful field of inquiry.

I owe special debts to Nancy V. Ashmore, James L. Baughman, Bertram Wyatt-Brown, William B. Catton, Donna Chiccone, Elizabeth Dozier, Elizabeth Edgar, Christian Kolbe, Charles Kovacik, John P. McWiliams, Jr., Alan Stokes, Ephraim Ulmer, and Janet Beers Winker for their assistance in various stages of this project. With typical generosity of spirit, Craig M. Simpson gave unselfishly of his time in reviewing manuscript drafts. Claire Wilson, whose skill and keen understanding of the scholarly process is surpassed only by her effervescent good humor and unusual patience, provided critical technical assistance. Jean Blodgett and Kerry D. Skeffington helped with the typing. Beverly Jarrett, now at the University of Missouri Press, gave me much encouragement at the crucial early stages of this project. I remain deeply grateful. At Louisiana State University Press, Margaret Fisher Dalrymple, Catherine Landry, and Julie Schorfheide expertly guided me through the long editorial process. My thanks to them, also.

The pleasant conditions and excellent staff at southern libraries and archives have contributed, I am sure, to the growing interest in the region among historians. My thanks go to those who have helped me with such efficiency at the South Caroliniana Library and the Thomas Cooper Library of the University of South Carolina in Columbia; the South Carolina Historical Society in Charleston; the Georgia Historical Society in Savannah; the City of Charleston Archives, where Susan King, Gail McCoy, and Ernestine Fellows made the many hours I spent there a pleasure; the Charleston Library Society; the Robert Scott Smalls Library at the College of Charleston; the Charleston Public Library; South Carolina

State Archives, Columbia; the Egbert Starr Library at Middlebury College (especially Fleur Laslocky, of the Inter-Library Loan Department); the Virginia Historical Society and Virginia State Library in Richmond; the Southern Historical Collection, Wilson Library, University of North Carolina at Chapel Hill; and the William R. Perkins Library, Duke University. Thanks also to Robert Leath, of the Historic Charleston Foundation, Lisa Denisevich, of Gibbes Museum of Art, and to Jane Brown, associate curator of the Waring Historical Library of the Medical University of South Carolina.

Travel and research were made possible through generous grants from numerous sources. I have received assistance from the Department of History and the Institute for Southern Studies at the University of South Carolina, the Charleston Scientific and Literary Fund, and the Association of American Colleges through their program to support research on philanthropy. My year at the National Humanities Center, Research Triangle, North Carolina, was an extraordinary opportunity, and I am deeply grateful to those who made it possible. Middlebury College has been exceptionally supportive in providing funds for research and travel to conferences as well as granting leaves.

My greatest benefactors have been my family. My parents, Mary and George Bellows, have supported me in all ways from the very beginning. My heartfelt thanks go to them and to George and Patricia Bellows. Ann Rockefeller Roberts and T. George Harris have provided unfailing encouragement.

Finally I thank my husband, Steven Clark Rockefeller, whose devotion to his own scholarship has been an inspiration, whose friendship has been sustaining, and whose love makes everything worthwhile.

Benevolence
Among
Slaveholders

I

CHARLESTON IN AN AGE OF BENEVOLENCE

> At first it is of necessity that men attend to the public interest, afterward by choice.
>
> —Alexis de Tocqueville

The founding of Charleston in 1670 coincided with the dawn of England's Age of Benevolence. The preceding two hundred years had produced a dramatic transformation in British ways of thinking about the poor. Destruction of the feudal system had forced thousands of peasants off the land and into a vagabond life. In rags and tatters, disorderly and angry, they lined the highways leading away from the countryside and crowded into cities. As peasant devolved to pauper, poverty evolved into an urban phenomenon. With landlords no longer responsible for their workers and monasteries stripped of their ability to distribute alms, the English struggled to reconceptualize the relationship between the poor and society.

The shocking realities of poverty horrified the sensibilities of the English middle classes. Their newly gained prosperity empowered them to act upon the principles of Christian stewardship. Their concern for public order forced them into deliberate action. By the end of the Elizabethan era, the right of all persons to a basic subsistence was written into law. The state assumed limited responsibility for the public welfare, but individuals and benevolent associations bore the brunt of the burden of the poor. The English also explored the use of wills, trusts, and foundations to facilitate innovative private philanthropy. Experimenting with methods to eliminate future dependency among the able-bodied, reformers fell into a fury of institution building to shelter the deserving poor, punish the vicious degenerate, and educate subsequent generations out of the cycle of hopelessness. By 1700, unusual agreement reigned among the English of all political persuasions from high Tory to Whig that the degree of compassion shown to the poor provided the "true test of a civilization." Consensus also existed on the point made most clearly by the author of the Carolina Constitution, John Locke, that charity endowed one with control. Guided by these twin precepts of English philanthropy,

Carolinians charted their own course in dealing with the poor in the New World.[1]

Charleston never knew a time without poverty. Debilitation and early death from endemic infection or epidemic disease almost destroyed the settlement in its first decades. In the steamy, near tropical climate where rattlesnakes thrived, British settlers on the first townsite endured perhaps the highest mortality rate of all colonists in North America. Suffering only increased as they pressed up into the fertile lands around the headwaters of the Ashley and the Cooper rivers.[2] Cargo ships that imported sugar and slaves also carried yellow fever from the West Indies. In late summer and fall of 1699, epidemics hit both Charleston and Philadelphia with stunning force. To the horrified Carolinians, the unremitting suffering and loss of life could compare only to the bubonic plagues that had crippled London earlier in the seventeenth century. All trade and other business ceased for five weeks while survivors dedicated themselves to the all-consuming tasks of dispensing medicines, feeding the ailing, and digging graves. By the time the first killing frost subdued the disease-bearing mosquitoes, Charleston had lost almost one-sixth of its population of some three thousand. This epidemic was the first of many that would periodically sweep over Charleston and other ports along the Atlantic during the next sixty years, leaving both poverty and grief in their wake.[3]

The hostile environment of the Carolina coast thus shaped the early social policy of the colony. Natural disasters forced colonists to quickly define their relationship with one another and establish procedures for collection and distribution of relief. In contrast to diseases such as malaria and dysentery that routinely struck down the weak, epidemics snatched away the strong, took breadwinners and protectors. Their survivors, blameless for their predicament, fell upon the mercy of the com-

1. Wilbur K. Jordan, "The English Background of Modern Philanthropy," *American Historical Review*, LXVI (January, 1961), 401–404; Gertrude Himmelfarb, *The Idea of Poverty: England in the Early Industrial Age* (New York, 1984), 6; Merle Curti, "American Philanthropy and the National Character," *American Quarterly*, X (Winter, 1958), 425.

2. Among first-generation natives fortunate enough to survive to the age of twenty, 40 percent would die before age fifty and most would be dead before sixty. The second generation, living from about 1721 to 1760, enjoyed only a slightly enhanced chance of reaching middle age. Harry Roy Merrens and George D. Terry, "Dying in Paradise: Malaria, Mortality, and the Perceptual Environment in Colonial South Carolina, *Journal of Southern History*, L (November, 1984), 534, 541, 543; St. Julien Ravenel Childs, "Notes on the History of Public Health in South Carolina, 1670–1800," South Carolina Historical Association *Proceedings* (1932), 15.

3. John Duffy, "Yellow Fever in Colonial Charleston," *South Carolina Historical and Genealogical Magazine*, LII (October, 1951), 191.

munity. Defending Carolina from the Spanish and overcoming Indian resistance also exacted a high cost in human life. The Yamassee War of 1715, which brought the colony to the threshold of destruction, resolved the immediate threat but threw large numbers of widows and orphans upon an impoverished community. The dramatic and seemingly random afflictions visited upon individuals by such unpredictable forces as hurricanes or wars set a precedent in Charleston for public involvement in personal tragedy.[4]

The primary challenge facing Charlestonians in the first decades was how to meet their acknowledged obligations to the suffering without the institutional structure that existed in England. Charity had slipped away from the exclusive control of the church after the Reformation, but Protestants continued to understand benevolence as part of their personal religious practice.[5] In the first recorded wills, Charlestonians made specific bequests to the local poor. For example, Huguenot Arnaud France, "making profession of the reformed religion in the belief of which I have always lived and would die," bequeathed fifty shillings and the proceeds from the sale of his land to the "needy poor of the French Church." It then fell to the rudimentary local government rather than the church establishment to manage the numerous gifts and bequests. In 1695, the provincial government passed its first Act for the Poor, appointing a specific board of commissioners to administer the growing fund. The period during which voluntary donations alone supported the local poor proved very short. Within three years of the first act, the demand for assistance so outstripped contributions that the South Carolina Assembly passed its first colonywide poor tax.[6]

In 1704, the Charleston-based assembly merged all political and judicial districts with the parishes. Since South Carolina had no incorporated towns, endowed hospitals like those in England, or even trade companies that supported public services as in some other colonies, all responsibility for public health and relief fell to the parish government. With the establishment of the Anglican church two years later, responsibility for collecting taxes and distributing alms logically fell to the vestry and churchwardens of St. Phillip's Church. These "sober, discreet and substantial"

4. *Ibid.*, 196–97.

5. Wilbur K. Jordan, *Philanthropy in England, 1480–1660* (New York, 1959), 144–47.

6. Caroline T. Moore and Agatha Aimar Simmons, *Abstracts of the Wills of South Carolina, 1670–1740,* I (Columbia, S.C., 1960), 12; Thomas Cooper and David J. McCord, eds., *The Statutes at Large of South Carolina* (Columbia, S.C., 1836–41), II, 78, 116, 136.

men, elected by the freeholders every Easter, assumed powerful positions in the community as the chief parochial and civil officers for the provincial capital.[7] The overall creditable performance of the vestry's duties to the public in regulating markets, overseeing sanitation, setting and enforcing quarantines to forestall the spread of disease, hiring physicians for the poor, and encouraging local experimentation for new cures reinforced the Anglican establishment in Charleston and muted protests from Dissenters. The connection of poor relief to the parish government established a link between civic and religious duty never formed in Virginia or North Carolina, where the courts, remote and inchoate institutions, haphazardly distributed alms from the general tax fund to the most desperate. In Georgia, where political institutions lagged behind those of the other colonies, the response to social problems remained strictly a private affair, financed by voluntary donations until the nineteenth century.[8]

The expense of establishing even this rudimentary public welfare system in Charleston added to the growing antagonism between the town and the rest of the colony.[9] Rural parishes protested having to contribute to a general pool, as mandated by the 1698 tax act, because Charleston always drew the lion's share. Planters who already supported slaves resisted subsidizing the city's white poor. In response to growing dissension on this issue, the assembly revised the law in 1712, shifting responsibility away from the colony at large to the individual parishes. With this change, the colonial law more closely resembled the Elizabethan Poor Law of 1601 and the Settlement Act of 1662.[10]

The British poor laws (adopted in spirit by all the colonies), rationalizing the patchwork of provisions enacted over a period of three hundred years, were designed to ameliorate the social disruption of England's painful transition from feudalism to wage-labor capitalism. As the state

7. The parish system remained unchanged until 1868. Frederick Dalcho, *An Historical Account of the Protestant Episcopal Church in South Carolina* (Charleston, 1820), 27, 116–17; Elizabeth Clarke Hannum, "The Parish in South Carolina, 1706–1868" (M.A. thesis, University of South Carolina, 1970), 60.

8. The colonial patterns persisted until the Civil War. Richmond built a poorhouse, but the Hustings Court oversaw the fate of Richmond's orphans in a cursory fashion. Savannah's poorhouse was financed and operated by a private corporation that went bankrupt during the 1830s. Clarence L. VerSteeg, *Origins of a Southern Mosaic: Studies of Early Carolina, and Georgia* (Athens, Ga., 1975), 101; S. Charles Bolton, *Southern Anglicanism: The Church of England in Colonial South Carolina* (Westport, Conn., 1982), 7–8, 14, 141–42; Childs, "Public Health in South Carolina," 17–18.

9. Richard Maxwell Brown, *The South Carolina Regulators* (Cambridge, Mass., 1963), 51.

10. Cooper and McCord, eds., *Statutes of South Carolina*, II, 593.

gradually superseded the church as the primary dispenser of relief, Christian charity evolved into a force to stabilize the vagrant laboring population. The South Carolina variant of these laws, as first codified in 1712, followed the form but not the function of the English statutes. Establishing eligibility for poor relief forced lawmakers to define the parameters of the community. This first formal step in identifying "the public" coincided with the first provision for a free school for Charleston's children, in 1710. The law defined *inhabitant* as "*any person*" (except Catholics) who had been "quietly and peaceably" residing in a parish for three months as a "native, householder, sojourner, apprentice, or *servant*." The town bore no responsibility if petitioners established residency for strictly "private" reasons, such as being sick or lame and unable to leave the city for three months or lodging in town for seasonal work when one's real home was in another parish. Local overseers of the poor or churchwardens theoretically monitored all newcomers, assessed their potential as burdens, and expelled those indisposed or unable to join the productive work force.[11]

As would historically be the case, the sick poor dominated the rolls of parish dependents. Before the establishment of formal hospitals, the vestry advertised for private citizens to take in the homeless sick. Those afflicted with boils and sores, fevers and rheum, languished on pallets offered by the lowest bidders. As demand for medical care grew, the charges for this care soared. By the late 1720s, parish officers found themselves "obliged to take up with very poor Accommodations of Lodging," which caused great suffering among the sick and a burdensome expense for the taxpayers. In 1734, the St. Phillip's vestry petitioned the assembly to build a workhouse to serve as an infirmary, reduce the increasing costs of boarding the homeless, relieve the city of the embarrassment of beggars whose numbers grew every year, and provide a controlled environment to regulate the morals of the uninhibited. The assembly passed an act that same year authorizing the vestry to raise funds to build what was probably a simple wooden barracks and approved £1,000 for its annual maintenance. At the same time, however, a petition for a separate jail went down to defeat, probably because the pauper and the criminal blurred together in the public mind. The workhouse indeed functioned as a house of correction where indigent inmates might face shackles and "moderate whipping."[12]

11. *Ibid.*
12. St. Phillip's Episcopal Church, Vestry minutes, January 6, 1734, typescript in South Caroliniana Library, University of South Carolina; Joseph Ioor Waring, "St. Phillip's Hospital in Charlestown in Carolina," *Annals of Medical History*, IV (May, 1932), 284.

One of the truisms of social welfare history is that legislative acts for the poor are nearly always obsolete by the time of implementation. By 1738, not long after the first paupers moved into Charleston's newly constructed poorhouse, foreigners and native vagabonds pressed so aggressively upon the public purse that the assembly passed a law requiring all ailing or incapacitated immigrants to post security before entering any South Carolina port. Failing this, the masters of ships bringing in these undesirable settlers were responsible for the paupers' expenses if they established a three-month settlement.[13]

Every revision in local poor laws drew parish officers more closely into contact with the most unsavory and pathetic elements of the city, expanded their duties, and added to the burden of public service. The intangible rewards of authority, local recognition, and association with the town's leading figures balanced the tedium of these unpaid positions. Election as vestryman or churchwarden also provided an avenue for social and political advancement for rising merchants of the city. In contrast with the vestries of the surrounding parishes, where members of the same few plantation families served generation after generation, St. Phillip's Parish elected a diverse slate of officers. Among those eighty-four church officers serving from 1732 to 1770 who can be identified, fifty-five were merchants. Those who most enjoyed the rewards of the urban economy traditionally also served in local government. Although one might be excused from such service with a small fine, most bowed to public opinion and did their civic duty. Robert Pringle felt pressured to serve as a churchwarden, a position "attended with some Trouble, [but] there is no Dispensing with it as it comes in Course."[14]

Prominent Charlestonians such as Thomas Smith, George Seaman, and Benjamin Smith served as parochial officers during the late 1730s and early 1740s as they began their ascent in the business community. Each spent at least eighteen years in service to the community. Benjamin Smith, a planter and merchant, served two terms as churchwarden and twenty-six as vestryman, and left the largest estate in the history of the colony at his death in 1770. Public figures like Governor Robert Johnson and Sir Egerton Leigh, judge of the vice-admiralty court and attorney general, also regularly attended vestry meetings. Charles Coatsworth Pinckney, destined for fame at the Constitutional Convention and twice

13. Cooper and McCord, eds., *Statutes of South Carolina*, III, 155–56.
14. Richard Waterhouse, "South Carolina's Colonial Elite: A Study in the Social Structure and Political Culture of a Southern Colony, 1670–1760" (Ph.D. dissertation, Johns Hopkins University, 1973), 241; Robert Pringle, *Letterbook of Robert Pringle*, ed. Walter B. Edgar (Columbia, S.C., 1972), II, 211.

a Federalist presidential candidate, volunteered his services, as did William Loughton Smith, future South Carolina congressman and heir to one of the colony's greatest fortunes. The fabulously wealthy Gabriel Manigault faithfully sat for sixteen terms as vestryman and twenty-two as firemaster. Seventy-five percent of those elected before the city's incorporation in 1783 served multiple terms; probably all were slaveholders, even the few craftsmen elected to office. Rather than elevating "public authority over private privilege," as David J. Rothman has contended, designation of St. Phillip's vestry as almoners of the poor *merged* the two and gave increased potency to the rising merchant elite of the city.[15]

With few written instructions, parish officers guided the city directed only by what Pauline Maier has described as an "immediate sense of local sentiment."[16] And local sentiment clearly mandated care for the poor. Charged with oversight of church silver as well as town paupers, parish officers judiciously dispensed annual assessments for the poor to the indigent widow and injured mechanic, subsidized apprenticeships with urban artisans, paid wet nurses for motherless children, found homes for orphans, paid transport for the disappointed back to their own parishes, fed the hungry, clothed the naked, and punished the wicked. With equal facility, vestrymen handed out charitable alms with one hand and lent parish money at interest to local entrepreneurs with the other. Operating from their room at St. Phillip's Church, they set the precedent for public benevolence that would change little for the next century and a half.

The decisions the parochial officers made about punishing drunks or forcing support from wayward fathers for bastard children endowed them with some of the coercive powers of the reviled British ecclesiastical courts. Most, however, took the role of the impartial magistrate rather than of morality police as their model. Performance of these duties melded harmoniously with the movement toward a more emphatically paternalistic culture in Charleston. Participation in the symbols, as well as the substance, of poor relief insinuated members of the evolving elite into the lives of independent producers who fell outside their traditional purview. By faithfully fulfilling their responsibilities to the laboring

15. Waterhouse, "Colonial Elite," 240; Walter B. Edgar and N. Louise Bailey, *The Commons House of Assembly, 1692–1775* (Columbia, S.C., 1977), 642, 607, 627, 430, Vol. II of *Biographical Directory of the South Carolina House of Representatives*, 3 vols.; David J. Rothman, *The Discovery of the Asylum: Social Order and Disorder in the New Republic* (Boston, 1971), 12; Christopher Hill, *Society and Puritanism in Pre-Revolutionary England* (New York, 1964), 270.

16. Pauline Maier, "Popular Uprisings and Civil Authority in Eighteenth Century America," *William and Mary Quarterly*, 3rd series, XXVII (January, 1970), 7.

classes in times of need, the town fathers hoped to establish the bonds of mutual obligation and reciprocity. On one occasion in 1765, the commissioners of the market discovered local bakers using unfair scales, and in a gesture not without theatrical quality, they confiscated nine hundred loaves to redistribute among the poor "with their own hands." In 1767, Nathaniel Russell, who would rise in the coasting trade to become one of the wealthiest men in the city, wrote to Ezra Stiles in Newport of an incident in which the wardens of St. Phillip's raised subscriptions of more than £200 sterling in two days, as well as food, clothing, and blankets, for a group of newly arrived Belfast immigrants in great distress when they landed in Charleston. When Russell visited the barracks where they were housed, the Irish Protestants expressed "their Gratitude in very moving Terms and seem astonished at the Kindness of the People & I think not without Reason." [17]

Charleston leaders embraced an irenic view of the world as they moved toward greater community inclusiveness. Harboring few illusions about the perfectability of men and society, they well understood that the good order and social harmony of the town depended upon linking the interests of the white Protestant population. Their view of the relationship between the poor and society contrasts with the increasingly restrictive attitude developing in Boston. [18]

In a departure from John Winthrop's "Modell of Christian Charity," Puritans, repelled by the depravity of man and worldly politics, turned inward, sifted through the population to find the elect, and limited their stewardship to virtuous church members. While the Puritans grew increasingly preoccupied with the relationship between man and God, liberal Anglican theologians argued that the true test of a religious life lay in one's relationship with the world. Many prosperous Charlestonians rejected the gloom preached by John Calvin and adopted the optimistic and benign teachings of the Latitudinarians, who argued that redemption, not original sin, more accurately defined human experience. Moral progress, then, could be furthered by their contributions to benevolent causes. With the development of humanitarian institutions in the city, some saw the unfolding of God's will in history. [19]

17. South Carolina *Gazette,* February 2, 1765; Nathaniel Russell to the Reverend Ezra Stiles, July 19, 1767, in Historical Society of Pennsylvania, Philadelphia.

18. Darrett Rutman, *Winthrop's Boston: Portrait of a Puritan Town, 1630–1649* (Chapel Hill, 1965), 217–19; Robert M. Weir, *Colonial South Carolina: A History* (New York, 1983), 221.

19. David Brion Davis, *The Problem of Slavery in Western Culture* (New York, 1966), 349–50, 362.

The goals of charity also differed between Boston and Charleston. The Puritans, believing poverty directly related to degeneracy, used their wealth to encourage virtue among the poor. They laid the foundation for the modern concept of philanthropy, which aspires to be unsentimental and systematic and assumes that a far-reaching reformation of society may be achieved through individual transformation. American philanthropy, as it has evolved from its Puritan antecedents, rests upon firm ideas about entitlement and equality.

In comparison, benevolence as understood and practiced in Charleston retained an Old World aristocratic tone animated as much by noblesse oblige as Christian charity. Suppliants did not have to be pure in heart, but they did have to be appropriately humble. Charleston's leaders lived at ease with the existence of poverty even as they tried to blunt some of its most painful aspects. That some were comfortable while others suffered was a product of God's ineffable world order, not their flawed social system. Relief for the poor, consequently, was usually reactive and provided short-term material solutions to immediate problems such as beggars on the streets, epidemics, or temporary economic dislocations. The relationship between giver and recipient reinforced the local hierarchy and acknowledged sympathy or duty rather than admitting social injustice.[20]

The contrasting views of poverty, its sources, and its cure in Charleston and Boston during the colonial period underscored a fundamental difference in the way citizens of both communities viewed the concept of sin, the malleability of human nature, social organization, and individual agency. In both towns, public-spirited citizens would have described their relationship to the poor in religious terms, but exactly how benevolence affected an individual's relationship to God proved one of the most explosive theological issues of the mid–eighteenth century. The emotion-laden debate over whether one finds salvation through good works or through election by God's grace followed the Puritans to America and by the 1730s threatened the stability of communities across New England. The lines drawn around this question ultimately transcended theological doctrine. Enthusiastic revivals propounding the personal rather than institutional relationship between man and God provided an outlet for animosities against the Anglican church and those who wielded its authority. The energy of this movement seared across New England and ignited a series of revivals that touched every colony and became known collectively as the Great Awakening.

20. Calvin Woodward, "Reality and Social Reform: The Transition from Laissez-Faire to the Welfare State," *Yale Law Journal,* LXXII (1962), 300–303.

The Great Awakening was primarily a movement of the urban North and the rural South that fed on popular discontent with an overly intellectual, often remote clergy. Charleston alone among southern towns caught fire, and large numbers of its citizens (not noted for living the closely examined life) found themselves alternately weeping and shouting at meetings held by the great exhorter George Whitefield. His stinging criticism of the high-living Anglican clergy reawakened in Dissenters and French Huguenots lingering animosities over taxation in support of the established church long repressed in the interest of political and social harmony. St. Phillip's rector Alexander Garden (chastised by Whitefield for his indulgence in dancing and other local revelry) publicly attacked the eclectic theology of this enthusiast, who professed to be an Anglican while preaching the "old and exploded Doctrine of Calvinism" in a style reminiscent of German pietism. The Scottish-born Garden echoed beliefs held by New England liberals. He paired the power of individual agency with God's mercy to gain salvation and warned his congregation that heaven could not be won by cataclysmic rebirth or "instantaneous regeneration." The reward of eternal life, Garden insisted, required a lifetime dedicated to Christian acts. One could not simply give alms, for example, but had to meditate and reflect upon motives.[21]

Whitefield appeared in Charleston at a most opportune time. His revivals, which reached their frenzied peak in 1742, brought release to citizens tottering on the edge of an emotional precipice. At numerous times during the preceding five years, Charlestonians thought their end might truly be near. Rumors of Spanish invasion, particularly virulent epidemics, a violent slave uprising, and finally the Great Fire of 1739 convinced merchant and laborer that the time to repent was at hand. A visiting New England revivalist seized the opportunity to instruct Charlestonians on the "Burning of Sodom with its Moral Causes."[22]

---

21. Alexander Garden, *Regeneration and the Testimony of the Spirit . . . Two Sermons Lately Preached in the Parish Church of St. Phillip, Charles Town, in South Carolina* (Charleston, S.C., 1740), 2; David J. Morgan, "The Great Awakening in South Carolina, 1740–1775," *South Atlantic Quarterly*, LXX (Autumn, 1971), 596–99; Sidney E. Ahlstrom, *A Religious History of the American People* (New Haven, 1972), 390–92. Whitefield harangued Charlestonians for their sinfulness in not providing religious instruction for their slaves. Clearly taking this criticism to heart, Garden himself violated a law newly passed in 1740 after the terrors of the Stono Rebellion, not only teaching two young slaves to read the Bible but also raising money to open a school where the teenagers instructed other slaves in the basic tenets of Christianity.

22. Josiah Smith, "The Burning of Sodom with its Moral Causes, Improved in a Sermon in Charleston, November 1740," in Smith, *Sermons on Several Important Subjects* (Boston, 1757), 5; South Carolina *Gazette*, November 11, 1740.

Whitefield transcended mere haranguing of his guilt-ridden audiences. His message to Americans had more potency than that of Jonathan Edwards or any of the other voices rising during the Great Awakening. Rather than manipulate irrational human fears, he reminded men and women of the good in them all and urged them to act on it. Whitefield prescribed active participation in Christian charity rather than passive remorse as the way to a new life. Part of his revolutionary message was that *everyone*, not only the upper classes, had the ability and the responsibility to help the unfortunate. So that others might practice what he preached, Whitefield even founded Bethesda Orphanage in Georgia for the most destitute population of the most destitute colony and began a whirlwind fund-raising campaign in both America and England. His ambition to build an elaborate institution based on German Pietist August Hermann Francke's asylum in Halle, Germany, near Savannah foundered on economic realities of the struggling colony. In one of the cruel ironies that haunt southern benevolence, Whitefield invested some of the donations in a South Carolina plantation; the harder his drivers pushed the slaves, the larger the orphans' endowment. In the interest of maximizing profits from the lands belonging to the orphanage, he strenuously lobbied the Georgia Assembly to amend its charter to legalize slavery.[23]

Charleston's religious frenzy waned with Whitefield's departure, while the pervasive ill ease lingered on. Emphasis on the spirit receded, but the political dilemmas remained. The issue of the black-slave majority loomed largest in the public mind. Perhaps no other single factor would have such an important impact upon the town's policy toward poor whites. Immunity from the yellow fever that decimated white indentured servants during their first years in the colony made slaves, from Africa or the West Indies, the most economical form of labor. By 1690, slaves outnumbered white servants; in less than twenty years, blacks would outnumber all whites in Charleston and the surrounding districts.[24] The tragic consequences for the blacks have been extensively documented, but the impact of slave labor upon the propertyless whites remains largely unexplored. Even though South Carolinians adopted slavery directly

23. Robert H. Bremner, *American Philanthropy* (Chicago, 1988), 19–22.
24. Peter Wood, *Black Majority: Negroes in Colonial South Carolina from 1670 through the Stono Rebellion* (New York, 1974), 36. The population of South Carolina consisted of 1,360 free men, 900 free women, 110 white male servants, 90 women servants, 1,200 white children, and 4,100 blacks. The rate of change may be observed through comparison with the 1703 census that showed 1,460 freemen, 110 male white servants, and 3,000 blacks (Evarts B. Greene and Virginia D. Harrington, *American Population Before the Federal Census of 1790* [Gloucester, Mass., 1966], 173).

from Barbados, a limited "plastic" period existed in the early eighteenth century, as it had in Virginia, during which time a passing traveler might have seen white servants standing in the knee-high brackish water of rice fields along with West African blacks. Spared the ultimate hopelessness of the slave, white servants in South Carolina (especially the non-English), as in all colonies, suffered violations of their contracts and endured corporeal punishments. When real wages in England began increasing by 1680 and the British government placed tighter restrictions upon the emigration of skilled artisans and mechanics, Irish Protestants, orphans, and paupers desperate for work rushed in to fill the void. Seldom skilled, much less articulate about their rights than better-educated craftsmen, their indentures were bought, sold, traded, and even gambled away. Husbands were separated from wives, mothers from children. Women endured the predations of their masters.[25] One newcomer, inconsolably despondent over the hopelessness of his situation, "dispatched" himself into the Black River, where in short order "half a Score of Alligators . . . made no Scruple of working upon the Poor Fellows Carcase pretty sufficiently."[26]

Although many notable exceptions have contributed to the legend of mobility in the New World, the majority of white indentured servants found only limited opportunities. One study shows that over half of the 241 servants who came to South Carolina by 1680 died or disappeared from public record. Of those whose fates are known, 15 percent remained propertyless. A total of 40 percent of all servants who tried their luck in the colony owned land, compared with an 80 percent rate among free immigrants. In 1726, the South Carolina Assembly passed a law designed to enrich opportunities for the landless and better secure the colony against slave uprising by requiring all plantations, even those with only a solitary slave, to have a white servant on the premises—more, if slaves numbered over twenty. By creating demand for white servants in the rural districts, it was hoped that "more industrious, laboring men" would opt to leave Great Britain and take their chances in South Carolina.[27]

25. David W. Galenson, *White Servitude in Colonial America: An Economic Analysis* (Cambridge, Mass., 1981), 166–67; VerSteeg, *Southern Mosaic,* 109; Marcus W. Jernagan, *Laboring and Dependent Classes in Colonial America, 1607–1783* (New York, 1960), 55.
26. Quoted in Theodore D. Jervey, "The White Indentured Servants of South Carolina," *South Carolina Historical Magazine,* XII (October, 1911), 168–69.
27. Lois Green Carr and Russell R. Menard, "Immigration and Opportunity: The Freedman in Early Colonial Maryland," in *The Chesapeake in the Seventeenth Century: Essays on Anglo-American Society,* ed. Thad W. Tate and David L. Ammerman (Chapel Hill, 1979), 206–42; Aaron M. Shatzman, *Servants into Planters, The Origin of an Ameri-*

But where there were no black slaves, poor whites fell even more deeply into peonage. Georgia prohibited slavery to create greater opportunities for poor English debtors, but all the hard labor of clearing dense forests, planting, weeding, and harvesting then fell to indentured servants and free whites. Unwilling to withstand conditions often worse than those they escaped in England, tired of ceaseless bending and stooping and working in regimented gangs, the most venturesome filled the Georgia night with the sound of their fleeing footsteps. One planter admitted to James Oglethorpe that only with leg chains could he maintain control of his white work force. By the 1740s, custom dictated that "Negroes did all the [plantation] work" in South Carolina, so many of those who skulked through the Lowcountry swamps often made their way to Charleston, a city just at the dawn of its golden age.[28] Wagons crowded the roads bringing goods from the plantation districts. City wharves sagged under the weight of Lowcountry bounty—deerskins, rice, indigo, and Sea Island cotton bound for England and the international markets. Georgia runaways, usually arriving at the town line "in a miserable beggarly condition," found work in an economy hungry for workers, black or white.[29] Busy ropemakers, coopers, cordwainers, carpenters, and painters all actively recruited apprentices and hired help. Once in the cosmopolitan city, the runaways blended into the population of the landless or unskilled who also drifted into urban centers. Tenements offered cheap rooms, well-dressed citizens might give a shilling to a beggar, and dark alleyways offered the safety of anonymity.

Attempts by the colonial government to attract more white settlers to balance the rising black majority inadvertently accelerated the problem of poverty in Charleston. In 1731, Governor Robert Johnson created eleven new townships stretching in a protective arc around the Carolina capital from the Savannah River to the North Carolina border and offered white European Protestants incentives of land and money to settle there. The scheme to create a class of independent yeomen and insulate Charleston from marauding Indians or rebellious slaves enjoyed some

---

can Image: Land Acquisition and Status Mobility in Seventeenth-Century South Carolina (New York, 1989), 131–32.

28. Georgia legalized slavery in 1755. Colonial Records of the State of Georgia (Atlanta, 1732–52), V, 559; Cooper and McCord, Statutes of South Carolina, III, 272.

29. Johann Bolzius warned that Georgia's poverty would deepen with slavery. Wealthy Charleston merchants would travel south in droves, he correctly predicted, buy up the best plantation lands, and as they did in their own colony, "refuse to pay a greater price to the white people for their Labour than Negroes, by which, they can't possibly subsist or maintain themselves" (Colonial Records of the State of Georgia, XXV, 168).

limited success, but in the long term large numbers failed to transform their red clay or sand-hill holdings into productive farms. Some never even left the town. Unsuccessful Swiss, Germans, and Scotch-Irish retreated to the relative safety of the city and swelled the growing ranks of those in need. Requests for new appropriations for the relief of poor Protestants and complaints over these expenses filled colonial records for the next twenty years.[30]

Concern over the large black population burst into panic in 1739. That September, nearly a hundred slaves threw off their bonds and for several weeks marched through the Lowcountry with banners, guns, and drums. Twenty whites lay dead in their wake as they made their way toward Georgia and freedom. The band was apprehended before they reached their destination. After the fury of trials and executions subsided, the South Carolina Assembly tried to sort out the causes of the Stono Rebellion, the largest to occur in any colony, and concluded that the overwhelming numbers of fractious African-born slaves and poor management by whites precipitated this revolt. The planter-dominated assembly moved quickly in 1740 to set high tariffs that virtually prohibited importation from Africa for the next decade. They also passed a battery of more restrictive laws providing the framework for a slave code that would remain little changed until emancipation. In 1751, the assembly further directed that a percentage of the import duty on slaves be used to help attract poor Protestants to the Lowcountry, even though experience showed this would only increase the costs of relief. Long before the end of the colonial period, Charlestonians had already linked black slaves and poor whites together. Understanding this linkage not only provides the key to the development of the relief system but also illuminates the evolution of class relations in Charleston.[31]

Charleston harbored a heterogeneous population of black and white, slave and free, poor and rich, unknown in the rest of the region. Fate distributed its bounty unevenly among them: only 10 percent of the population held 50 percent of the wealth.[32] In addition to luckless indentured servants and homeless immigrants, laborers and craftsmen from other colonies added to the diversity of Charleston's white population.

Geographically removed from the hardships of the French and Indian War, Charleston's economy boomed with increased demand for its prod-

30. Robert L. Meriwether, *The Expansion of South Carolina, 1729–1765* (Kingsport, Tenn., 1940), 17–30; Weir, *Colonial South Carolina,* 194–95.

31. *Ibid.,* 208–209; Edmund Morgan, *American Slavery, American Freedom: The Ordeal of Colonial Virginia* (New York, 1975), 338–62.

32. Weir, *Colonial South Carolina,* 214.

ucts, especially naval stores. After 1763, the northern colonies continued to suffer when a postwar depression cut their shipping and trade. High food prices hit the urban laboring classes of the larger cities particularly hard. More than a thousand paupers crowded Boston's poorhouse. During the 1760s, when the cost of living doubled in both Philadelphia and New York, Irish and German immigrants perceived South Carolina as the "best poor man's country" despite the ubiquity of slave labor. Natives and immigrants flowed south into Charleston at a time when its taxpayers already supported more poor people than all other parishes combined. Attempts to provide subsistence for those on Charleston's economic margins drove the poor rate up from £5,000 current money in 1762 to £8,000 in 1770.[33]

Instability of the world market, wars with the French and Indians, widespread depression, and the constant influx of immigrants all contributed to the incidence of indigency in Charleston, yet competition with slaves was most commonly blamed for the presence of beggars among the city's merchant princes. As early as 1744, Charleston shipwrights agitated for what may be called a "split economy," with blacks legally locked out of all but the most menial jobs. The South Carolina *Gazette* offered its support and argued: "The great fundamental principle should be that the slave should be kept as much as possible to agricultural labors. . . . There should be no black mechanics or artisans, at least in the cities."[34]

Craftsmen inveighed against competition with slaves, it should be noted, but not against slavery. This tactic was only one of several devices used in their attempt to regulate the labor market. During the 1760s, all classes of workingmen, from black chimney sweeps to white master carpenters and bakers, experimented with combinations to fix prices and set minimum wages.[35] In a 1765 letter to a local newspaper, "A Trader" called upon local government to insulate the working classes from "forestallers" or extortioners, who created artificial scarcities in Charleston. With the vital resources of the town going to the highest bidder, he

33. Gary Nash, *The Urban Crucible: Social Change, Political Consciousness, and the Origins of the American Revolution* (Cambridge, Mass., 1979), 53. In 1759, for example, Charlestonians paid a poor tax of £6,000 current money while the churchwardens of St. John's Colleton assessed their parishes' needs at about £348 (Waterhouse, "Colonial Elite," 239).

34. South Carolina *Gazette,* quoted in Richard Morris, *Government and Labor in Early America* (New York, 1947), 187.

35. By 1800, the average Charleston laborer commanded wages that ran from 10 cents to 25 cents higher than those in any other city (Robert Walsh, *Charleston's Sons of Liberty: A Study of the Artisans, 1763–1789* [Columbia, S.C., 1959], 133).

warned, "we shall soon be obliged to build more Almshouses to receive our poor distressed inhabitants; for it is past a Doubt that an Industrious Man, who does not earn Thirty or Forty Shillings in the day (and few do that) cannot possibly pay house rent, cloath and feed his family and pay Five pounds out of his poor pittance to purchase a cord of firewood and that ill-measured." The "Trader" demanded greater protection for "the many who are placed by Providence in lower stations." He implored the governor to restore the moral economy of the past and once again rule "his people with the tenderness of an indulgent parent." [36]

Nostalgia for the days when the merchant elite of the town monitored and enforced standards of a fair wage and good measure signaled a decline from earlier paternalistic intervention. By the 1760s, Charleston merchants, struggling against mercantilistic restrictions, moved toward liberal ideals of laissez-faire and free trade. Commissioners of the market, responsible for enforcing the practice of fair value and just prices, began ignoring rising prices and let vendors charge whatever the public would bear. Liberal sentiments also affected the giving practices of Charleston's charitable associations. The South Carolina Society, one of the most prestigious and generous of the numerous benevolent groups in the city, began modestly in 1737 as the Two-Bit Club with a few French immigrants meeting in a tavern and making small pledges to help other Huguenots get started in Charleston. The fortunes of the hard-driving and enterprising Huguenots rose with those of their adopted city, and they emerged as leaders in the business community. By 1722, Huguenots composed 20 percent of the city's population.[37] Using their own experiences as models, the self-made men of Charleston folded liberal assumptions about the power of individual agency into their attitudes toward the white poor. Education of poor children won most enthusiastic support among French Protestants. However attached Charleston's elite were to the forms of a patriarchal society in their relations with women, children, and slaves, in their dealings with white laborers they adopted the competing liberal mode of demanding that workers act as free agents.

Frequent complaints that local leaders neglected their civic obligations opened an avenue for a group of ambitious men anxious to push into the governing strata of the city. By the 1760s, numerous artisans had accumulated sufficient wealth to buy their own shops, and many tried to fol-

36. South Carolina *Gazette*, February 2, 1765.
37. Frederic Cople Jaher, *The Urban Establishment: Upper Strata in Boston, New York, Charleston, Chicago, and Los Angeles* (Urbana, Ill., 1982), 326.

low the path of the reigning colonial gentry to social recognition and political power. Some, like Daniel Cannon, who worked his way from prosperous carpenter to planter, eventually won a position of public trust on the St. Phillip's vestry, but most of the urban artisans served only on increasingly ineffective regulatory committees. Determined to participate in one of the most important rituals of the city, artisans formed their own social and benevolent club, the Fellowship Society. Adopting the rhetoric of Enlightenment ideals, Charleston artisans claimed they were bound to the poor not only "by the strictest ties of social duty" but also by the "distinguishing faculty [of] Reason." Members of the Fellowship Society exuded energy and claimed high moral purpose at a time when most of the other benevolent associations, such as the South Carolina Society, were in their second generation and more focused upon pursuing good society than the social good. The Fellowship Society dedicated its efforts to the creation of an institution to house the insane and mentally disordered of the community, a part of the population scandalously ignored by the Anglican vestry. The founding members, many of whom fell in with the radical Sons of Liberty, criticized the vestry and churchwardens for shirking their obligations to the poor. They challenged the moral authority of the elite by struggling to establish an independent hospital under their control. Although the Fellowship Society failed in this goal, the debate it inspired likely influenced the assembly's decision to build a new workhouse in 1768. This lesson in the potential power of voluntary associations to influence public policy no doubt impressed future revolutionaries of the city.[38]

The grand jury and St. Phillip's vestry ultimately agreed with the Fellowship Society that the moldering workhouse and hospital, now thirty years old, violated even eighteenth-century standards of human habitation with its putrid smells, filthy, crowded rooms, and indiscriminate mixing of poor widows, prostitutes, and thieves. The Commons House of the assembly began its own investigation into the shadowy world of Charleston's poorest citizens in 1767 and found 129 (2.5 percent of the population) incarcerated in the dismal confines of the workhouse, 67 pensioners living on their own, and 33 children between the ages of five and twelve being educated with public funds. Even though the colonial government absorbed the costs of transients and nonresidents, the parishes of St. Phillip's and St. Michael's spent £6,515 on the local poor alone, an

---

38. Rules of the Fellowship Society, quoted in Walsh, *Sons of Liberty,* 28, 30; Cooper and McCord, eds., *Statutes of South Carolina,* IV, 293.

increase of 500 percent over twenty years. The most dramatic rise had been in the years since 1755, when the annual assessment was £3,000 and the population 9,000.[39]

How had these expenses for poor relief swelled just when Charleston and the Lowcountry enjoyed unprecedented prosperity? The report cited five reasons for the increase in dependency. Primarily, the investigators concluded, the parish had been too expansive in disbursing assistance. The insouciance of the vestry and churchwardens toward banishing the opportunistic and transient poor back to their home parishes before they qualified for aid forced Charlestonians to bear a disproportionate share of the burden. The large number of poor Protestants who lingered behind the safety of the city fortifications instead of venturing out to the dangers of the Carolina Backcountry added to the numbers of non-Charlestonians receiving aid. The widows and orphans of militiamen, all agreed, made irrefutable claims upon public benevolence. Depressed conditions in other colonies forced northern colonists southward. Stagnation of commerce due to the Stamp Act in 1764 exacerbated the sufferings of the poor in all port cities. Finally, the report singled out the "overabundance" of taverns and "tipling Houses" where undesirables could ruin their health while establishing the three-months residency necessary to dip legally into the public trough.[40]

At the time of the discussion of the new poorhouse, Henry Laurens wrote James Grant that evidence of Charleston's promising civic destiny was everywhere: "We are regulating our Port and Harbour, going to build a sumptuous Exchange and Customs House, extending fine streets . . . building a new Hospital and enquiring into the State of the Poor." The creation of a public hospital and inquiry into the "State of the Poor," as the London-educated Laurens well knew, placed Charleston in step with England's Age of Benevolence, a time when humanitarianism would become fashionable.[41] Among the dominant classes, the term *compassion* had begun shoving aside *duty* in discussions of their relationship to the poor. Laurens meant no irony when he linked the elegant Ex-

39. J. H. Easterby, ed., "Public Poor Relief in Colonial Charleston: A Report to the Commons House of Assembly About the Year 1767," *South Carolina Historical and Genealogial Magazine,* XLII (April, 1941), 83–86.

40. *Ibid.;* Peter A. Coclanis, *The Shadow of a Dream: Economic Life and Death in the South Carolina Low Country, 1670–1920* (New York, 1989), 114. St. Michael's Parish had been created in 1751 to accommodate the growing population of the city, but the collection and distribution of alms remained the responsibility of the St. Phillip's Vestry.

41. Henry Laurens to James Grant, March 23, 1767, in *The Papers of Henry Laurens,* ed. George C. Rogers and David R. Chesnutt (Columbia, S.C., 1968–), V, 238; Himmelfarb, *Idea of Poverty,* 37.

change Building, the center of commerce, with the functional new poor-house and hospital. The Charleston merchant did not relate the city's vigorous commerce, with its dependence on volatile world markets, to the creation of poverty and dependence, as later republican theorists would.[42] Laurens believed instead that the wealth generated by trade permitted Charlestonians to indulge their higher sentiments toward a class that had been with them always. He thought Charlestonians necessarily harbored more highly developed sensibilities toward the suffering (abundant evidence suggests otherwise), for they were both among the richest and the most generous of all Americans. On the eve of the American Revolution, when nine of the ten most wealthy British colonials lived in Charleston or its surrounding plantation district, Charleston already enjoyed a reputation as a city that was "open hearted and exceeding most . . . in acts of Benevolence, Hospitality, and Charity."[43]

The Revolution had little impact upon the practical functioning of Charleston's poor-relief system. After the city's incorporation in 1783, responsibility for the indigent (greatly increased in the wake of the war) passed to the commissioners of the poor appointed by the city council. The same urban elite continued their "gratuitous execution of many branches of power" after the American Revolution as before, though successful artisans and mechanics increasingly participated in the public ritual of meeting with the poor and granting boons.[44] The face-to-face method of dealing with the poor persisted and blended with the larger sense of "personalism" that characterized southern social relations.[45]

What would change, and change dramatically, would be the relationship of Charleston and the South to the rest of the nation. The ideals of the Enlightenment that spurred America to take its stand against England lingered on after the last shots were fired. Slavery, at cross purposes with liberty and equality, thrust the South into a minority and defensive position. The hierarchical society that the Charleston elite struggled to carve out of the Carolina frontier grew stagnant as the city's importance as an international entrepôt declined and the value of its surrounding agricultural lands decreased.

At the beginning of the nineteenth century, Charleston had little to

42. See Drew McCoy's discussion of the problems of wealth and virtue, poverty and dependence in *The Elusive Republic: Political Economy in Jeffersonian America* (New York, 1980), especially 48–75.

43. Rev. William Hollinsead, *An Oration Delivered at the Orphan House of Charleston, October 18, 1797* (Charleston, S.C., 1798), 6.

44. Governor William Bull the Younger, quoted in Weir, *Colonial South Carolina*, 262.

45. David Potter, *The South and the Sectional Conflict* (Baton Rouge, 1968), 17–30.

offer the "common man" whose voice was beginning to be heard throughout the new Republic. Opportunities for social mobility, for land and slaves, lay to the west. The necessity to provide relief for unemployed whites pressed hard upon the leaders of the city, who understood the threat to their institutions that would come with murmurings among the nonslaveholders and who were still very much tied to the culture of benevolence that was so important to the way Charlestonians understood themselves. Even as its economic position continued to deteriorate, Charlestonians joined with other Americans in forming voluntary associations dedicated to reforms of all kinds (except abolition) to improve urban life, anxiously trying to stay abreast of the "spirit of the age."

II

THE SPIRIT OF THE AGE

The spirit of the age is . . . the spirit of SOCIAL ENTERPRISE, abounding in energy and enthusiasm, in wisdom and benevolence. That spirit lives and moves everywhere; and with the aid of the Bible and the Tract, of the Missionary and the Sunday School, is traveling through the whole earth.
—Thomas Smith Grimké, 1831

With political independence secure by 1815, Americans began the difficult process of sorting through traditional values of the past and forging new responses to changing social and economic relationships. During the first decades of the new Republic, the southern clergy detected the same disorder, ungodliness, and detachment from the larger social good in the South that infected northern cities. Many established limited partnerships with the New England ministry in their moral war to create a "benevolent empire" in America and helped set the nation on an unprecedented course of social and moral reform.

A national movement to send missionaries to local slums rather than distant lands began about 1802 with the founding of the Massachusetts Bible Missionary Society. Southerners also embraced this movement to deliver the nation from its sinful ways. Public drunkenness, Sunday revelry among immigrants, and the shocking inability to read the Bible among the children of the city all brought Charlestonians into the circle of national reform. From 1815 to 1830, this conservative desire to ground the nation in Christian principles forged one of the most enduring cultural ties between North and South. As long as reform remained unpolitical and focused upon personal morality, southerners enthusiastically supported the Home Mission movement, Bible and tract societies, and temperance unions. Even peace societies found support in Charleston. By the time of Andrew Jackson's election, however, a "romantic revolution" engineered by a New England "power elite" rocked American theology. As widespread acceptance of the democratic notion that everyone could achieve salvation replaced determinism, hopes for the perfectibility of society through regeneration of individuals swept through New England with the Second Great Awakening.[1]

1. John L. Thomas, "Romantic Reform in America, 1815–1865," *American Quar-*

Until this new definition of Christian America as a country without slavery ultimately excluded southerners from national reform groups, Charlestonians remained imbued with the "spirit of the age," the application of religious principles and natural law to social problems. In 1826, Robert Mills surmised that Charleston stood in the "centre of a vast circle" of benevolence that wreathed the entire nation.[2] Charlestonians, basking in the fading light of the great rice boom, initially participated fully, along with conscientious citizens of Philadelphia and Boston, to excise the wen of immorality on the Republic. An agent for a northern benevolent society believed he was going to bring light into the darkness on a venture into the heart of the South but found Charlestonians both prosperous and openhanded. "I was never in a place where so many people might give largely, without abridging any luxury, as here," remarked a very surprised Jeremiah Evarts, head of the Boston-based American Board of Commissioners, who also shocked the folks back home with the news that "the mass of them give more liberally than the mass of people with the same wealth as New England." Historian David Ramsey, who belonged to both the Charleston Dispensary for the Poor and the local Bible society, half complained that Charlestonians actually carried charity "rather to excess."[3]

At this time, sin was understood as having its origins in poverty. Americans directed their formidable moral energy toward freeing the poor from the slavery of their benighted condition. Reformers found nineteenth-century urban poverty different from the quiet, hidden poverty of the countryside or the sentimentalized poverty of the widow and orphan. They now confronted the angry, roiling, criminal poverty of the hopeless unemployed, the rootless immigrant, and the unrepentant drunk. As "God's Will" faded as an explanation for social inequity, the more remote forces of urbanization, immigration, and industrialization were blamed for the disorder caused by poverty's children—intemperance, licentiousness, sabbath breaking, ignorance of the Scriptures.

The decline in domestic manufacturing and the rise of more specialized production for the national and world market, with their unpredict-

---

terly, XVII (Winter, 1965), 656–61; Elwyn Smith, "The Forming of a Modern American Denomination," Church History, XXXI (March, 1962), 89.

2. When Mills made his survey of Charleston, the city supported more than fifty public and private institutions, relief associations, and tract and Bible societies (Robert Mills, Statistics of South Carolina [1826; rpr. Spartanburg, S.C., 1972], 435).

3. Evarts quoted in John Wells Kuyendal, Southern Enterprize: The Work of the National Evangelical Societies in the Antebellum South (Westport, Conn., 1982), 37; Ramsey quoted in Jaher, The Urban Establishment, 395.

able surges and slumps, created chaos for the American worker just as new technology forced more and more into wage labor. The threshing machine, for example, reduced farm tenancy by making short work of the task that had once employed hundreds of unskilled laborers swinging flails during the barren winter months in the warmth of northern barns. As the need for year-round labor decreased, farmers began hiring seasonal workers who had to find their own shelter between harvest and spring planting. Fluctuations in the demand for labor and low wages made it difficult for workers to accumulate savings. Their constant search for employment so disrupted ties with their families that in the event of a calamity or even a brief sickness, increasing numbers had to choose between public charity or crime to sustain themselves. Although slavery provided the major source of labor in the South, white workers in cities of the Cotton Kingdom suffered from the same forces eroding the position of wage earners throughout the nation. Northern workers joined disappointed German and Irish immigrants who drifted south where warmer winters promised more work days.[4]

As the poor assumed a new and often hostile face, former allies regarded them as social problems rather than individual objects of pity. Clergymen across the nation detected rot in the nation's moral and spiritual center. Evidence of a descent from past standards haunted the observant not just in Philadelphia, Boston, and New York but in Charleston, Richmond, and Savannah. Even in smaller inland towns such as Columbia, Petersburg, and Augusta, the possibility of disorder frightened the alert. No class escaped blame as Sunday after Sunday, churchmen preached to empty pews about the evils of intemperance, sabbath breaking, and the sacrifice of duty to pleasure.

Similarities in the early years of religious benevolence in the North and South have been obscured by historians who insist upon depicting the period of cooperation as a doomed prologue in the continuum that began with prayer societies and ended with abolition. However, Charleston's experience casts doubt upon the presumption that this evolution was either absolute or inevitable. In discussing the connection between philanthropy and abolition, David Brion Davis has noted the blithe indifference of the liberally disposed in England, who throughout the seventeenth century erected institutions and orphanages with little thought to the plight

4. Joanne Hannon, "Poverty in the Antebellum Northeast: The View from New York State's Relief Rolls," *Journal of Economic History*, XLIV (December, 1984), 1009; Michael Katz, *In the Shadow of the Poorhouse: A Social History of Welfare in America* (New York, 1986), 6; Paul Boyer, *Urban Masses and Moral Order in America, 1820–1920* (Cambridge, Mass., 1978), 1–4.

of the slave or guilt over their profits from the African trade. Slavery became a topic of British concern only during the late eighteenth century. In America, the institution survived the Enlightenment, the Great Awakening, and the Revolution. Capitalism, Davis argues, achieved what rationalism, Christianity, and republicanism could not by successfully challenging the whole realm of feudal social arrangements, including paternalistic responsibility, as inefficient and unprofitable.[5]

By first focusing on abolition of slavery, a symbol of patriarchal power practiced in distant lands, British, and later, northern American emancipationists, enjoyed the advantage of long-distance liberalism by watching the explosion of a social system from a sheltered place. But this is not to say they were cynically pursuing the economic interests of the rising middle class; abolitionists were experimentalists, not crude materialists. Capitalism helped many find "a recipe," to use Thomas Haskell's apt term, to resolve one of the most perplexing moral problems of the nineteenth century, particularly thorny because it enjoyed the sanction of both church and state. By mobilizing against the horrors of the colonial plantation system that uprooted Africans and forced them into the harsh discipline of gang labor, British reformers could strike a blow against the same alarming "insecurity and mobility of labor in a profit-oriented market" that accompanied the industrialization of their society without endangering their own progress and social harmony. The association of precapitalist systems with the degradation of labor and anti-Christian attitudes rather than the image of benign paternalism reduced nostalgia for the world lost to the English peasantry and smoothed the transition into the modern industrial world.[6]

Similarly, during the first half of the nineteenth century when America was going through its own economic transformation, the public image of the South with its traditional agrarian folkways declined, partially through the efforts of abolitionists and partially through the slaveholders' own truculence. Instead of a charmed land renowned for its openhanded generosity and contributions to republican thought, the South gained the reputation as an evil roadblock to fulfillment of the national destiny. As early as 1815, Elijah Parish, exhorting from a New England pulpit, bemoaned the fact that "the southern section of this country, once irradiated with the gospel of Jesus, now all is dark and hideous."[7]

5. Davis, The Problem of Slavery, 13.
6. Ibid., 335–37; Thomas Haskell, "Capitalism and the Origin of Humanitarian Sensibility," American Historical Review, XC (April, 1985), 359–61.
7. Elijah Parish, A Sermon Preached at Ipswich, September 29, 1815, at the ordination

Parts of the South had clearly experienced spiritual decline after the Revolution. The Virginia elite floundered in a religious vacuum after Jefferson succeeded in his crusade for disestablishment. The Episcopal church fell into a shambles. Until revivalism swept across the South after 1800, the plain style of evangelical denominations held small attraction for the aristocracy. Deism and skepticism took hold of the Virginia elite, causing alarm among the New England righteous, but tidewater Virginia differed from Lowcountry South Carolina. In the more Protestant Charleston, where the Anglican leaders had traditionally shared power with members of their own class among wealthy Presbyterians and Congregationalists, the Episcopal church maintained its standing. After the Revolution, Charlestonians appeared more outwardly pious (especially the women) and faithful in church attendance even as they reveled in the pleasures of their remaining prosperity. The local oligarchy, with its demonstrable devotion to the public good, survived challenges from an aspiring middle class during revolutionary upheavals. In the succeeding decades, Charlestonians felt quite secure about participating in the national movement for a moral reform that brought into sharp relief those social problems caused by the hard edge of capitalism piercing through the fabric of northern free society. According to the major sources of authority of the time—the Constitution, the Bible, and the common law—slavery was not wrong. Many southerners experienced a deep personal piety and brought genuine enthusiasm to their benevolent work. However, convictions about the deep nature of sin in the human heart tempered their expectation for an imminent millennium. Even those attracted to religious liberalism remained unconvinced by transcendentalism, questioned the possibility of religious perfection as preached by Charles Grandison Finney, and rejected the utopianism of Robert Owen. All three of these powerful forces ultimately helped transform moral reform into the call for immediate abolition by New Englanders.[8]

In the early decades of the benevolent crusade, Charleston's missionary associations invited some of the most single-minded graduates of New England theological schools to work among their white poor. Southern clergymen of deepest social conscience found their ministry among local slaves. Charleston's Female Domestic Missionary Society, organized in 1818, the first in the South, actively recruited graduates of Andover

of Rev. Daniel Smith and Cyrus Kingsbury, as missionaries to the West (Newburyport, Mass., 1815), 11. On the effects of disestablishment in Virginia, see Rhys Issac, The Transformation of Virginia, 1740–1790 (Chapel Hill, 1982), 285–93.

8. Henry F. May, The Enlightenment in America (New York, 1976), 136–37, 143–44, 149; Thomas, "Romantic Reform in America," 658–59.

Theological Seminary. Founded to uphold Congregational orthodoxy when Unitarianism overtook Harvard, Andover developed into one of the "driving wheels" of "the New England engine" propelling a sinful America to its true Christian destiny.[9]

City missionaries, who eschewed silk vestments and high-toned congregations for "the outcast, the sick, the miserable, and the despairing," constituted a unique breed. Some simply could find no church of their own; others believed they had a special calling. Part social workers, part pastors, they not only bridged the gap between the stolid theologians and the vast sea of the unchurched but also served as a connection between those living "in the dirtiest and most disgusting hovels" and those on the broad-porched mansions of the city. When dedication to a common good still transcended sectional politics, Charleston ladies found these earnest young men especially effective because they had a keen eye for sin and moral corruption. One New England missionary sent to labor in the Charleston vineyard reported to his sponsors that immorality and pleasure-seeking thrived as a "fearfully prevalent and increasing evil amongst us." The corruption of the sabbath proved his case: "Crowds frequent, on the Lord's Day, the Coffee Houses and dram shops; the half-concealed traffic in places of petty trade; the unoccupied pews in most of our Churches; the rattling of public conveyances; the multitudes that throng the streets and public walks on excursions of pleasure; the groups to be seen on the wharves or sailing in the harbour."[10]

These enthusiastic young men also embraced an emotional style that resonated with the spiritually destitute. One admittedly reveled in the "delicious emotions" that he experienced "while preaching in Christ's stead" to the sinners at the Charleston almshouse. Trusting that the special heartaches of dealing with such a hopeless class brought them closer to God, they frequently compared their labors among the despised with Christ's work. Systematically, they interviewed the forgotten men and women of the city "in as delicate a manner as possible" about their character and "moral condition," church affiliation, and state of their children's education. They played on their guilt, hopes, and fears, as one missionary explained his tactics: "I have endeavored, either by reproof, by instruction or by exhortation, to arouse their consciences, and to awaken in their minds an interest in regard to the concerns of eternity

9. John C. Dann, "Humanitarianism Reform and Organized Benevolence in the Southern United States, 1780–1830" (Ph.D. dissertation, College of William and Mary, 1975), 159–67; Smith, "The Forming of a Modern American Denomination," 89.

10. Rev. Thomas McGruder, *Report Presented to the Female Domestic Missionary Society of Charleston, South Carolina* (Charleston, S.C., 1837), 18.

and of the soul. In many instances, I have witnessed indications of deep impression. Tears suffusing the eye, have on many occasions, given demonstration, that the sensibilities of the soul were deeply touched."[11]

Religious benevolence in Charleston reflected the presence of multiple traditions: the social ethic of the Anglicans; the drive for proselytizing voluntary associations among Evangelicals; Jewish benevolent practices; the search for acceptance by Catholics. On a stop in Charleston while gathering information for his *Impressions of America,* George Lewis confirmed that "the Episcopal Church here has the greater part of the wealth . . . [while] the Methodists and Baptists have the masses, both white and colored." More harmony and less stratification existed among denominations than his analysis might suggest.[12] Charleston's economy had offered not only opportunities for comfort but considerable wealth to artisans and tradesmen. Abstemious Baptists and hardworking Methodists often found their virtue rewarded. Doctrinal concessions by both the Baptist and Methodist churches, calculated to increase their popularity in the South, muted the strident antislavery position of these denominations during the revolutionary period. This change not only allowed their members to reap the profits of bonded labor but also greatly reduced a potential cause of community friction.

Continuing the outward toleration that had characterized the formative period of the town's history, local leaders retained Anglicanism's comprehensive social vision of the organic unity of public life. This approach was more often institutional than evangelical, inclusive rather than discriminating. This attitude might be seen in the actions of the commissioners of the poorhouse, a body of prominent citizens appointed by the city council who assumed many of the duties of the colonial churchwardens. In 1810, they refused the request of Episcopal minister Theodore Dehon to build a chapel adjacent to the almshouse. In this "school for heaven," he believed, a pauper might learn patiently to "lay at the gate of the rich man, and meekly bear his neglect patiently." Although convinced from their experience with slaves of the subduing possibilities of religion, these civic leaders resisted the temptation to use it so blatantly for social control of whites. A decade later, as the Second Great Awakening touched the hearts of Charlestonians, the commissioners also rejected constant demands from Evangelicals that all children on the

11. *Ibid.,* 1–3, 7, 8, 14; Cranmore Wallace, "Reports of Charleston City Missions," *Southern Episcopalian,* III (August, 1856), 267, II (August, 1855), 490–91.

12. Samuel S. Hill, Jr., *The South and the North in American Religion* (Athens, Ga., 1980), 3–11; Rev. George Lewis, *Impressions of America and the American Churches* (1848; rpr. New York, 1968), 109.

city's bounty be forced to attend Protestant Sunday school. Children brought to the Charleston Orphan House unbaptized remained in that spiritually perilous state until they reached the age of discretion because the commissioners wanted to avoid scrupulously the appearance of choosing one denomination over another. Years of administering public charity had taught them that any hint of coercion only caused "great disquiet" among the white poor. The commissioners of the poor agreed that it was "advisable not to interfere in religious matters." [13]

Catholics endured an uphill struggle for a share in the public life of Charleston, and church officials monitored the city's relief system for all signs of discrimination. John England, first bishop of South Carolina, worked tirelessly to parry all attempts to use public monies as a lever to push the poor toward Protestantism. In 1825, he charged the commissioners of the Charleston Orphan House with failing to provide proper religious instruction for their Catholic charges. The commissioners quickly responded to his demand that "poverty shall not deprive its victims of religious rights" and began inviting local priests to join the Protestant ministers who took turns preaching in the orphans' chapel on Sunday afternoons. [14]

Sophisticated Catholics understood that co-option into the civic culture of Charleston posed the same threat to the integrity of their faith as the "zealous sectarians" who lurked in their neighborhoods and tried to seduce their children into Protestant Sunday schools with offers of new shoes and books. Though demanding their rights, most remained aloof from the attempts by the community to sponsor joint projects for the poor. Charleston's *Catholic Miscellany* warned priests that the frequent invitations they received to join public ceremonies and parade arm in arm with ministers of "twenty discordant sects" did not necessarily indicate respect for their faith. Instead, this form of public theater seemed "in accord with certain republican principles, often falsely understood in a civil point of view and still more falsely applied to the *one* Religion of

13. Christopher E. Gadsden, *An Essay on the Life of the Right Reverend Theodore Dehon, D.D.* (Charleston, S.C., 1833), 168–69; Minutes, April 24, 1820, in Charleston Poor House Records, City of Charleston Archives, Charleston, South Carolina (hereinafter cited as CPH); *Gospel Messenger*, VIII (January, 1831), 6. In 1851, a group of Episcopalians succeeded in their longstanding desire to establish an orphanage under their complete control, since the city orphan house maintained such a firm policy of nonsectarianism ([Rev. T. C. Dupont], "Report of the Mission of St. Stephen's Church," *Gospel Messenger*, XXII [August, 1845], 241–42; James Warley Miles, "Address Before the Church Home," *Gospel Messenger*, XXIX [October, 1852], 193–201).

14. Minutes, June 23, 1825, in Charleston Orphan House Records, City of Charleston Archives, Charleston, S.C. (hereinafter cited as COH).

one God, and his *one* Christ and the *one* eternal priesthood of Christ." In ecumenical overtures, Catholic leaders detected an attempt to fulfill a political ideal of order and harmony.[15] The two Irish benevolent associations, the Hibernian Society (1801) and St. Patrick's Society (1821), which devolved into social clubs open to bon vivants of the entire community for merriment and comradeship, illustrated to many Roman Catholics the homogenizing tendencies at work in the city.

In contrast with the experience of the Catholic community, the Jews of Charleston, who were as a group more prosperous, found the benevolent traditions of Charleston congenial with their practices of gift giving and charity. The Sephardic and eastern European Jews migrated first to Savannah in 1730 and began moving to Charleston during the next decade. By 1820, Charleston's Jewish community of about five hundred formed one of the largest in America. Though certainly not exempt from earnest proselytizations of Christians, many felt they had found a home amid the easy tolerance of the cosmopolitan city then enjoying its commercial heyday. A significant number of Charleston Jews advocated adapting the ancient codes of their faith to their life in the New World and unsuccessfully tried to recruit Isaac Mayer Wise, leader of the Liberal Reform movement, as their rabbi. Accepting slavery and fully participating in the life of the community as merchants, teachers, and journalists, Jews administered their own charities and sat on the boards of public institutions. The constitution of Charleston's Hebrew Orphan Society, founded in 1801, the oldest incorporated Jewish charity in America, celebrates the combination of "liberty and philanthropy" at work in the city.[16]

In Charleston, the traditions of the Anglican church survived disestablishment and continued to stand for "moderation, comprehensiveness, liberality of doctrine, and stability of custom." Remaining staid in the midst of revival fever and clinging defiantly to its hierarchical structure against the sweep of democratic sentiment, the Episcopal church, in many ways the denomination most accepting of an imperfect world, worked to reconcile duty to the poor with the sentiments of elite congregations. Resistance of the national Episcopal church to the modern pas-

15. *United States Catholic Miscellany,* December 1, 1849; Aaron I. Abell, *American Catholicism and Social Action: A Search for Social Justice, 1865–1950* (New York, 1960), 19–20.

16. Thomas J. Tobias, *The Hebrew Orphan Society of Charleston, S.C., Founded 1801: An Historical Sketch* (Charleston, S.C., 1957), 2, 4, 7, 12; Barnett A. Elzas, *The Jews of South Carolina from the Earliest Times to the Present Day* (Philadelphia, 1905), 131–32, 285.

sions of temperance and abolition also strengthened its position in the South. Even though local vestries probably did represent the "southern aristocracy at prayer," the practical effect of their sense of noblesse and paternalism was a willingness to challenge reluctant clergy and to use the church to work out what they conceived to be civic and Christian obligations of the church.[17]

Charlestonians, especially the Protestants of the nonliturgical denominations, threw themselves wholeheartedly into the vogue of voluntary associations that served as bridges between religion and culture. Voluntarism, the freedom of citizens to associate that stands at the heart of democratic society, has historically been a mighty force for social change in America. These "workshops of republicanism" operated at full capacity in Charleston and most other southern cities. In the critical early years of the Republic, voluntary associations provided another vehicle for expression of the public will. Voluntarism empowered the individual. At the same time, however, it promised to act as a palliative to the atomistic tendency of democratic society. The freedom to join with others to create new institutions or critique existing ones introduced the possibility for a new alignment of power in society. With control over one's own soul, any person could be a general in the moral revolution brewing in America. Or, as one Charleston reformer phrased it, even if a man "be a farmer, a day laborer, a seaman, yet has he influence on all with whom he associates." The myriad organizations formed by private citizens amazed Alexis de Tocqueville during his American travels. From these he deduced that in democratic societies no one person was in "a position to force his fellows to help him," so "if they want to proclaim a truth or propagate some feeling by the encouragement of a great example, they form an association."[18]

The doctrine of free association had first provided the energy for disestablishment and later for separation of church and state in America. When Protestant ministers hesitated to leave the spiritual realm and enter the affairs of "the world" when social problems such as intemperance

17. May, *The Enlightenment in America,* 74; Kuyendal, *Southern Enterprize,* 43; Bruce Mullin, *Episcopal Vision/American Reality: High Church Theology and Social Thought in Evangelical America* (New Haven, 1986), 128–29.

18. James Luther Adams, "The Voluntary Principle in the Forming of American Religion," in *Voluntary Associations: Socio-cultural Analyses and Theological Interpretation,* ed. Ronald Engle (Chicago, 1986), 172–73; Lois W. Banner, "Religious Benevolence as Social Control: A Critique of an Interpretation," *Journal of American History,* XL (June, 1973), 40; Thomas Smith Grimké, *Address on the Patriotic Character of the Temperance Reformation* (Charleston, S.C., 1838), 31; Alexis de Tocqueville, *Democracy in America* (1832; rpr. New York, 1969), 513–14.

seemed to threaten the Republic, lay activists took up the campaign against immorality. In so doing, they assumed much of the power of regulating public behavior that the clergy had once held. Communicants of urban churches, North and South, began focusing their energies upon the problem of poverty and sin in the city rather than in their souls. "Social duty," declared the *Southern Christian Advocate,* has emerged as "a branch of morality as clearly defined as any other." The Methodist journal cautioned its readers that the time had gone when Christians could be self-absorbed: "You are not your own, you are bought with a price." Living the Christian life demanded "other responses than just a pious sigh, or a liberal subscription." Systematic benevolence, the regular donation to the poor through an association of citizens, was touted as a "scheme of Christian beneficence devised in heaven."[19]

As voluntary associations gained political power through the united exertions of lobbying for sumptuary laws, for example, moral reform gained prestige for its patriotic and religious value. With this shift came a decline in the emphasis upon good works and salvation replaced by the equation of moral reform and patriotism. Thomas Smith Grimké described the temperance crusade as "preeminently Christian and American . . . one of the noblest and fairest forms, in which the principle of individual responsibility and social justice has ever been manifested. It rests on the obligation of each to think, to judge, to act for himself. It ilustrates, while it enforces the comprehensive obligation that each is bound to combine with others, in promoting not only his own immediate good, but, to the utmost of his ability, the good of his fellowmen, whether living or unborn. No individual can rightfuly withhold his own from the common stock of social influence."[20]

Churching the rowdy and salvaging the lost appealed to citizens of the seaport towns especially. Bible societies and Sunday school unions won active supporters, as did movements for world peace and, until the Missouri Compromise in 1820, the colonization of free blacks in Africa. Regarded during the 1820s as a model of benevolent enterprise (by other southern towns at least), Charleston claimed private and public relief systems dedicated to every human need from foundling homes to burial societies and to every worthy cause from assisting Jews ostracized for embracing Christianity to educating Chickasaw Indian children. Robert

19. "The Position of the Church to the Working Classes," *Southern Christian Advocate,* June 20, 1851.

20. Grimké, *Address on the Temperance Reformation,* 29, 31. This quotation preserves Grimké's simplified style of spelling devised to facilitate the teaching of reading to poor children, who had little time to spend in school.

Mills, the architect who gave concrete expression to Charleston's civic aspirations, compiled a long list of the city's benevolent institutions in 1826. He found the citizens of his hometown the most charitable in the young Republic.[21] An English traveler, Captain Basil Hall, also included Charlestonians in his praise of zealous and liberal Americans of wealth, who, though they could not prevent the poverty and suffering found in cities, were "universally ready, not only with their money, but with their personal exertions to relieve the distress of their less fortunate fellow creatures." The one flaw in the human condition overlooked by Charlestonians was hubris; even sympathetic neighbors in Savannah tired of persistent boasts about South Carolina's "magnanimous, chivalrous people," which they had repeated so often over the years "that they have persuaded themselves of their reality."[22]

The first voluntary societies focused upon local mission work. They gained power through merger into regional, then national systems. Ladies' missionary societies and children's Sunday school classes from across the country began sending their collections to Boston, Philadelphia, or New York, to the central headquarters of the various associations. When improvements in communications and transportation combined with the religious enthusiasm of the Second Great Awakening, moral reform groups, which were beginning to collect huge annual revenues, now had the potential to evangelize across the country and produce religious tracts by the thousands. For the national leadership of the American Bible Society, founded in 1816, or the American Sunday School Union, which began its work in 1824, this meant not only the opportunity to further the Lord's work but also the chance to create a truly national religious culture. The New England clergy (dubbed the "Protestant Jesuits" by one detractor) saw this as an opportunity to impose their vision on the rest of the country and actively tried to dictate the goals of the "benevolent empire."[23]

Trying to surmount rising sectional tensions, the national evangelical associations embarked upon their "Southern Enterprize" during the 1830s just as the antislavery forces were solidifying their campaign in the

---

21. Mills, *Statistics of South Carolina*, 426–35. Even when the town's prosperity waned with the passing of the great rice and cotton fortunes, citizens continued and even accelerated their benevolent efforts, switching emphasis from religion and education to economic amelioration through fuel and garment societies.

22. Basil Hall, *Travels in North America* (1829; rpr. Graz, Austria, 1964), III, 166–67; "Savannah and Charleston," *De Bow's Review*, XIII (March, 1850), 245.

23. Adams, "The Voluntary Principle," 195; Smith, "The Forming of a Modern American Denomination," 77–78, 89; Calvin Colter, *Protestant Jesuitism* (New York, 1836).

North. The American Sunday School Union also initiated a campaign in the South and other "destitute places" lacking effective public schools. Wherever "wild and wandering children of ungodly parents" ran riot, "the Sunday School appeared to be *the* saving institution of our future." Advocates thought of the Sunday scholars as tiny funnels through which they might introduce lessons of middle-class morality into the homes of the poor. Evolving as almost a distinct denomination, urban Sunday schools attracted teachers from a variety of churches who felt the need to do mission work. "In the Lanes and bye ways which shrink from the light of the Sun, among Sabbath breakers and Sabbath-rioters," they sought the young so that "some truths of Divine love may be sown in their tender consciences." One of the most beneficial features of their work was to remove children from the hopeless environment of their homes "in order that their hearts and heads may be supplied, if possible, with something they can take back for the good of the household. A right principle in the heart, a simple hymn in the memory, or a pleasant little book in the hand, may be as a light to shine in a dark place." It was in this way, explained a writer for the *Southern Christian Advocate,* that "we gently and effectually introduce the Gospel, unmixed with human philosophy and speculation into the homes of the people; and is not this the true remedy for social evils, introduced at the right time and place and operating upon the right class of persons?" [24]

Only the lissome and elusive street waif could hope to escape the well-meaning who prowled the alleys and paths of the most disreputable sections of the towns seeking new faces to scrub and uncorrupted hearts to inculcate with the lessons of the Sunday school. The envoy of Charleston's Female Domestic Missionary Society regularly rounded up all the "vagrant and neglected children of our city" to enroll them in these "nurseries of sacred learning." To preserve the paupers' pride, a Charleston Baptist church established a Garment Society, which suited up "little vagrants" for church with cast-off clothing. Every organization had a story like the one related by a Charleston teacher about the little seven-year-old boy who listened to the lessons under open windows or lingered around the doors and when asked to join the other children, replied, "Oh yes Sir, if Mother will only dress me to come, I will try very hard to get my 'ed-i-ca-tion.'" [25]

The image of mothers among the lower classes in the literature of the

24. American Sunday School Union, *The Union Annual, 1837* (Philadelphia, 1837), 33; Kuyendal, *Southern Enterprize,* 66–67; "Sunday School for Children," *Southern Christian Advocate,* July 11, 1851.

25. Charleston *Mercury,* October 9, 1852; Miscellaneous file, May 4, 1850, in COH.

benevolent societies contrasted sharply with that of the domestic angels of the upper classes. A spokesman for the Sunday school sponsored by Charleston's Marine Church recounted the story of the ten-year-old boy who was so impressed with the temperance messages he had heard there that he caused quite a stir by approaching every customer at the restaurant where he worked to sign the pledge and even began refusing to serve liquor if the patrons insisted on ordering it. His conscience forced him to quit before his angry boss fired him, but his mother sent him back.[26]

The American Bible Society and the American Tract Society also established branches in the South and hired colporteurs, who knocked on the doors of both the rich and the humble in towns and wearily rode through dense backwoods to reach isolated cabins. By 1855, the American Tract Society had a hundred agents canvassing the scriptural wasteland of Virginia and the Carolinas. In Virginia alone, colporteurs sold over forty thousand tracts, gave away fifteen thousand to the poor, and began the tradition of placing Bibles in hotel rooms. Charleston remained one of the few bright spots in the South, and agents found in 1841 that through the efforts of four independent Bible associations "the wants of the poor . . . are so constantly developed mainly by kind and anxious agency of ladies, that the individual must be culpably careless and indifferent who is without a Bible." In contrast, the agent working in Savannah reported moral and material conditions among the poor "perfectly appalling" but saw their grateful reception as a cause for hope. Another Savannah worker who had once been an "Anti Missionary Baptist" told how the poor sought him out, racing down the streets to catch up with him or anxiously waiting at the crossroads to get their Bibles. They thanked him profusely, but he quickly said, "No it is not I, it is the Bible Society of Darien and Savannah that have sent you these holy books of God that you may live and die in happiness." Upon hearing this, the agent reported, they would reply, "Well, God Almighty, bless those good gentlefolks."[27]

Often more rugged than the urban missionaries, these "bookmen" intrepidly invaded grogshops to press into shaky hands of "poor haggard

26. American Sunday School Union, *Annual Report, 1857*, quoted in W. B. Kennedy, *The Shaping of Protestant Education: An Interpretation of the Sunday School and the Development of Protestant Educational Strategy in the United States, 1789–1860* (New York, 1966), 69; *Southern Christian Advocate*, April 2, 1857; Commissioners' file, n.d., in COH.

27. *Report of the Executive Committee of the Bible Convention, November 25, 1841* (Charleston, S.C., 1842), 7; Bible Society of Georgia, *Annual Report* (Savannah, 1841), 97–98.

victims of alcohol" tracts such as *The Afflicted Man's Companion* and Edward's *History of Redemption*. They also reported destitution to local ministers wherever they found it, directed children to the nearest Sunday school, and reproved "sin-hardened, self-righteous old women" for their cynicism. God's footsoldiers took particular delight in pressing tracts upon Catholics, often quoting a very precise "body count" in their reports.[28]

For southerners, this nationalizing trend had ominous implications quite apart from the antislavery sentiment among the leadership of these expanding organizations. Already alerted to the flow of capital out of their region by the tariff debates surrounding Henry Clay's proposed "American system" of 1824, hardworking southern associates of groups like the American Bible Society were enraged to realize that their region was perceived as a mere colony in the benevolent empire. In true imperial style, representatives from the national organizations (Philadelphians particularly) frequently engaged in blatant "spiritual swindling" by siphoning off the hard-earned donations from earnest southerners and diverting them to projects in the North.[29]

Even in the face of such centrifugal forces, northern and southern moderates worked exhaustively to mediate differences because most understood they worked for an even larger cause than social reform. By the 1840s, when the Protestant denominations split over slavery, membership in the moral reform groups such as the American Sunday School Union (ASSU) was among the few enduring ties southerners had to national culture. The mission of the ASSU won such enthusiastic approbation that hopeful partisans saw it as not only a soul-saving but also "a Union saving institution" that forced South Carolina and Massachusetts "to exchange the kiss of peace and to work shoulder to shoulder in this great cause of Christian love." The American Tract Society, which claimed to know "nothing of North or South, East or West," and the Bible society clung to their southern missions, though radical forces on both sides of the slavery question labored furiously to break these connections.[30]

28. Clifford S. Griffin, *Their Brothers' Keepers: Moral Stewardship in the United States, 1800–1865* (New Brunswick, N.J., 1960), 92; American Tract Society, *Report of Colportage in Virginia, North Carolina, and South Carolina for the Year ending March 1, 1855* (New York, 1855), 3–4.

29. Kuyendal, *Southern Enterprize*, 39–40.

30. American Sunday School Union, *Union Annual, 1837*, 33; American Tract Society, *Twentieth Annual Report* (New York, 1845), 13. In 1845, proslavery Methodists formed the Methodist Episcopal Church and Southern Baptists formed their own convention. Seven

Despite outward similarities in organization and even goals, fundamental differences dating back to the colonial period reappeared under
the stresses imposed by the slavery debate. Early in their campaign, abolitionists had won the rhetorical battle with skilled and evocative use of
language; by appropriating terms such as *benevolence* and *reform* first,
they promoted their cause as the sine qua non of progress. Abolitionists
scored an important victory in 1817 when Ohio proponents of immediate abolition named their journal the *Philanthropist*. They worked tirelessly and in the end successfully to make their cause synonymous with
philanthropy, not only souring southerners on the term but also making
it impossible for slaveholders to claim a stake in the benevolent empire.
Attacks upon slaveholders as personally reprehensible accelerated during
the national debates over the spread of slavery into the Missouri Territory
in 1820. Spokesmen for the South drove abolitionists to greater furies
by insisting that their own peculiar institution was the ultimate poor
law, providing cradle-to-grave care for their laborers. They denounced
abolitionists and all their works as "false philanthropy," shabby and
misguided, in contrast to their own "Christian charity." Pro-slavery
apologists leveled similar charges against "the pseudo-philanthropists of
England and the Northern United States," who had weakened "an institution of God's appointment" by their weeping "over the imagined wants
and sufferings of those who are far better provided for and far happier
than their own poor." As long as the debate focused on the material
conditions of chattels, slavery's defenders could muster damning evidence
about the abysmal state of factory workers in free society. When loss of
personal freedom emerged as the major objection to slavery, this argument lost its power. Immediatists pressured other moral reform groups
such as the American Bible Society to exclude slaveholders and alienated
southerners who otherwise longed to participate in the "spirit of the age"
by applying Christian principles and natural law to social problems.[31]

The very term *philanthropy* came to anger some southerners, who
thought it only a guise used by abolitionists to infiltrate southern hearts
with their cant. A writer in the *Southern Literary Messenger* bemoaned
the "overcivilization" of Christianity and corruption of its mission away

---

years earlier, the Presbyterians had also split on theological issues that followed sectional
lines.
    31. "Christianity versus Philanthropy," *Southern Literary Messenger,* XXXIV (Septem-
ber–October, 1862), 574–76; Rev. Samuel Cassells, "The Relation of Justice to Benevolence in the Conduct of Society," *Southern Presbyterian Review,* VII (July, 1853), 90; "The
Charities of the Church," *Gospel Messenger,* XXVII (November, 1850), 233; Kuyendal,
Southern Enterprize, 79, 134–36.

from saving souls. He cautioned those seeking to walk in the path of Christ to remember that Jesus "proposed no legislative reforms," nor did he attend "a scientific, literary, or philanthropic assemblage." When Christian institutions mixed with "social and economic and material reforms, the world is left without a soul." Philanthropy as practiced by the Beechers and Phillipses of the North, the author concluded, "has been alike the canker worm of Christianity and the curse of the age. What care the philanthropists of Boston for the souls of men?" Referring to the relentless efforts of thrifty Bostonians to economize on their services to the poor, William Gilmore Simms condemned the impersonal treatment in which "the poor are made to assemble at set places, undergo examinations and be fed on soup." [32]

Catholics deeply distrusted what they saw as self-created, quasi-religious associations competing with the authority of the church. In their eyes, Protestant laymen had formed an unsanctified ministry "ignoring . . . the Church of Christ and its Sacraments for the sake of some machine of human invention." Holding up the American Sunday School Union as an example, the *Catholic Miscellany* condemned every "union of men" who claimed to translate the Scripture into social action. Conservatives of all denominations shared this concern. During the debate whether the Episcopal church should endorse the Young Men's Christian Association in Charleston, opponents expressed skepticism about voluntary associations. Although they performed social good, they were all of "modern date" without either biblical or historical precedent and threatened to evolve into a new and mongrelized denomination. [33]

Pressure to make the church an instrument of social change caused great ambivalence among clerics. Ministers of evangelical denominations especially deplored the decline of spirituality during the first half of the century and suspected that some deep corruption had entered the church. Haunted by the slavery issue, many southern ministers harbored deep reservations about involving their churches in questions of politics or economics and would have preferred to limit the benevolent activity of the church to spreading the Word among the poor and lost sheep of the city. Some felt repulsed by the corruption and dissipation of the most vicious among the poor and the lack of receptivity of the virtuous whose souls were as downtrodden as their bodies. Still others were

---

32. "Christianity versus Philanthropy," 574–76; Charleston *City Gazette*, February 4, 1831, quoted in William H. Pease and Jane H. Pease, *The Web of Progress: Private Values and Public Styles in Boston and Charleston, 1828–1843* (New York, 1985), 145.

33. *United States Catholic Miscellany*, April 18, 1857; "Young Men's Christian Association," *Southern Episcopalian*, IV (October, 1857), 364–66.

reluctant to tamper with God's mysterious ordering by providing material relief. Few visitors could enter the miserable homes of the underclass devoid of heat, furnishings, and food and leave not at least equally concerned about ameliorating the pain of their earthly existence as well as their eternal fate. The frenzy of activity among the various benevolent associations, many feared, diverted the generous from scrutiny of their own souls.

And the activities of these quasi-religious groups all required cash. To pay for their good intentions, charity organizations plunged deep into the money culture. To appeal to pleasure-loving Charlestonians, they sponsored frivolous parties and fairs and even held raffles and lotteries. Critics among the evangelicals decried this falling away from the path of Christ as fundraising pushed aside visitations to the poor, and bookkeeping skills became more important than winning souls.

Early in the nineteenth century, as more Baptists and Methodists found prosperity in southern towns, they inadvertently dissociated themselves from their churches' historic mission to the reviled of the earth, black slave and poor white. Their clergy adopted prevailing ecclesiastical fashion as more donned flowing robes to speak before increasingly well-dressed congregations. Methodists also succumbed to stained-glass windows and imported organs. In 1818, just before a period of inflation and recession, Charleston Baptists commissioned Robert Mills to design a spacious and elegant church that set the standard for good taste as the city moved into its Greek Revival period. All of these luxuries cost money and forced churches to assume mortgages. Raising money rather than preaching to the poor increasingly siphoned off the energy of ministers who expanded their canvass to include not just the pious but also the "outside citizens and generous sinners." [34]

The press of raising money to support benevolent enterprises opened up a new arena of competition among the denominations. Since Catholics attempted to operate a charity system completely free of city funds and city control, they aggressively solicited aid from private citizens. Even though much of the operating capital for their small orphanage and school came from the personal sacrifices of working-class Catholics, their energetic fund-raising in Charleston fueled the animosity of Protestant groups. Of all the southern churches, the Catholic faced the greatest challenge in financing its charities because it had the largest demand and the fewest resources. About half the priests assigned to urban dioceses left

34. Brooks Holyfield, *The Gentlemen Theologians: American Theology in Southern Culture, 1795–1860* (Durham, 1978), 7–25, 49.

after only a few years because of the "trials and privations of their poverty-stricken mission." John England, bishop of Georgia and the Carolinas, chastised Protestants for succumbing to the temptation to sell pews to pay for their luxuries and thus creating "a very painful and galling distinction" between the classes that caused "pride and conceit in one, and mortification and shame in the other where both ought to be on a footing of equality before their common maker."[35]

England, who probably built the "low and rough" St. Finbar's Cathedral from his own personal funds, hit on a particularly sensitive point.[36] Under the press of growing debt, quite a few evangelical churches joined Episcopalians in charging pew rents, a time-honored and to some minds invidious device belonging to the Old Regime rather than the new Republic that not only excluded many true believers but brought the lines of class from the street into the sanctuary. The wealthiest, who could pay as much as $500 a year, heard comfortable words from comfortable seats nearest the altar (presumably nearest to God); those with more modest incomes occupied the rear hoping to move up someday; the poor, who attended at no charge, sat where they were told, usually on hard benches on the periphery; and slaves in their gaudy finery sat in the galleries. Inclusion of the poor in traditional churches raised delicate political as well as spiritual questions. The balconies had historically and symbolically been designated for slaves, and the pews in the sanctuary were for rent only, so the white poor had to slip into "free benches," which advertised not only their poverty (their clothes usually did this) but also their marginality in relation to the rest of the white community.

Episcopalians, the Charleston denomination most articulate about the connection between religious virtue and social cohesion, tried to win more broad-based popularity by creating "free chapels." When Episcopal bishop Theodore Dehon failed in 1815 to have the city build a chapel next to the almshouse, he turned to the private citizens of Charleston and began soliciting pledges of $30 a year to build a church for the poor "in

35. *United States Catholic Miscellany,* April 18, 1857; "The Diurnal of the Right Reverend John England, First Bishop of Charleston, S.C., 1820–1823," in *Records of the American Catholic Historical Society* (Philadelphia, 1895), VI, 202–203; Patrick Carey, "Voluntaryism: An Irish Catholic Tradition," *Church History,* XLVIII (March, 1979), 50–51. Even before the influx of immigrants into the cities in the 1840s, Catholicism carried such a heavy social, not to mention political, stigma that many of the affluent, especially among the Germans, denied their faith and joined Lutheran churches (John J. O'Connell, *Catholicity in the Carolinas and Georgia* [1878; rpr. Spartanburg, 1972], 163).

36. "The Abiel Abbot Journals: A Yankee Preacher in Charleston Society, 1818–1827," ed. John H. Moore, *South Carolina Historical Magazine,* LXVIII (October, 1967), 235.

the most economical manner." He found Episcopalians preferred under-writing what they candidly called "cheap churches" to welcoming in their own the ragged, who stumbled through the liturgy and put greasy knee to velvet prayer stool. Many were quite happy to support efforts to bring the church closer to the poor as long as the church did not bring the poor closer to them.[37]

Struck down by yellow fever in 1817 when he was just forty-one, Dehon, who was from Boston, only lived to see a couple of pews dedicated to the use of the poor in the new Church of St. Paul in the suburb of Hampstead. However, his wife, Sarah Russell Dehon, daughter of wealthy Yankee merchant Nathaniel Russell, had shared his dream fully and worked tirelessly to establish the first Episcopal Free Chapel in America. In fact, Sarah Russell Dehon may well have actually been a driving force behind his commitment to improving the religious life of the poor. Educated in Medford, Massachusetts, in one of the most prestigious women's academies in America run by Ann Newton, the sister of artist Gilbert Stuart, she belonged to a family of forward looking women who were deeply involved in the benevolent life of Charleston. Her mother, Sarah Hopton Russell, whose brother and brother-in-law ran a large slave-trading firm before having to flee Charleston as Tory sympathizers, brought a large dowry to her marriage to Nathaniel Russell, a Rhode Island native who reigned over the city's merchant princes by the 1790s. The first president and leading benefactor of the New England Society, founded in 1819 to provide charity for northerners in need, Nathaniel Russell enjoyed a well deserved reputation for good works, and so did his wife. In 1813, Sarah Hopton Russell and her sister, Mary Christiana Hopton Gregorie, provided leadership in the formation of the Ladies Benevolent Society, a pioneering association dedicated to providing home health care to the sick poor. Responding to the increased suffering in the port city caused by the War of 1812, this nondenominational group adopted as their motto "I was sick and you visited me." As their acquaintance with the lives of the white poor grew more intimate, the women of the society observed that the indigent suffered from spiritual as well as material destitution. In a reversal of the customary evolution of reform societies, where the souls of the poor were traditionally of more interest than their material well-being, selected members of the Ladies Benevolent Society seeing this need formed in 1818 the Charleston Fe-

37. *Gospel Messenger*, XI (January, 1834), 12–15; Stephen Elliott, *Journal of the Proceedings of the Twenty-Seventh Annual Convention of the Protestant Episcopal Church of Georgia* (Marietta, Ga., 1849), 9; Christopher E. Gadsden, *An Essay on the Reverend Theodore Dehon*, 197, 170.

male Domestic Missionary Society, dedicated to bringing the comforting words of the church to the outcast. Already enjoying a reputation for both her prudence and piety, Sarah Russell stepped forward as the missionary society's primary benefactress and enabled her "pious and zealous" friends to recruit the newly ordained Reverend Edward Phillips to start an outreach ministry in a rented room that welcomed both black and white.[38]

In 1824, Theodore Dehon's successor, Bishop Nathaniel Bowen, consecrated St. Stephen's Free Chapel, built on a Guignard Street lot donated by Sarah Russell. By 1828, Rev. Phillips had provided religious instruction to more than 300 young people, baptized 225, and confirmed 56. In recognition of this quiet and productive work among the city poor, Charlestonian Frederick Kohne bequeathed $10,000 to the mission in 1829. The mission reduced its debt, established a library with more than four hundred volumes, and secured a burial ground to spare their communicants the ignominy of the unconsecrated paupers' field.[39]

With the founding of what is widely considered the first "free" Episcopal Church in America, a dual parochial system evolved in Charleston with satellite urban missions administering sacraments from baptism to burial to both blacks and whites and operating day and Sunday schools for children of the poor but having no elected vestry of their own. The board of directors of the Charleston Female Domestic Missionary Society continued to underwrite the mission and direct its operations in consultation with the rectors of the three local Episcopal churches who served as the board of trustees for St. Stephen's. The services retained the traditional liturgy that was thought to contain all the lessons of "evangelical morality" needed by the "poor and lowly," but were made more accessible by additional scriptural instruction. Charleston's devastating fire of 1835 claimed this first building, but an even more substantial structure was constructed on Anson Street.[40]

With the resignation of Edward Phillips, several interim missionaries

38. Albert Sidney Thomas, *A Historical Account of the Protestant Episcopal Church in South Carolina, 1820–1957* (Columbia, S.C., 1957), 14, 261; Charles Brooks, *History of the Town of Medford, Middlesex County, Massachusetts* (Boston, 1886), 298–99; W. Robert Higgins, "Charles Town Merchants and Factors Dealing in the External Negro Trade, 1735–1775," *South Carolina Historical Magazine*, LXV (October, 1964), 206; William Way, *History of the New England Society of Charleston, South Carolina, for One Hundred Years, 1819–1919* (Charleston, S.C., 1920), 12, 25–30. Sarah Hopton Russell (1753–1832) and Sarah Russell Dehon (1792–1857) are both memorialized in St. Stephen's Chapel.

39. Thomas, *The Protestant Episcopal Church in South Carolina*, 262–63.

40. *Ibid.; Gospel Messenger*, XI (January, 1834), 12–15.

served until Paul Trapier, who had revived churches in St. Andrew's and St. James's parishes outside of Charleston, was "induced" to accept the call to come to St. Stephen's in 1834. Trapier obviously found the invitation one he could not refuse. Two years earlier, he had married Theodore Dehon's seventeen-year-old daughter. Since Sarah Russell had died that same year, the young couple moved directly into the magnificent Federal-style mansion on Meeting Street (built by Nathaniel Russell in 1808) to be with Sarah Dehon Trapier's mother, Sarah Russell Dehon, who had returned to her family home upon Bishop Dehon's death. It was within this house, perhaps the finest private home in the South, that plans to spiritually elevate Charleston's poor had coalesced. Sarah Russell Dehon and her sister, Alicia Hopton Russell Middleton (wife of Arthur Middleton of Stono), sat on the board of directors that oversaw Trapier's work and encouraged him to expand his efforts into the northern reaches of the peninsula, where a mixed population of poor whites and free blacks desperately needed his services. In 1839, the Female Domestic Missionary Society opened St. John's Mission in Hampstead, which was heavily subsidized by Sarah Russell Dehon, a "mother in Israel."[41]

Trapier reluctantly left mission work in 1840 to accept the prestigious and many times more lucrative position as rector of St. Michael's Church at the "opposite extreme of Charleston," and regretted it for the rest of his life. His ministry to the privileged became embroiled in endless conflicts with the powerful and independent vestry, who no doubt presented a vastly greater challenge to his authority than had been the case at St. Stephen's. He later remembered that "however salutary the discipline of humiliation may have been to me, I should have been spared a great deal of mental suffering had I remained in my comparatively humble sphere among a people who were becoming more and more attached to me and deriving apparent benefit from my labours among them."[42]

Trapier's eventual successor at St. Stephen's was one of those rare urban missionaries who retained his youthful optimism despite low pay and the arduous task of bringing light into so much darkness. A Dartmouth graduate born in New Hampshire, Cranmore Wallace spent a decade teaching in a remote South Carolina school before moving to Charleston as principal of a girls' academy. Ordained in his mid-thirties by the Episcopal church, he served as the rector of the Episcopal Church Home, as well as missionary-in-charge at St. Stephen's. He enjoyed great success

41. Paul Trapier, *Incidents in My Life: The Autobiography of the Reverend Paul Trapier, S.T.D.,* ed. George W. Williams (Charleston, S.C., 1954), 62, 19–21; Thomas, *The Protestant Episcopal Church in South Carolina,* 222–23, 263.
42. Trapier, *Incidents in My Life,* 20–21.

among the humble of Charleston because he understood they had "a pride at least equal to that of the rich." The little chapel often overflowed at Wallace's service because he modified the formal liturgy and experimented with extemporaneous discourse for those who could neither read nor respond to the elegant language of the Book of Common Prayer. He found success with the catechism devised by Paul Trapier for use with illiterate slaves. Energetic and selfless, he made over a thousand visits to the sick poor during a typical six-month period. He shamelessly pursued the wealthy all over the city whenever a widow needed rent money or a child a pair of shoes. This northerner not only secured contributions from the gentry but won their respect. Always "quick to detect lying tears and sharp in reprimanding the false and unworthy," Wallace, one Charleston journal noted at his death in 1860, was "the favorite almoner of the rich."[43]

The example of the three Sarahs—Sarah Hopton Russell, Sarah Russell Dehon, and Sarah Dehon Trapier, who also became involved with the Ladies Benevolent Society—illustrates the depth of involvement by women in the religious benevolence of Charleston. Wealthy women gave generously to charity and used their social connections to win support for their favorite causes. Those from the middling classes, wives of clerks and printers, for instance, worked more directly with their churches, doing the hard labor of raising money among those with the least to spare. Charleston women of leisure did much more than busy themselves in a whirl of hanging crepe paper and arranging flowers for charity fairs. They engaged in substantial projects with important though seldom dramatic results for the sick, abused, uneducated, ill-clothed, and unemployed. But what impact participation in public activities had upon these women personally remains unclear. Most likely they enjoyed whatever power came with association and relished friendships with one another. Many, like Mary Smith Grimké, mother of eleven, probably found temporary relief from irresolvable domestic quarrels. Scant evidence exists, however, to suggest that Charleston women gained any new "consciousness" or insights into the restrictions upon their own lives in this decidedly patriarchal society. In fact, seeing white seamstresses bent, blind, and alone, made some married women reflect upon their own good fortune. Individual women found opportunity for public action as leaders of those incorporated voluntary associations through which they enjoyed a legal standing to hold, buy, and sell property that they did not often

43. Cranmore Wallace, "Reports of Charleston City Missions," *Southern Episcopalian,* II (August, 1855), 289; Charleston *Courier,* February 4, 1860.

have in their private lives.[44] Despite "networks" with other women and expansion of their "spheres," no glimmerings of abolitionism or feminism (as it is currently understood) come to light. What does come clear is that in their benevolent lives women did not operate in a different moral universe than men. Their motives, as they expressed them, were both religious and patriotic. Their perceived interests scarcely differed from those of the larger culture. Women raised money for incorrigible sailors, and men established schools for orphan girls.[45]

Unlike the experience of most southern cities, Charleston's system of private benevolence and public poor relief coalesced during the colonial period before the roles of men and women became as rigidly defined as in the nineteenth century. Women had the private means to participate in benevolence because through their fathers and husbands, they shared in the city's extraordinary wealth. For example, in 1775, only five estates in Boston were valued at £1,000, whereas in Charleston during the same year there were a total of thirty-six, of which four were the estates of widows.[46] By the 1820s, women's associations competed successfully for charitable dollars with venerable male groups such as the South Carolina Society. The idea of poverty as a problem of individual morality rather than God's will gained acceptance early in the nineteenth century just as the notion of a separate woman's sphere found expression. Female nature, pious and nurturing, seemingly suited women perfectly for visiting the poor, tending the ill, and distributing religious tracts, but men retained control of institutions and public policy. The religious rather than the political aspects of helping the poor did open the door to women as active participants in civic life. When piety declined as the leading force behind benevolence during the depression of the 1840s and the city government once again superseded voluntary associations as the most important source of local relief, the role of women in the public life of the community waned.

The Charleston experience was unique. In small southern towns founded after the Revolution, such as Petersburg, Virginia, an indifferent local government considered both poverty and its relief a woman's problem.[47] New Orleans supported charitable institutions but did not place as much public value on the practice of benevolence. In Savannah and

44. Lori D. Ginzberg, *Women and the Work of Benevolence: Morality, Politics, and Class in the Nineteenth-Century United States* (New Haven, 1990), 48–53.

45. For a different view, see Susan Lebsock, *The Free Women of Petersburg: Status and Culture in a Southern Town* (New York, 1984), 142–43, 195–236.

46. Jaher, *The Urban Establishment,* 326.

47. Lebsock, *Free Women of Petersburg,* 203.

Richmond, busy merchants and other town leaders dedicated themselves exclusively to their businesses and left the nurturing aspects of charity to women. Charleston men, on the other hand, had time on their hands. After 1820, the port's slack economy threw even the ambitious into "tiresome lives of half-employment."[48] Sitting on boards of charitable institutions, investigating matters of public health, or presiding over benevolent societies filled the days of prominent Charlestonians with meaningful and respected occupation.

It was from this milieu of voluntaristic benevolent activity, it should be remembered, that abolitionists and agitators for women's rights, Sarah and Angelina Grimké, emerged. They formed their opinions and developed their sensibilities in a Charleston home filled with slaves, among frivolous friends, with parents who combined the Puritan ethic with the industry of the French Huguenot.

A shocking character in Sarah Grimké's rather thinly disguised "testimony," drawn from accounts of her family and friends, was a gentlewoman who weekly visited the white poor across town with baskets of food and Christian sentiments, and with the same regularity beat her black servants until they bled. Though according to Grimké this person enjoyed repute as "a charitable woman and tender hearted to the poor," over a period of time she had ordered several teeth extracted from a slave girl's mouth and fashioned an unspeakably horrid spiked collar for her to wear around her neck. If this woman had suffered from some terrible perversity and kept her victim locked in a dormer room, Grimké and history may have been more understanding, but her wrath fell upon the black seamstress of the house. Day in and day out, the mistress gazed upon the girl's "lacerated and bleeding back, her mutilated mouth and heavy iron collar" with no apparent remorse.[49] Family friends (including some of the city's most distinguished and benevolent) passed this servant without comment; her owner exhibited no shame. Instead—and this is what enraged the Grimké sisters—because of her good works to the poor, she deported herself as if assured a place in heaven and enjoyed the praise of local society.

Sarah Grimké wrote with particular venom of those slaveholding matrons who engaged in benevolence, those "Janus-faced women" dedi-

48. The languid economy continued to enervate enterprising men throughout the 1850s. See James J. Pettigrew to W. S. Pettigrew, March 12, 1853, quoted in Robert N. Olsberg, "A Government of Class and Race: William Henry Trescot and the South Carolina Chivalry, 1860–1865" (Ph.D. dissertation, University of South Carolina, 1972), 30.

49. Testimony of Sarah Grimké, in Theodore Dwight Weld, *American Slavery as It Is: Testimony of a Thousand Witnesses* (1839; rpr. New York, 1969), 22–23.

cated to winning the affection of the white poor while tyrannical or negligent toward their own slaves and children. In them one can now see the twin threads that comprised the warp and woof of southern society, pulling here, binding there, and coming unraveled in another spot. The contrasting strands of benevolence lay alongside indifference; generosity merged with rapaciousness; the beautiful interspersed with the shabby and made the old "slave capital" of Charleston respected by some and loathed by others. What the sisters Grimké could not abide about their hometown (or their family) was the easy accommodation to the complex mixture of good and evil in the human heart.

Slaveholding blunted southern sensibilities only selectively. Contrary to many northerners' contention that owning slaves tended to "harden the heart, to dry up all the fountains of human sympathy, to make one callous to the wrongs and the woes of those around him," slavery coexisted with moral reform in the same way that the benevolent Charleston lady could, without feeling intellectual or moral contradiction, beat her slave in the morning and minister to the poor in the afternoon. Grimké's account vividly portrays a paradox of the southern system, where good coexisted comfortably with evil and occasionally rose above it.[50]

Angelina peeled back the layers of morality, piety, benevolence, and noblesse oblige to show that beneath the riddle of paradoxical southern behavior was the question of control: "These seeming contradictions vanish when we consider that over *them* she possessed no arbitrary power, they were always presented to her mind as unfortunate sufferers, towards whom her sympathies most freely flowed; she was ever ready to wipe the tears from *their* eyes, and open wider her purse for *their* relief, but the others were her *vassals* thrust down by public opinion beneath her feet." Angelina further condemned a respectable woman, "the head of the fashionable elite" professing religion during the revivals of 1825, who held prayer meetings, family vespers, and her own thrice daily devotionals in the same room where she laid cowhide on her slaves. The place that was hushed for evening prayer had echoed with screams only hours before.[51]

Mary Smith Grimké was considered by her daughters "a very devout woman of rather narrow views and undemonstrative in her affections"

50. Charles G. Parsons, *An Inside View of Slavery* (Savannah, 1874), 153; Robert Bunch, British consul to Charleston, quoted in Laura White, "The South in the 1850s as Seen by the British Consuls," *Journal of Southern History,* I (February, 1935), 33; Gerda Lerner, *The Grimké Sisters of South Carolina: Rebels Against Slavery* (Boston, 1967), 1–67.

51. Testimony of Angelina G. Weld, in Weld, *American Slavery as It Is,* 52–57.

toward her family. She provides a perfect example of the pious church-woman who found both approbation and escape in her ministrations to the poor. In contrast to her husband, state supreme court justice John Faucheraud Grimké, who developed over the course of their married life into an exceedingly cultured gentleman and respected legal scholar, Mary Grimké's large family consumed all her energies and prevented her from pursuing her passion for serious reading in theology. Over twenty years, she bore fourteen children and raised eleven to adulthood. As her domestic responsibilities multiplied, she became increasingly "nervous, exhausted and irritable," constantly feeling she lacked control over both children and slaves. "God is a God of order," she reminded her youngest daughter, Angelina, "and cannot approve of violence and discord." Mary Grimké was desperate for order and peace in her own life as well as in the cosmos, but the louder she shrieked and the greater the punishments she imposed, the less respect the children showed her. The slaves mimicked the young heirs, and as Angelina later admitted, "The servants were just what the family was," rivaling the children in rudeness and disobedience. Sarah and Angelina blamed Mary Grimké for their personal unhappiness and withheld their affection from her. Sarah criticized not only her failure to acknowledge the "deplorable state of our family" but her imperviousness when confronted with "her own faults" and "how miserably she has brought us up." Only at the end of Sarah's life did she feel her heart "very sore" when remembering the harsh manner, "destitute of the spirit of love and forbearance," with which she had dealt with her unhappy mother.[52]

Too conscience-stricken to take to her couch and lose herself in devotional reading, Mary Grimké ironically found comfort beside the sickbeds of the poor and in the dark cells of sinful women. At least once a week she closed the door of her troubled home on Meeting Street and embarked on a mission to fulfill "man's duty to God" by visiting her unfortunate neighbors as a member of the Ladies Benevolent Society. This group, thought to be the oldest woman's organization in continuous operation, is notable for its early attempt to deliver home health care in a systematic and "scientific" fashion. Its members, mostly wealthy and well-connected Episcopalians, determined from the outset not to be another mere auxiliary financed and directed by men; their charter specifically states that the treasurer must be an unmarried woman. Local minis-

52. Catherine Birney, *The Grimké Sisters: Sarah and Angelina Grimké, the First American Women Advocates of Abolition and Woman's Rights* (1885; rpr. Westport, Conn., 1977), 14–16.

ters—Protestant, Catholic, and Jewish—preached a special sermon every February and donated the collection to the society. Both men and women who practiced charity beyond the grave often named the Ladies Benevolent Society to administer their legacies to the urban poor. By 1861, it possessed an endowment prudently invested in local stocks that yielded $4,000 annual income. Pushing outside the boundaries of their own parlors, society members often met in the public spaces traditionally reserved for men, usually in the commissioners' conference room of the Charleston Orphan House.[53]

To counter the criticism every benevolent group encountered, that their gifts only encouraged idleness, the 1820 annual report of the Ladies Benevolent Society insisted that "every system of charity, which takes the rich among the poor, must be particularly efficacious and beneficial, it improves the condition of one party, the feelings of the other, and the virtues of both." Emphasizing head over heart in their dealings with the suffering poor, visitors rotated the cases among themselves to prevent forming attachments that might cloud their judgment. Tough-minded and unwilling to support those feigning illness, the ladies demanded a doctor's certificate before extending aid so they might be spared the potentially embarrassing task of surprise visits to see whether the symptoms were genuine. More than just a nineteenth-century Junior League, the society personally visited the virtuous and profane, white and free black. One chilling February night, Sarah Russell ventured deep into the very heart of the urban darkness, down to the tenderloin district, to answer the call of a dying prostitute to take care of her child. In 1835, Mary Grimké personally oversaw the care of twenty-four patients and distributed $110 in goods.[54]

Seeing the state of abandoned women who once had comfortable lives,

53. From 1814 to 1828, the collections from St. Michael's alone totalled nearly $2000 (Margaret S. Middleton, "The Ladies Benevolent Society of Charleston, South Carolina," in *Yearbook of the City of Charleston, 1941* (Charleston, S.C., 1942), 216, 218; "Ladies Benevolent Society," in *Yearbook of the City of Charleston, 1896* (Charleston, S.C., 1897), 414–18).

54. "Ladies Benevolent Society," in *Yearbook of the City of Charleston, 1896*, 414–18. At a meeting at Mary Grimké's house in 1835, members of the Ladies Benevolent Society received notice that J. M. Hopkins had set up a trust for the sick and infirm among the free blacks of Charleston and its suburbs to be distributed by the society. The same rules applied to both races, but the free blacks had to have an endorsement by a "responsible" white person. Since the Ladies Benevolent Society worked only in the city, they shared the responsibility with the Female Charitable Association of Charleston Neck (Ladies Benevolent Society Minutes, December 15, 1835, typescript in South Caroliniana Library, University of South Carolina; *Southern Episcopalian*, IV [December, 1857], 488).

still owning a silver spoon, a leather-bound volume, or a superannuated slave, must have deeply affected these privileged women and provoked reflection about the vulnerability of all women's lives. Surely Mary Grimké empathized with a patient such as Mrs. Cowle, who raised and educated two children "by the labour of her own hands" and was abandoned by them to suffer alone with the festering ulcers of leprosy. Denounced by her daughters as a miserable failure as a mother, Mary Grimké won high praise from her coworkers in benevolence as an "active, efficient, *devoted* officer." Upon her death in 1839, she was eulogized in the Ladies Benevolent Society minutes as "descriminating in her intercourse with the class of people with whom she had to deal, firm and decided in her dealings with them, [and] untiring in her visits." The eulogy continued, "While she ministered to their bodily wants, the concerns of the immortal soul were never forgotten & works of Christian counsel never failed to accompany those of sympathy and kindness. Such was our friend!"[55]

The model of the Ladies Benevolent Society stayed very much in the minds of the Grimké sisters. Somehow the kindness and magnanimity shown to powerless whites magnified the community's contrasting negligence and meanspiritedness toward slaves. Almost ten years after leaving Charleston, Angelina, herself once a member of the Ladies Benevolent Society, recalled with bitterness the story of a visiting commissioner who "allowed" a free wife of one of her slaves to leave her employment to nurse her husband during a long illness and offered her no compensation, when it was the policy of the society to pay a nurse's wages to families of poor whites so they might not suffer loss of income. Angelina confided to her journal that she wanted to dedicate herself to "exposing the awful sin of professors of religion."[56]

While Angelina "starved on the cold water of Episcopacy," her brother, Thomas Smith Grimké, drank deeply and was refreshed by the High Church theology of St. Phillip's Episcopal Church. Sarah, Angelina, and Thomas adhered to the "old religion" of salvation by works and were held tightly by the force described by their biographer, Catherine Birney, as the "iron bands of a religion that taught the crucifixion of every natural feeling as the most acceptable offering to a stern and relentless God." Sarah's charitable work, visitations to the sick, and even kindnesses toward family members during her Charleston years were calcu-

55. "Ladies Benevolent Society, Annual Report," *Southern Evangelical Intelligencer,* II (1820–21), 244–47, quoted in Dann, "Humanitarianism Reform," 149; Ladies Benevolent Society Minutes, December 22, 1855; Ladies Benevolent Society Minutes, July 29, 1839, quoted in Middleton, "Ladies Benevolent Society," 229.

56. Birney, *Grimké Sisters,* 43.

lated "to avert from herself the wrath of her Maker." The Grimkés embraced an ideal for a Christian America that was rooted in adherence to the ancient Scriptures rather than in any creations of the modern age and drew upon the truths of the Protestant Reformation rather than the revelations of the Enlightenment.[57]

Thomas Grimké remained the beloved brother even though he held many slaves. His usually uncompromising sisters seemed to accept this flaw in him in ways they could not in their aged mother. Unlike Mary Grimké, he did not argue with them but always promised to explore the subject at some future date. They believed Thomas, who maintained a large plantation south of the city and thought it was his paternal duty to care for these workers, while they insisted that their mother clung to the five servants inherited from her husband strictly through perversity. Upon Thomas' unexpected death, Sarah and Angelina wrote a sketch of his life in which they quoted, without irony, the Charleston Bar Association's praise of him as a "kind and patient master."[58]

Thomas Grimké had received one of the best classical educations available to Americans of his time. Industrious and deeply pious even as a young man, his apparent superiority over his classmates at the College of Charleston encouraged his parents to send him to Yale. While in New Haven, he won the friendship and admiration of Timothy Dwight. Their association undoubtedly influenced Grimké's decision to enter the ministry when he graduated in 1807. His father, however, pressed the young scholar to choose the more lucrative legal profession. The elder Grimké believed that in the event of his early death, the entire family would turn to Thomas for financial support. In obedience to the patriarch's wishes, he laid aside his dreams and diligently studied law with Langdon Cheves, but "literature, benevolence and piety" remained his lifelong passions. Grimké found the practice of law steeped in "fraud and injustice," and devoted whatever time he could to pro bono legal assistance to the poor of the city. In partnership for a time with Robert Y. Hayne, Grimké developed a lucrative practice and faithfully gave not a tenth but a half of his income to charity. Too devoted to the principles of law to make any exceptions for the circumstances of those who stood before him when he sat on the bench, he sometimes secretly reimbursed poor persons for the amount of the judgment he had imposed upon them.[59]

57. *Ibid.*, 72, 27.

58. [Sarah and Angelina Grimké], "A Sketch of Mr. Grimké's Life," *Calumet*, II (January–February, 1835), 137. See, for example: Thomas Smith Grimké, *Address at the Dedication of the . . . Depository for Bible Tracts* (Charleston, S.C., n.d.).

59. [Sarah and Angelina Grimké], "Mr. Grimké's Life," 133–34; James H. Smith,

Thomas Smith Grimké devoted his life to the law and reforming his hometown with the same passion his sister Sarah summoned in attacking it. In his social thought, Thomas Smith Grimké seems almost as radical as his sisters. Yet where they alienated, he attracted; where they fell out of favor with family and friends, he won election to local office and enjoyed national popularity as an advocate of avant-garde causes such as world peace, temperance, Sunday schools, and educational reform. Combining "the simplicity of the child with the moral courage of the martyr," the genial and winsome Grimké won the respect if not the total approbation of the community. Unlike his sisters, who felt isolated and alone because they eschewed "scenes of sinful frivolity and amusement" so commonly identified with Charleston, Thomas, aesthetic in his habits but congenitally full of "zest and unvary'd cheerfulness," found a place in the public life of the city. His work and experience illustrate that Charleston nurtured another dimension of discourse beyond the gossip at the St. Cecilia Ball and chitchat of Race Week.[60]

The conflicts Grimké's sisters had in the community and in the family were, of course, related to their gender and the rigid local interpretation of the role of women. But the difference in the experiences of brother and sisters also suggests that the city tolerated criticisms only within certain parameters. In the early years of the Republic, southerners might concede the evil of slavery as long as it was paired with the evil of poverty as two equally intractable and historic problems of mankind. As late as 1859, Baptist minister Basil Manly, Sr., pleaded with the American Tract Society to curb the "restless faction" of abolitionists who insisted that slavery be condemned as a sin of the human will instead of a symptom of "the present fallen state of humanity."[61] Abolitionists like O. B. Frothingham never relented. Pauperism, he contended, "is an old fact resulting from

---

Eulogium on the Life and Character of Thomas S. Grimké. Delivered March 10, 1835. Before the Literary and Philosophical Society of South Carolina (Charleston, S.C., 1835), 5; Adrienne Koch, "Two Charlestonians in Pursuit of Truth: The Grimké Brothers," *South Carolina Historical Magazine*, LXIX (July, 1968), 160–61.

60. [Sarah and Angelina Grimké], "Mr. Grimké's Life," 134; "The Honorable Thomas Smith Grimké," *Calumet*, II (January–February, 1835), 132.

61. Moderates of the New York–based American Tract Society pursued a conciliatory position with the southern branches, and suppressed the radical faction until the abolitionists bolted and heated up their presses in Boston with fiery indictments. Clinging to the ties with the national group, southerners censored unwanted materials (South Carolina Branch of the American Tract Society, *Reports and Resolutions in Reference to the Action taken on Slavery* [Charleston, S.C., 1857], 4–5; Charleston *Mercury*, January 7, 1859; Griffin, *Their Brothers' Keepers*, 181–83).

man's ignorance, error and general imperfection, and . . . from its nature involves no direct Guilt. Slavery is essential Guilt."[62]

Unlike his sisters, Grimké held out the hope for social change even among the hard-bitten sinners of their hometown and focused his attention upon individual and curable failings. Dubbed the "Father of the temperance movement in South Carolina" and author of its constitution, he saw the attitude of Charlestonians change from scorn to enthusiasm for his cause. He described the voluntary societies of his day as indomitable machines for "remodeling public opinion and changing public feeling on many points." The associations' power came from their basis in Christianity, "the mightiest system for the regeneration of the nations that man has ever conceived."[63]

As a young man, he proved himself willing to "throw the gauntlet in the very teeth of public opinion" by condemning dueling. Despite his radical ideas, he escaped ridicule, except from elegant Charlestonians, who laughed at the shabby clothing he wore in self-denial and to save money for charity. Like most Charlestonians deeply engaged in the national moral reform societies, he opposed Nullification but was unique in his abilities to dissect its arguments. After an impassioned critique of the "sophistries" of its supporters in the state senate, Grimké faced threats at home. Sending his wife and six sons from town, he defiantly sat on his piazza waiting for the mob. Seeing him unmoved by their harrying hoots and catcalls, the mob lost interest and drifted into the chilly winter night.[64]

Grimké's experience with the rowdy Nullifiers paled in comparison with the viciousness of the academic world when he challenged the emphasis that Yale and other leading colleges placed upon the classics as symptoms of an antiquated and aristocratic system that excluded talented sons of the poor who lacked training in ancient languages. Oblivious to the reputation that he was gaining as a troublesome "educational gadfly," he pressed for other changes in speeches he made across the nation. His advocacy of the study of American history and literature attracted much more interest than his argument for the return to a Bible requirement as a guide to moral life. Although Grimké dabbled in local politics and took strong positions on controversial issues, he always saw himself as an individual working out his own salvation, not a "public man." He confided to a friend: "I have lived in private life, and for private life . . . and I wish

---

62. O. B. Frothingham, "Pauperism and Slavery," *Liberty Bell,* XIII (1853), 169–70.
63. [Sarah and Angelina Grimké], "Mr. Grimké's Life," 134–35.
64. *Ibid.,* 136–37; Birney, *Grimké Sisters,* 102.

no public honors." A founding member of the American Peace Society, Thomas Grimké modeled his life upon the lessons of the Sermon on the Mount. Most important for understanding his benevolent and charitable career was his strong attachment to the doctrine of the Atonement. "Deeply feeling the depravity and corruption of the old nature in himself," his sister wrote, using his revised method of spelling, "he lookd to the blood of Jesus Christ to cleanse him from all sin." Feeling himself a sinner at heart, he had enormous compassion for those who also faltered. Christian community, he believed, was inclusive. He shared with his sisters enormous sympathy for the Cherokees in Alabama and Georgia, and mourned with many Charlestonians in his reformist circle in the 1830s when Andrew Jackson's policies sent them on their Trail of Tears to inhospitable lands in Oklahoma.[65] In 1835, Grimké contracted cholera in Ohio while on a lecture tour advocating his educational reforms among the new states. His brother Frederick, a judge in Ohio, reached his brother at the moment of his death and declared that forty-eight-year-old Thomas had "sacrificed himself in the cause of Religion and Philanthropy."[66] His eulogists bemoaned his passing before his time, but in fact his time had already passed.

Andrew Jackson's election in 1828 signaled America's move from the age of humanitarianism to the age of capital. Southerners, warned one Nashville orator speaking to a local benevolent society, should brace themselves for a change; they were spinning inexorably toward "a fast age—a mercenary age—its wing is lightning, its ruling spirit gain." Contrary to Thomas Grimké's optimistic prediction, the true spirit of the times would be grounded in the ethic of competition rather than Christian cooperation.[67]

The triumph of capitalism, with its emphasis on free labor and individual agency, also redefined the problem of poverty in ways that thrust more responsibility upon the poor to help themselves than on the rich to share their good fortune. During the 1820s, charity lost much of its direct connection with Christianity in the North and became more an instru-

65. Smith, *Life and Character of Thomas Grimké,* 8; [Sarah and Angelina Grimké], "Mr. Grimké's Life," 133–38. When asked how would he defend Charleston if he were mayor and the city were to be attacked by pirates, Grimké said he would "call together the Sunday-school children and lead them in procession to meet the pirates, who would be at once subdued by the sight" (Birney, *Grimké Sisters,* 103).

66. Koch, "Two Charlestonians," 167.

67. John M. Bright, *Charity: A Lecture Before the Robertson Association, Nashville, Tenn., October 14, 1858* (Nashville, 1858), 7.

ment of public policy than personal salvation. Poverty as a "positive good" even gained credence among those who believed that forging a Christian America required not only love and brotherhood among its citizens but also self-control. The whip of hunger would, according to those who believed in the rationality of labor, force the idle and licentious to drop the bottle to feed themselves. Charleston's Ladies Benevolent Society operated on the premise that "by doing too much, the independence and energies of the object are destroyed." The South embarked uncertainly on its own poorly marked path toward bourgeois capitalism.[68]

That hardheaded hunchback Thomas Cooper rejected "idiot sensibility" and "morbid tenderness of mind" toward the poor as "the ethics of sentimental novelists." A report from Philadelphia incorporated with great zest by Cooper, the English-born president of South Carolina College, in his textbook *Lectures on Political Economy* (1828), concluded that the poor laws not only had a deleterious effect upon those assisted but also removed the impetus for private charity. After years of reading, thinking, and fretting about one of the most pressing issues of the day, Cooper concluded that "the mischiefs of poverty can be counteracted by no form of charity dispensed by the rich, but by the conduct of the poor alone." Salvation of the poor lay not with bleeding hearts of the religious or even well-meant intervention of politicians but in the time-tested instrument of capital accumulation, the savings bank with its compounded interest and friendly advisers. "In this country, there is no man so poor as not to be able to invest a small weekly sum" in a savings bank, Cooper argued. The poor needed the habits of "temperance, of saving, and self denial."[69]

As the antislavery reformists began calling for immediate abolition, southern churchmen like the Reverend Thomas H. Taylor at the 1830 diocesan convention of South Carolina urged both clergy and laymen to

68. "Regulations for Visiting Committee," Ladies Benevolent Society Constitution of 1852, copy in South Caroliniana Library, University of South Carolina.

69. Thomas Cooper, *Lectures on the Elements of Political Economy* (Columbia, S.C., 1826), 308–11. Cooper, a man of contradictions, had a varied career. Disillusioned with the violent aspects of the French Revolution, he sought asylum in America, where he hoped to establish a utopian community with his friend and fellow Englishman Joseph Priestly. An outspoken Jeffersonian, he was punished under the Sedition Act, later gained and lost a judgeship, and gained and lost a teaching position. When he was named a professor of political economy at South Carolina College in 1820, he promptly acquired slaves. During his tenure as president of that institution, he maintained a precarious balance between his unpopular outspoken anticlericism views and his well-received attacks upon banks, corporations, and monopolies (Paul K. Conkin, *Prophets of Prosperity: America's First Political Economists* [Bloomington, Ind., 1980], 142–47).

inquire more closely into the needs of the white "labouring class."[70] During the next generation, Charlestonians shifted their focus from the religious and moral aspects of poverty to the political and economic implications of rising numbers of white paupers. The concept of "Christian charity" or benevolence that had largely enjoyed a suprapolitical status transcending both sectional politics and local prejudices was dragooned into active service on both those fronts.

70. "Diocesan Convention of South Carolina," *Gospel Messenger,* VI (February, 1830), 88.

Sarah Russell Dehon, 1792–1857
  Courtesy Historic Charleston Foundation

Mrs. John Faucheraud Grimké (Mary Moore Smith, 1764–1839) (watercolor on ivory, 1791)

Christopher G. Memminger, 1803–1888
From Henry D. Capers, *The Life and Times of C. G. Memminger* (Richmond, 1893).
Courtesy South Caroliniana Library, University of South Carolina

W. Jefferson Bennett, 1808–1874
From Henry D. Capers, *The Life and Times of C. G. Memminger* (Richmond, 1893).
Courtesy South Caroliniana Library, University of South Carolina

Bishop John England, 1786–1842
From Peter Keenan Guilday, *Life and Times of John England, First Bishop of Charleston*
(New York, 1927). Courtesy South Caroliniana Library, University of South Carolina

Charleston Orphan House, after renovations of 1854–1855
Courtesy South Caroliniana Library, University of South Carolina

Girls' High School and Normal School, built 1858–1859, later renamed the Memminger School.
From Arthur Mazÿck and Gene Waddell, *Charleston in 1883* (Easley, S.C., 1983).
Courtesy South Caroliniana Library, University of South Carolina

Roper Hospital
From *Ballou's Pictorial Drawing Room Companion,* August 8, 1857, from the Waring
Historical Library Collection, Medical University of South Carolina, Charleston, S.C.

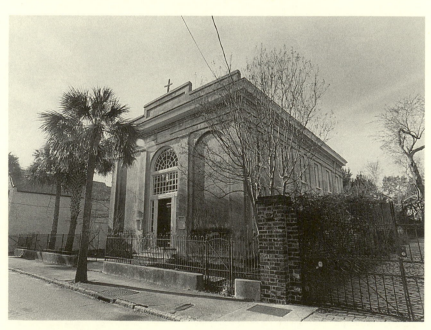

St. Stephen's Episcopal Chapel, built in 1835
Photograph by George Bellows, Jr.

The Cathedral of St. John and St. Finbar, 1850–54 (etching by Patrick Keely)
From *Harper's New Monthly Magazine*, XV (June, 1857). Courtesy Carolina Art Association/Gibbes Museum of Art

Nathaniel Russell House
Photograph by Louis Schwartz. Courtesy Historic Charleston Foundation

𝕿𝕳𝕴𝕾 𝕴𝕹𝕯𝕰𝕹𝕿𝖀𝕽𝕰, made the *third* ———— day of *October* —— in the year of our Lord one thousand eight hundred and *twenty two,* —— and in the *forty seventh* ———— year of AMERICAN INDEPENDENCE, WITNESSETH, That *John* —— *Fordham* — of *Charleston* —————— aged *Eleven years* —————— by and with the consent of *Rich W Cogdell C.O.* —— hath placed and bound *himself* to the Commissioners of the Orphan-House, (for the time being) established in the said City of Charleston, in the State aforesaid, and by an ordinance of the honorable the City Council, ratified on the 18th day of October, in the year of our Lord 1790, entitled, "An Ordinance for the establishment of an Orphan House in the City of Charleston, for the purpose of supporting and educating poor orphan children, and those of poor, distressed and disabled parents, who are unable to support and maintain them," to be subject to all such ordinances, rules and regulations, as now are, or hereafter shall be in force, touching and concerning said Institution; to dwell and continue in the said Orphan-House, until *he* ———— shall be of sufficient age to be bound as apprentice to such profession, trade or occupation as may be suited to *his* ———— genius and inclination, and from thence to dwell, continue and serve with such person to whom these Indentures shall be transferred from the day of the date thereof, from thence next ensuing, and which will be completed and ended on the *third* ———— day *October* ———— in the year of our Lord one thousand eight hundred and *thirty two* ———— During all which term the said *John* —— *Fordham* — shall demean *himself* agreeable to the said ordinances, rules and regulations, until the said transfer shall take place; and from thence *his* said *Master* ———— well and faithfully shall serve, *his* secrets keep, *his* lawful commands every where gladly do; hurt to *his* said *Master* ———— shall not do, nor willingly suffer to be done by others; the goods of *his* said *Master* ———— shall not embezzle or waste, nor lend them without *his* consent to any. From the said Orphan-House, or from the service of *his* said *Master* ———— shall not at any time depart or absent *himself*, without leave from one of the Commissioners, or from *his* —— said *Master* ———— but in all things shall well and faithfully demean *himself* during the said term.

In WITNESS WHEREOF, we have hereunto interchangeably set our Hands and Seals, the Day and Year first above written.

[signatures]
Elias Kingman

Richard W Cogdell c.o.
John Fordham

John Dawson
Commiss.r

THIS INDENTURE, made the *eighteenth* ————————— **day of** *March* ———— in the year of our Lord one thousand eight hundred and *twenty four* —— WITNESSETH, that the Commissioners of the Orphan-House, by virtue and in pursuance of the before written instrument of writing, and by, and with the consent and approbation of the said *John Fordham* ————————————————————————————— (testified by *his* ———————— being made a party to, and signing and sealing this present Indenture) Have given, granted, assigned, transferred, and set over, and by these presents do fully and absolutely give, grant, assign, transfer and set over unto *John Leek* ——————— of *Laurens District, Farmer and Blacksmith* ———— —————————————————————————————————— the foregoing Indentures, and all right, title, duty, and term of *his* service and demand whatsoever, which the said Commissioners have in or to the said *John Fordham* ——————— or which they can, may, or ought to have in *him* by force and virtue of the powers and authorities in them vested. And the said *John Leek* ——————————————— *his* said Apprentice the said trade, science, or occupation of a *Farmer and Blacksmith* ———— which *he* now uses, with all things thereunto belonging, shall and will teach and instruct, or otherwise cause to be well and sufficiently instructed, after the best way and manner that *he* can; and shall and will also find and allow the said Apprentice, meat, drink, washing, lodging and apparel, both linen and woollen, and all other necessaries in sickness and in health, meet and convenient for such an Apprentice, during the term aforesaid; and at the expiration of said term, shall and will give to *his* said Apprentice (over and above all *his* other clothing) one new suit of apparel, and FORTY-THREE DOLLARS; to be paid to the Commissioners for *his* use, and a hat, one pair of shoes and stockings, with suitable linen, as fit and usual for such an Apprentice, and furnish *him* with clean linen at least twice a week. And it is hereby further agreed, by and between the said Commissioners and the said *John Leek* ——————————————— that should he the said *John Leek* ——— dismiss the said *John Fordham* from *his* service before the expiration of the aforesaid term, or return *him* to the Orphan-House, without the consent of the said Commissioners, then and in that case, the said *John Leek* ——— shall pay to the said Commissioners the sum of ONE HUNDRED DOLLARS as liquidated damages. ——

In WITNESS WHEREOF, we have hereunto interchangeably set our Hands and Seals, the day and Year first above written.

Witness
Elias Kingman

John Leek
John Fordham

Dan.l Stevens
Commissioner

Charleston Orphan House indenture
Photograph by Terry Richardson. Courtesy City of Charleston Archives

TRANSIENT SICK AND CITY POOR.

ADMITTED INTO THE HOUSE.

Date of Admission.	NAMES.	By whose Order.	Place of Nativity.	Age.	Occupation.	Time of Residence in Charleston.	Date of Discharge.	Date of Decease.	Length of Time in the House.	Date of Removal to Hospital.	REMARKS.

Charleston Almshouse record book

Photograph by Terry Richardson. Courtesy City of Charleston Archives

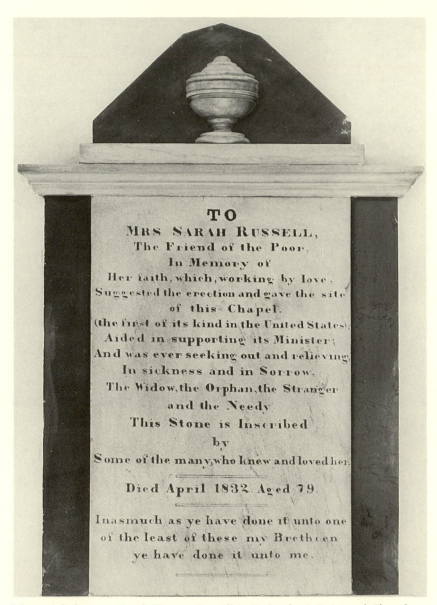

TO
MRS SARAH RUSSELL,
The Friend of the Poor,
In Memory of
Her faith, which, working by love,
Suggested the erection and gave the site
of this Chapel,
(the first of its kind in the United States);
Aided in supporting its Minister;
And was ever seeking out and relieving,
In sickness and in Sorrow,
The Widow, the Orphan, the Stranger
and the Needy.
This Stone is Inscribed
by
Some of the many, who knew and loved her.

Died April 1832. Aged 79.

Inasmuch as ye have done it unto one
of the least of these my Brethren
ye have done it unto me.

Memorial plaque to Sarah Hopton Russell in St. Stephen's Episcopal Chapel
Photograph by Terry Richardson

III

THE PROGRESS OF POVERTY

The great problem which posterity has to solve is, how to distribute more equally and more beneficially among the whole mass of the community the wealth in all ways accumulated.
—Thomas Cooper, 1826

When Andrew Jackson became president in 1828, urban poverty hung like a shadow over the new Republic, clouding its democratic promise. A British traveler noted at the time that "pauperism and destitution of various kinds are fast becoming heavy loads upon the public purse of all the States bordering on the Atlantic." Homelessness and criminality among urban whites posed an ideological challenge to the northern free society and raised uncomfortable questions about racial supremacy in the small urban enclaves of the South.[1]

In addition to its moral dimension, poverty persisted as a political problem. The Charleston Poor House, a familiar landmark for almost a century, no longer stood as a symbol of community aspiration. Its grim facade, now intruding into a residential area, loomed as a constant reminder of the erosion of Charleston's place in the national hierarchy. The local economy stumbled during Jefferson's Embargo of 1807 and the subsequent War of 1812 and collapsed in the Panic of 1819. Decline in the price of short staple cotton from Carolina's worn-out fields during the early 1820s delayed recovery. The development of the steamship made old trading patterns with Europe obsolete and dashed the future prospects of the city. New York City benefited most from this new technology and superseded Philadelphia as the nation's leading port city. Within one Charlestonian's lifetime, the decline in coastal trade nudged the city from fourth among American cities after the Revolution to sixth in 1830; on the eve of the Civil War, it plummeted in a breathtaking descent to twenty-second. The shocking deterioration of South Carolina's leading city compared to the boom times of New York City made the tariff protecting American industry a particularly bitter issue for Charlestonians. Many agreed with a local newspaper's contention: "We have no ob-

---

1. Hall, *Travels in North America,* III, 165; Daybook, February, 1827, in CPH.

jection to the North being enriched by our riches, but not from our poverty."[2]

Charleston languished into obsolescence with its demotion from regional entrepôt to mere depot, "a sort of West Indian town." The decline in economic functions performed in the city robbed Charlestonians of the numerous opportunities for advancement they had once enjoyed. By 1828, the value of city real estate had decreased by half since the beginning of the decade. Talented and enterprising Charlestonians reluctantly fled their failing home. Retail trade shriveled; unemployment hit artisans and laborers alike; houses stood empty; building contractors fell idle. The Charleston *Mercury* asked, "What is become of the thriving, industrious mechanics who swarmed about our streets twenty years ago, full of hope and energy, marrying and rearing up families to take their own places in public and private usefulness?" The answer might have been found by looking in the Charleston Poor House that had given shelter during the winter months of 1827 to 162 men, women, and children, a number that would not be equaled until the deep agricultural depression twenty years later.[3]

By the 1830s, southerners held up the northern poorhouse as a monument to free labor. But Charlestonians had run their own poorhouse basically along the same model as similar institutions in New York, Boston, and Philadelphia. With the rising numbers of poor and the growing secularization of Charleston society, religious benevolence and voluntary associations receded in importance in Charleston just as they were gaining their greatest political influence in the North.[4] The municipal government began shedding its old-fashioned eighteenth-century forms to deal with the problem of poverty and other urban issues with greater efficiency.[5]

Treatment of the poor, however, continued to reflect important cultural, historical, and political differences in the moral economy of American cities. The structure of the labor market, the social composition of urban leadership, and the population demographics all contributed to the dynamics between the powerful and the powerless. In northern cities,

2. Allen Kaufman, *Capitalism, Slavery, and Republican Values: Antebellum Political Economists, 1819–1848* (Austin, Tex., 1982), 124; Robert R. Russel, *Economic Aspects of Southern Sectionalism, 1840–61* (New York, 1960), 22, 23–32; Coclanis, *Shadow of a Dream,* 115–16; Kenneth M. Severens, *Charleston: Antebellum Architecture and Civic Destiny* (Knoxville, 1988), 64; Charleston *Mercury,* October 4, 1827.

3. Charleston *Courier,* March 13, 1828; Charleston *Mercury,* October 4, 1827; Daybook, February, 1827, in CPH.

4. Boyer, *Urban Masses and Moral Order,* 3–21.

5. In 1836, Robert Y. Hayne became the first salaried "mayor," a departure from the tradition of having an "intendant" preside over the city with no compensation.

the propertyless increasingly melted down in the public mind into "the masses."[6] With the well-integrated residential patterns of Charleston—black and white, rich and poor, living close to one another—interaction between the classes occurred regularly. Successful applications for public or private charity depended upon endorsements by well-known local figures. A poor woman could not commit her child to the orphan house without corroborating male signatures, though any poor man could. Thus, the fortunes of the poor depended upon the bonds they could forge with wealthy citizens. Before large-scale foreign immigration began in earnest during the 1840s, public men and women of Charleston continued to know and be known by those down on their luck. The local poor routinely approached them on the street or rang their doorbells late at night for a few dollars to leave town, post bail, or feed a sick child. For the poor of Charleston, the "charity of the world" was at best meager and restricted to those meeting a number of criteria, including sometimes as much as a year's residency. At no time during the nineteenth century did a "golden age" of benevolence exist when neighbor cared for neighbor or churches and private associations perfectly met the needs of the deserving.

Slavery, of course, also gave a unique twist to the way Charlestonians thought about the poor and, to a lesser extent, the way they worked toward their relief. Poverty among whites posed a special dilemma for southerners, whose political culture was historically one of "mutual bonds and reciprocal duties" characteristic of a deferential, paternalistic social order. The republican tradition, as interpreted in this predominantly agricultural region, equated political liberty and personal independence with owning property. The prevailing definition of freedom as the ability to live on one's own terms had deep roots in the British past. During the Tudor period, the English defined slavery in terms of power relationships rather than race; those unable to defend their liberty did not deserve to enjoy it. As liberty emerged as the "central idea" during the colonial period, southerners made mastery over others rather than self-control a key element in their interpretation of the ideal citizen. Americans also connected free will and conscience with the right to self-government; in a republic, the virtuous and independent, guided by their own discretion, served as the foundation of the commonwealth.[7] As poverty and slavery

6. For a discussion of the erosion of this concept of community that accompanied urban expansion in the North, see Boyer, *Urban Masses and Moral Order*, 56–57.

7. Jack P. Greene, "'Slavery or Independence': Some Reflections on the Relationship Among Liberty, Black Bondage, and Equality in Revolutionary South Carolina," *South*

became increasingly conflated, so did labor and subjection. To hoe another man's field or sew the shirt of another woman's husband unfailingly decreased an individual's standing. In a slave society, the aristocratic ideal considered work degrading rather than ennobling. Freedom meant freedom from labor. Southerners living in the rural districts continued their preoccupation with individual freedom as defined in these terms and consequently projected those who hired out their labor as creatures of circumstance, less free than the propertied, less worthy of citizenship, somehow, than other whites. Changing demographics, however, compelled Charlestonians and other urban dwellers to reconsider the political necessity of including the white servant, the Irish driver, or the German peddler in the larger urban community.[8]

The formation of a white working class forced Charlestonians and other southerners to modify some of the axioms of southern thought. Interest in mobilizing the underutilized labor of poor whites ebbed and flowed with the economy, the price of cotton, and the cost of slaves, but among taxpayers and city officials there persisted a constant preoccupation with the languishing and idle poor as wasted resources.[9] Just as planters rechanneled creeks to more productive use, town fathers hoped to redirect the poor out of hopeless, dead-end, and nonproductive jobs into a disciplined labor force where regimentation and economy of effort would have an enhanced effect for individuals and society. One of the issues surrounding the operation of the Charleston Poor House was whether, as the British had long contended and codified in their poor laws, there truly existed a duty for all citizens to labor, given the unique labor structure of the South.[10] Should the white poor be forced to work, to hoe and plant in poorhouse gardens, crack rocks, and spin cotton? The answer was emphatically yes.

In 1842, when Charleston's commissioners of the poor conducted a

Carolina Historical Magazine, LXXX (July, 1979), 207; J. G. A. Pocock, The Machiavellian Moment: Florentine Political Thought and the Atlantic Tradition (Princeton, N.J., 1975), 119–34; William J. Cooper, Liberty and Slavery: Southern Politics to 1860 (New York, 1983), 14–15.

8. This notion found its highest expression in James Henry Hammond's "Mudsill Speech," delivered before the United States Senate in 1858: "The man who lives by daily labor and scarcely lives at that, and who has to put out his labor in the market, and take the best he can get for it, in short your whole hireling class . . . are essentially slaves" (Congressional Globe, 35th Cong., 1st Sess., App. 71).

9. Robert Starobin, Industrial Slavery in the Old South (New York, 1970), 205.

10. The best book on this debate is Edgar Furniss, The Position of the Laborer in a System of Nationalism: A Study of the Labor Theories of the Later Mercantilists (New York, 1965), 90–95.

thorough investigation of the poorhouse, their spokesman expressed astonishment at the total "absence of almost everything like organized industrious effort within the institution." They worried lest the lives of the virtuous poor were "suffered actually to rust out for want of employment." The ragtag unemployed lived their lives in a whirlwind: "When out they consume their substance in riotous living, only to return, get sobered, and after a brief enjoyment of leisure here at the public expense return again to prey upon its charity, or offend its decency." The commissioners understood their duty clearly. The public deserved compensation; the dissipated must "be compelled to labor." [11]

In the discourse revolving around the white poor, paternalism often receded. The talk usually ran to individual responsibility for one's misfortunes and the correspondence between rewards and merit. In these ruminations, one can see how southerners embraced contradictory notions of social relations and split the white laborers from the black. The fondest desire of city governments from Boston to Savannah was to transform the idle into the industrious. Whatever truth may be attached to the devaluation of labor in the minds of the southern elite, there was agreement that the white poor should work, and work hard. [12] Every October, when the Charleston City Council reviewed the year's expenditures for the poor, debt-ridden city officials would cast their eyes toward the crippled and gnarled, wheezing and weary, lying on the corn-shuck pallets in the poorhouse, and wonder if these idlers were doing as much as they might for their own maintenance.

Debate arose over the best method of harnessing pauper power, but most agreed that almshouses should at least be self-sufficient. Efforts to turn poverty into profit included making orphans assemble fruit crates, alcoholics hammer coffins, and "fallen women" take in laundry. Some of the projects succeeded in the short term, especially the coffin making, but the very nature of the institution meant that inmates were either too inept or too unwell to participate in productive work. During the 1830s, the city started buying crushed rock from the North and having local carpenters rather than inmates pound together rough pine slabs to transport thin corpses from the poorhouse to potter's field. [13]

11. Minute book, November 12, 1842, in CPH.
12. The classic study of the southern attitude toward work and leisure is David Bertleson, *The Lazy South* (Westport, Conn., 1980).
13. In 1850, Richmond's Poor House and Hospital housed 199 inmates. Of these, 122 could perform no work at all, and the others spent their time in general maintenance—sweeping, washing, and sewing (Richmond Overseers of the Poor, Annual Returns, 1850, in Virginia State Archives, Richmond, Va.).

The first initiative to use pauper labor for a city project arose from the scarcities suffered by the city during Jefferson's disastrous Embargo of 1807. Fearing a shortage of textiles, a group of local leaders underwrote the ill-fated South Carolina Homespun Company. Displeased because the company had to recruit in the North for skilled operatives, the city council (as part of an attempt to make the whole town self-sufficient) demanded that all those able to work in the poorhouse be taught to spin cotton thread or suffer solitary confinement. In 1809, the factory did hire some of the inmates to "moat," or knock the impurities from the cotton, but among the ninety-odd inmates, only eighteen were fit enough to pick, card, or spin. The reopening of European trade and the increasing demand for space for the sick poor ended the first formal experiment. In 1813, however, the Ladies Benevolent Society appealed to the charitable of the city for donations of raw cotton for their training program teaching poor women trying to live on their own to spin. In 1816, the commissioners of the orphan house bought a "Pleasant Spinner," which rusted in the basement.[14]

Within a decade (and coincident with the 1828 "Tariff of Abominations") renewed enthusiasm for cotton manufacturing moved the commissioners of the poor to install a fly-shuttle loom in the almshouse. Promoters of the scheme imagined endless advantages; this new avenue of activity promised to turn the idle and unemployed into contented workers and save the city the sums it had been spending on their support. In addition, the cotton material they produced could liberate southerners from paying ransom to northern manufacturers. The commissioners paid a northern weaver $1.50 a day to give lessons for a month, but few of the paupers were trainable. The commissioners had hoped to bring those on out-relief into the institution to give them employment but dismissed as futile any attempt to compel them to work regularly. The men of the almshouse continued the work they did best, picking oakum (recycling old tarred ropes into caulking for ships) and breaking rocks. Some of the women brought their more nimble, though unskilled, fingers to the loom, enticed by premiums of extra tea and sugar. But this attempt, like Charleston's other large-scale ventures into commercial textile production, failed.[15]

The transient nature of the Charleston Poor House population and the

14. Minutes, August 29, 1809, in CPH; Mrs. St. Julien Ravenel, *Charleston: The Place and the People* (New York, 1922), 418–19; Clerk of Council files, June 3, 1816, March 17, 1829, in Charleston City Council Records, City of Charleston Archives, Charleston, S.C.

15. Minute book, February 12, August 13, 1829, both in CPH.

superintendent's lack of managerial skill doomed all efforts at productive labor. Except for the chronically ill, most inmates stayed only a short period, usually a season. The idea of work was actually self-defeating. The poorhouse, designed as a place of punishment or deterrent to the idle, discouraged long stays. Most programs, especially spinning and weaving, depended for their success upon inmates having the time to learn a skill. The superintendent, whose duties ranged from praying with the paupers at meals to beating them for violations of the rules, scarcely had time to oversee a spinning and weaving operation. Hopes that women and children of the outdoor pensioners might want to supplement their small incomes by learning the simple tasks of weaving also collapsed. This population avoided even coming near the Poor House, with the same disdain they later showed toward cotton factories on the peninsula. The disappointed commissioners discussed methods of coercion but could find no way.[16]

In all historical studies, the gap between theory and reality is often wide, and in few areas is this more often the case than in analyses of poor-relief policies. Official statements vowing tighter restrictions on behavior, more stringent distinctions between the worthy and the vicious, and earnest promises to weary taxpayers that budgets would be cut to the bone and the idle made productive usually gave way to the difficulty of managing a population that was for the most part very young, very old, diseased, or intemperate. *Social control*, a term popularized by sociologist E. A. Ross in the early twentieth century to explain the means of synchronizing the social order, holds little descriptive power for historians any longer. It swung back into fashion during the 1960s as a pejorative term wielded by historians seeking to emphasize the conflictual nature of the past rather than the organic and evolutionary "neo-Whig" interpretation. They merged their voices with leftist criticism of the contemporary welfare state by attempting to lay bare the darker motivations of American charity that an earlier generation of scholars had found so admirable. Nineteenth-century reformers who encouraged the poor to work hard, practice sexual restraint, and be temperate would be horrified to hear what they considered sound advice interpreted as "coercion." It should be remembered that efforts in Charleston and other cities focused on decreasing the numbers on the dole rather than recruiting them and bringing them under middle-class control. One of Charleston's most generously endowed aid societies maintained that "persons disorderly in

16. *Ibid.*

conduct, or who are of intemperate habits, having no family or reputable means of support when in health, shall be regarded as proper inmates of the poor house." Poorhouse stewards always questioned petitioners closely to ascertain if some relative, rather than the city, might take responsibility for the indigent.[17]

Charleston's experience with its poorhouse runs counter to the optimism surrounding the establishment of asylums in Jacksonian America. In 1768, the city celebrated the construction of a separate poorhouse for indigents distinct from the punishing rooms of the workhouse as an important landmark in the development of its urban form. Yet by the 1830s, with the same battered building still in use, there is little to suggest that anyone thought of the institution as little more than a necessary evil. A few optimistic souls believing in the uplifting effects of education did form a library in the poorhouse about 1829. Selections were limited to religious tracts and Charles Coatsworth Pinckney's collection, *The Gospel Advocate*. But it did have other volumes for paupers interested in *The Age of Benevolence, History of Poland*, or *Travels in Africa*.[18]

Dispensers of alms and Gospel-reading visitors to the poor undoubtedly wished to see a moral regeneration and transformation in the behavior of those they helped. Some distance, however, always existed between the wishes of the benevolent and the effect of their actions. They strove, for example, to limit their relief only to virtuous victims and the blind, lame, and halt, as prescribed by the Bible. Any close study of the almshouses and relief rolls of nineteenth-century cities reveals a mélange of the pitiable and perverse benefiting from the efforts of the charitable. The rhetoric was moralistic, but the practice expedient—removing beggars from public streets, sheltering illegitimate children, giving a drunk a pallet while he or she sobered up. Wild enthusiasm when public institutions made reform and control seem possible collapsed when increased poor rates were proposed. Any sort of systematic treatment of poverty was dashed by unwillingness to submit to increased taxation to

---

17. James Leiby, "Social Control and Historical Explanation: Historians View the Pliven and Cloward Thesis," in *Social Welfare or Social Control: Some Historical Reflections on "Regulating the Poor*," ed. Walter I. Trattner (Knoxville, 1983), 97–100; David J. Rothman, "Social Control: The Uses and Abuses of the Concept in the History of Incarceration," in *Humanitarianism or Control? A Symposium on Aspects of Nineteenth-Century Social Reform in Britain and America*, ed. Martin J. Wiener, Rice University Studies, LXVII (Houston, 1981), 12; Ladies Benevolent Society Constitution of 1852, p. 5, copy in South Caroliniana Library, University of South Carolina.

18. Rothman, *Discovery of the Asylum*, 130–54.

support such programs. Charlestonians of the nineteenth century, like other Victorians, vacillated between greed and generosity, paternalism and liberalism.[19]

Our clearest understanding about the relationship between town leaders and the poor comes neither from the hopeful pronouncements of the evangelical moral reformers or the blustery declarations by local politicians. It is the weary voice of John England, Catholic bishop of Charleston, whose long experience with the poorest of the city taught him that neither promise of heaven nor threat of the almshouse could "force this class of people" into conformity with middle-class values of sobriety, self-control, and savings banks. The poor of Charleston would not be coerced, England explained to the commissioners of the poor, "though we may win them and guide them and lead them."[20]

In Robert Mills's 1826 survey of South Carolina, he found a variety of local devices for relieving county paupers that ranged from hiring a supervisor who put them to work at various tasks in Edgefield to a system, found throughout the northern states, of simply letting them out to the lowest bidder in Newberry. These operations received poor rates ranging from 20 percent to 30 percent of the general taxes and were generally much more costly than institutionalization in Charleston. One county, for example, spent about $1,300 annually maintaining from 10 to 12 indigents, while the city of Charleston's total expenditure was about $4,400, which covered the 58 paupers staying in the house and 180 receiving outdoor rations. Mills estimated that Charleston had a population of about 27,000; somewhat fewer than half were white and bore much of the tax burden. About $12,000 in contributions from the state's "transient poor fund" relieved city taxpayers from the burden of nonresidents who took advantage of the public institution. In New York State, the poor farms cut costs so low, they could maintain a pauper for about 60 cents a week. Pennies were shaved from what was already one of the lowest expenditures in America. The most frequent directive from city council to the supervisors of the poorhouse was to retrench. During the 1830s, the commissioners finally protested that the "number of articles

19. David Roberts, "Dealing with the Poor in Victorian England," in *Humanitarianism or Control?*, ed. Wiener, 67–69; William Porcher Miles, *Report of the City of Charleston, 1857* (Charleston, S.C., 1858), 3.

20. John England to Commissioners, September 22, 1838, in Minute book, CPH. England was an Irishman who became bishop of Charleston in 1820. He established the first Catholic newspaper in America, the *Catholic Miscellany*, in 1826 and was the first Catholic invited to address Congress.

used are at their lowest possible point consistent with the comfort of the Inmates," and refused to make further cuts.[21]

In the summer of 1838, Democratic mayor Henry L. Pinckney, who had a large following among the working classes of Charleston, inquired into the state of the poorhouse and declared the general health of the institution good. Only one elderly inmate had died in the past year. In the previous ten months, 279 transients had passed through the asylum, compared to 24 local poor. The 46 adults and 75 children who lived outside the institution but depended upon the beef and bread rations from the city went four times a week to the local market and presented their coupons at the stalls of surly tradesmen. Pensioners could also send regularly to the poorhouse for a quart of the greasy soup dished up to the inmates. The hospital also kept busy during those months: Of the 168 patients treated there, 120 experienced cures and another 10 substantial relief; 5 chronic cases lingered, and 33 perished. Among the unfortunates in the "maniac" department, 23 returned to relative sanity, and 8 lingered on in confusion. During the winter quarter, the time of greatest pressure upon the resources of the asylum, the total cost of operation totaled $3,200. Only $600 went for food, $300 for clothing, and the rest for salaries and fuel. With an average of 115 inmates during the winter of 1838, the daily cost of feeding them averaged about a nickel apiece because the inmates subsidized their diet with a garden, with total maintenance at about 30 cents a day. The commissioners of the poorhouse charged the families of noncharity patients 37 cents a day for hospital care, 50 cents for the insane because they frequently destroyed their bedding and blankets. In comparison, the U.S. government paid local institutions that cared for incapacitated seamen 40 cents a day, and keepers of slave pens received 20 cents a day for each slave housed prior to auction. During the 1840s, the U.S. Army issued recruits one and a quarter pounds of beef and one and three-sixteenths pounds of bread. Slaves hired for canal building in one Georgia project received weekly rations of three and a half pounds of pork or bacon, and ten quarts of gourd seed corn.[22]

To evaluate the relative generosity of relief programs, economists sug-

21. In 1826, 390 transients resided in the poorhouse while 163 adults and 192 children benefited from outdoor relief. During the same year, Baltimore, with a population of about 70,000, spent $18,000 supporting 500 paupers, one-third of whom were foreigners (Mills, *Statistics of South Carolina*, 396, 432, 528, 628, 648, 733).

22. "Report of the Committee Appointed by the Board of Guardians of the Poor of the City and Districts of Philadelphia, 1827," in *The Almshouse Experience: Collected Reports* (New York, 1971), 5, 11–12, 13, 16; Rough minutes, May 15, 1837, February 21, 1838, in CPH; Minutes, November 3, 1832, May 23, 1837, in CPH; Hall, *Travels in North*

gest comparing the ratio of annual expenditures to potential earnings by common laborers. The benefit-earnings ratio reflects two important criteria in the process of public spending: the perception among taxpayers that their contribution actually relieves the suffering without encouraging idleness and the belief among the poor that relief is not a substitute for work. Based on Stanley Lebergott's estimates that from the mid–nineteenth century to modern times the average ratio of relief in America ranged from 22 to 31 percent of a laborer's earnings, the ratio of assistance offered in Charleston appears at least consistent with that of the rest of the country.[23] Few of the long-term pensioners actually had the option to work. Old men, sick and broken down, sometimes with their wives but mostly alone, dominated the rolls of the institution, and women with children constituted the majority on out-relief status.

A glance inside Charleston's poorhouses reveals a chaos belying the myth of orderly institutions. In contrast to the common practice at other public buildings in the city, few guides ever volunteered to show visitors the poorhouses, and even fewer visitors asked to see them. If they had, they would have been shocked at a scene combining the worst features of Bedlam and Babel. The dilapidated eighteenth-century building served as a "Bettering House" for town drunks and petty criminals, an asylum for the black and white insane, a haven for the homeless, and a hospital for the sick. The scene was so frightening that more than one applicant picked up his bundle and dashed away from the mélange of human misery. There, men and women exchanged their rags for pauper's ticking; dissipated prisoners from the Mayor's Court headed for the ground-floor cells; shifty-eyed inmates watched every unattended exit to escape to the revels of the street; abandoned women longed for the privacy of their lost homes as they washed the clothes of a hundred strangers; helpful friends carried in the sick, who, delaying this moment as long as possible, perished in the halls before a pallet could be laid; lunatics either roamed the house as "attendants" or wailed from their cells, "their unearthly whoopings and hallooings in the very ears of the sick."[24]

America, III, 169; Frederick Law Olmsted, *The Cotton Kingdom: A Traveller's Observations on Cotton and Slavery in the American Slave States* (1861; rpr. New York, 1953), 483–84.

23. Joan Underhill Hannon, "The Generosity of Antebellum Poor Relief," *Journal of Economic History,* XLIV (September, 1984), 811–13; Stanley Lebergott, *Wealth and Want* (Princeton, 1975), 57. The working year is considered to be 311 days, though in the South it may actually be higher. The average wage for common laborers averaged about $1.25 for much of the period under discussion.

24. Commissioners' minute book, November 12, 1853, in CPH.

The size of the poorhouse population rose and fell with the rhythms of the seasons. Winter's decline in port activity forced laborers from the docks to stay there for three months of middling warmth and greasy soups; in late summer and fall, the hospital wards often teemed with victims of the yellow fever or cholera epidemics that periodically disrupted the city and infected the newly arrived immigrants with particular ferocity. Christmastime found more drunks than usual in the basement cells; their revelry and cursing competed with the moans and shrieks of the insane confined nearby. High mortality among workingmen of Charleston and their inability to accumulate any substantial savings meant that their widows and children often ended up on the charity of the town.

Statistics about poverty based on admissions to the poorhouse are deceptive because the keepers of the daily tally made no distinction between true paupers and those paying patients admitted to the lunatic cells or the hospital wards. Their notations about gender were random, but information from individual years suggests that more men than women were likely to be inmates. Men generally constituted about 57 percent of the population receiving some form of public relief at the poorhouse. From 1830 to 1848, 7,320 men, women, and children resorted to the poorhouse. About 100 inmates lived there at any one time. Close to 400 passed through in the course of a year. Because of several waves of yellow fever during the 1830s, the death rate was twice as high as during the next decade. Most of the dead went to paupers' graves.[25]

Another category of the poor population consisted of the outpensioners. As expenses climbed during the 1850s, the poorhouse officials issued special coupons redeemable at designated stands in the market instead of having the pensioners come to the house. They also reduced the frequency of rations from four to three times weekly.[26] Charleston natives most often received this variety of assistance. Reflecting patterns in all port cities, the Irish and other foreigners were much more likely to be ordered into the Poor House than to enjoy outpensioner status. This fact has been interpreted as discrimination against immigrants and an attempt by the local government to subdue and unfairly incarcerate this rowdy class.[27] There may well be substance in this analysis, but there is an alternative possibility. Native Charlestonians,

25. J. L. Dawson and H. W. DeSaussure, *Census of the City of Charleston for the Year 1848* (Charleston, S.C., 1849), 48, 49.

26. *Ibid.,* 50. From 1830 to 1848, the number of people receiving provisions ranged from a high of 275 in 1832 to a low of 124 in 1840.

27. For one of the best discussions of the historical development of the poorhouse in America, see Katz, *In the Shadow of the Poorhouse,* esp. 16–19.

who always claimed at least 50 percent of the rations, had sufficient contacts in the city through relatives and friends to find shelter on their own. They could also more easily tap into church organizations and moral reform associations for assistance. Women, the majority of the outpensioners, often maintained their independence and kept their families together by piecing together slender livings from the charitable network of the city. Whatever bits of money they earned through home sewing or domestic service were often supplemented with rent money from their church or mission, clothes and materials from garment and flannel societies, and firewood from small groups dedicated solely to providing this service to the poor. Doctors at the Shirras Dispensary offered routine medical advice and drugs without charge. Beyond this, rations from the city tipped the scales in their favor. Catholic immigrants denied access to the services of Protestant benevolent societies or frightened away by their overtures, usually lacked an extended family network to give the occasional loan or help find a job that determined whether one could maintain a precarious independence.[28]

The steward of the Poor House kept close tallies on a third category, the "transient poor," because the state paid the expenses of those sojourning temporarily in the poorhouse, such as sailors or residents of other counties. Public relief institutions and private charities lured the poor to the city like a magnet. From 1830 to 1848, more than six thousand nonresidents had received assistance from Charleston's relief system. The ambitious may have headed west, but the broken went to town. The hope of finding a home for her three small children after a quarrel with her father-in-law drove the "high spirited" Susannah McMillan, a young widow of a blacksmith, to make the sixty-mile journey through dark Lowcountry swamp from Barnwell County to appeal to the commissioners of the orphan house. When Charleston police woke up a ninety-year-old North Carolina man sleeping on a bench on the outskirts of town, he told them he had walked fourteen miles for a place in Charleston's poorhouse.[29]

28. In 1830, those who were deemed the "permanent poor" numbered 347, a high for the period included in the 1848 census. The lowest number for this group was 150 in 1838. The Shirras Dispensary, founded with a bequest from Scotsman Alexander Shirras, received public funding and proved an attractive alternative to the hospitals because of the lower costs of having the sick stay at home.

29. Dawson and DeSaussure, *Census of Charleston, 1848*, 48; Henry A. DeSaussure to Commissioners of the Almshouse, n.d., in Commissioners' file, COH; Minute book, January 12, 1859, in CPH; Roper Hospital Casebook No. 2, May 11, 1860, in Waring Medical Library, Medical University of South Carolina, Charleston, S.C.

Our knowledge about the intimate life of the almshouse is restricted to the clues scattered through its well-preserved records. Inmates in this institution were almost identical to those in northern cities; there were more men than women, more old than young, and more walked in than walked out.[30] Most resisted the rules of the house, and their blatant violations tormented the steward and his wife. No proper fence enclosed the institution, so paupers slipped in and out of the cavernous building more or less at will. One came in and out more than 110 times; others went on sprees and were promptly "wheeled to the cage" at the city guardhouse. Inmates also had the freedom to leave on day passes. Some looked for work, visited families, or attended church. But a discouraging number went out to indulge in the pleasures of the city, only to return, like Elizabeth McCarthy, roaring drunk and lobbing rocks at the front windows of the institution.[31]

When not in the crowded wards, cells, or sickbeds of public institutions, the poor could be found in alleyways of the city—dark, hidden places more like backdrops to a Dickens novel than classic settings in the sunny South. Prostitutes, drunks, and vagrants found that anonymity suited their lives as they lurked in shaded corners. Every city had these sections, typically near the railyards, where the poor shared their pleasure and pain, as well as the occasional bottle of gin. Theirs were the lowest and least-healthy blocks that often flooded when high tide converged with the full moon, where decrepit shacks crowded along unlit unpaved paths, or tumbledown rooming houses indiscriminately offered shelter to families, sailors, and whores.

Although the poor, black and white, could be found in all quadrants of the city, they congregated in these pockets, adding complexity to the social geography of the town. Respectable residents of Charleston Neck complained bitterly about the lack of police protection as their neighborhood declined with infestations of "idle and spurious characters" and "the lowest and vilest class of grog shops." White hooligans mixed shamelessly with "our sable population." They celebrated the sabbath with "smoking and carousing together, quarrelling and fighting." Local authorities winked at the revels of the red-light districts, and the city benefited from taxing the "groceries" selling alcohol, but public outrage

30. From November, 1853, to November, 1854, 510 people were admitted to the poor-house hospital. Ninety-six died, 359 were cured, and the others were either relieved, remained, or removed to another institution (Minute book, November 12, 1854, in CPH).

31. *Ibid.*, May 29, 1861, August 17, 1861, January 6, 1831, May 14, 1862, May 15, 1860, April 25, 1859.

resulted when disorder spilled into the mainstream of urban life.[32] The Neck, shabby by day, became sheer pandemonium after sunset. There the poor spent hot summer nights lost in a reverie of street balls, flirting, and fighting. On cold winter days, they huddled around fires fueled by the broken bits of their tables and chairs.

Most of those living pained lives in the city had been born into poverty and stayed there. They came into the world of dependency with a quick knock on the door or a frantic tug at the bell. Slight figures dashed away into the night, leaving a wailing infant behind them. Chronicles of urban life repeat this story time and again. Unmarried women trying to hide their shame, poor women unable to feed another child, and others who just did not want to bother stood in shadows when the night patrol passed and left their children on doorsteps and stoops. Night porters checking on mysterious noises in the dark routinely found little baskets like the one left at Charleston's Akin Foundling Home holding a newborn with a scrawled note pinned to her clothes: "Alice/not christened/ Poverty the Cause." Others, less fortunate than little Alice, never even had names of their own and carried through life whimsical monikers given by public officials, like that of an infant abandoned in another city—Virginia Richmond.[33]

With such dismal beginnings, future prospects seldom brightened. Many ended up as victims. Sarah Adams Wilcox grew up in the Charleston Orphan House and had her long struggle to gain independence completely vanquished by a drunkard "husband who has rendered himself incapable of supporting his family."[34] Struggling from birth to death, living all their lives empty hand to empty mouth, those folk who escaped crime, disease, or accident often ended their days useless and alone, shaking with delirium tremens in poorhouses or jails.

The three major divisions within the Charleston Poor House reflected

32. Charleston *Courier,* June 23, 1847, September 16, 1845. The area including the Neck was incorporated into the city relief system in 1850 to reduce the bookkeeping problems of tracking the poor as they moved from one jurisdiction to another. In 1860, the city spent almost as much on out relief for the lower wards as for the upper. That year, 299 adults and children in the upper wards regularly received rations, compared with 321 in the lower wards south of Boundary (later Calhoun Street). For more on the relationship between the Neck and the lower part of the peninsula, see John P. Radford, "Race, Residence and Ideology: Charleston, South Carolina, in the Mid-Nineteenth Century," *Journal of Historical Geography,* IV (1976), 347–60.

33. William H. Gilliland to Mayor Charles MacBeth, January 1, 1862, in Indenture file, COH.

34. Application file, December 20, 1833, *ibid.*

the leading causes of institutionalization through the 1830s: disease, alcoholism, and insanity. Charity hospitals overflowed with the ailing. Even among the poor who had kindly friends or families to help them, the state of their so-called homes was even worse than the crowded, stinking pauper wards. Visitors to the sick poor described the shocking situation of those "swollen and inflamed with the pains of disordered rheum," miserably crouching in the corner of a "cold and damp cellar as tenable as your coal vault." They noted victims of burning fevers confined to a "close apartment, heated to stifling in preparing the evening meal on the shattered stove." The concept of home as a haven with clean linens and well-prepared medicines totally eluded the poor, who paid usurious rents to boardinghouse operators for closets "some ten feet square, in the attic, . . . narrow, crazy shelter, where the rain through the ill-made roof drops in upon the scanty bed, which a family of children are sharing with their consumptive mother."[35]

During the epidemics that regularly hit coastal cities, the unacclimated suffered yellow fever and smallpox; cholera presented a constant danger in the densely populated sections. Although the associations formed to give assistance during these periods never excluded the poor, unless someone in the household was well enough to summon help, volunteers often arrived too late. Cranmore Wallace, the worldly Episcopal priest who ministered to Charleston's poor, reeled at what he found in his investigations in the slums: "whole families, three or four of them sick with yellow fever and not a morsel of bread, or a cent of money or a billet of wood on the premises, or a nurse to hand a cup of cold water to the parched lips."[36]

Typhoid and syphilis, diseases of filth and promiscuity, also brought their victims in from the streets to beds many knew they would never leave. The majority were victims of poverty rather than self-indulgence. One such case was Cathy Kenny, a young Irish girl forced to sleep on the street and under houses, who washed clothes at the orphan house until crippled by rheumatism. Another was a German drayman who collapsed with sunstroke from working too hard in the unforgiving Carolina July and was saved by his horse, who delivered him home. Joseph Fermal, a Pennsylvania man who lived for two months in the same stables where he worked, arrived at the hospital "a very dirty fellow, his head . . . alive with lice—scalp and neck covered with sores, hair matted and very offen-

---

35. "Plea for a Church Hospital," *Gospel Messenger*, XXVIII (March 1851), 476.
36. Wallace, "Reports of Charleston City Missions," *Southern Episcopalian*, II (August, 1855), 490–91.

sive." With his head shaved and sores balmed, he went back to his chores.[37]

City doctors in Charleston's Roper Hospital jotted down observations as they walked the poor wards and looked into snaggletoothed and pock-marked faces contorted by years of deprivation and debauchery. Susan Potter, a thirty-eighty-year-old prostitute from Boston, glared up from her bed, "bloated and tremulous" from too much drink; James Miller, a Charleston native in his sixties, could only peek out through the one eye not swollen shut by the ulcers spreading across his head as vermin laid siege to his scalp; Irish prostitute Catherine Robson finally slept, having rolled fitfully, vomiting and "tortured the whole night with frightful fan-cies"; Ellen Passame, "a regular rum sucker," screamed hysterically and made the whole ward share her miseries.[38]

Poorhouse doctors saw a wide variety of ailments and gained experience in everything from nutritional deficiencies to pulling teeth. By donating their services, they played a crucial role in the relief system. Physicians from prominent local families, like Henry W. DeSaussure, whose father was for four decades a commissioner of the Charleston Orphan House, treated scabby and reeking paupers for eight years with no pay, "except the compensation of an approving conscience, and the blessing of the destitute sick."[39] Local workingmen endorsed Dr. Henry V. Toomer in his candidacy for physician to the poor of Charleston Neck because he always spoke "like a brother, to every poor man and mechanic of his acquaintance." With no thought to his own safety, Toomer frequently charged into "the night fogs of our swamps" and "the miasma of our rice fields to tend patients in need."[40]

Not until the technological advances in medicine developed during the Civil War began the movement toward the modern dual-health-care sys-tem did actual treatment differ significantly between the care of rich and poor. The options were limited to a few drugs from plants such as Peru-vian bark, from which quinine is derived, and simple procedures— bleeding, cupping with heated vessels to bring the blood to the skin sur-face, blistering, jalap and calomel purges, applications of hot flannels, and

37. Roper Hospital Casebook No. 2, March 14, 1860, June 16, 1862.
38. *Ibid.*, March 14, 1860, June 24, 1862, May 29, 1860, May 26, 1859.
39. William H. Inglesby, chairman of the commissioners of the Charleston Poor House, to Dr. Henry A. DeSaussure, November 1, 1847, copy in Rough minutes, CPH. As immi-grants began flooding into America during the 1840s, doctors in many northern cities, appalled by the lack of personal hygiene especially among the Irish, began distancing them-selves from the poor and referring them to the charity hospitals rather than have them come to their offices (Charles Rosenberg, *In the Care of Strangers: The Rise of America's Hos-pital System* [New York, 1987], 316–22).
40. Charleston *Courier*, September 6, 1847.

inhalants of steaming vinegar and water. Frequently reduced to alleviating symptoms rather than actually producing cures, doctors relied heavily on the soporific and soothing effects of opium and brandy-laced milk.[41]

When death came to the poorhouse, rather than liberating the sufferer, it sometimes proved the ultimate degradation. After unhappy victims fell into their last fits of delirium tremens or blackened with yellow fever, curious young doctors from the Medical College of Charleston unceremoniously probed the diseased remains. And this they did in full sight of those waiting fearfully for their own mortal fate. Charleston's commissioners of the poor expressed dismay that "when a patient died in the Hospital, not only are those around him saddened or depressed by witnessing the last gasps of life, or his convulsive struggles with death; but, when life is extinct, he is put into the Coffin before the eyes of all." To die in the poorhouse held special terror for Catholics. Until Bishop John England pressed the issue about 1840, the rattletrap hearse carted dead paupers straight to potter's field, never stopping at St. Finbar's Cathedral to permit a proper funeral despite the pleadings of distraught families. But to die alone in the miserable holes where many of the destitute lived had its own horror. Cranmore Wallace remembered seeing "men and women in the last agonies of death, or stiffened corpses laid out for the grave, and the husband or wife in a state of beastly intoxication in the same room."[42]

The majority of the men housed in the asylum suffered from the tangled afflictions of poverty, alcoholism, and disease. Although the connections between the three were undeniable, cause and effect remains even now a matter of debate. In 1829, Thomas Smith Grimké (then president of the South Carolina Temperance Society) wrote the commissioners of Charleston's poorhouse asking for information about alcoholics in the institution and an evaluation of the connection between intemperance and impoverishment. Clear in his own mind about the evils of strong drink, he sought evidence about the economic impact of alcoholism upon the whole community. The commissioners' matter-of-fact reply probably surprised him. At the time of his inquiry in June, usually a time of low oc-

41. Charles E. Rosenberg, "Social Class and Medical Care in 19th Century America: The Rise and Fall of the Dispensary," in *Sickness and Health in America: Readings in the History of Medicine and Public Health*, ed. Ronald L. Numbers and Judith W. Leavitt (Madison, Wis., 1978), 161; Joseph Pitt, "Observations on the Country and Diseases near the Roanoke River . . . ," *Medical Repository*, V (February, March, April, 1808), 337–42.

42. Minute book, November, 1852, in CPH; Bishop John England to Commissioners of the Poor House, September 22, 1838, *ibid.*; Wallace, "Reports of Charleston City Missions," *Southern Episcopalian*, II (August, 1855), 490–91.

cupancy, twenty-eight of the sixty-eight males suffered from intemperance, as did fifteen of the fifty women. The problem clearly went much beyond the individual sufferer in Grimké's perception; every self-indulgent sinner brought down his whole family with him. More than 20 percent of the women receiving rations from the city suffered destitution because of alcoholic husbands. Eight of the nineteen male inmates had lost their jobs from alcoholism. Of the eighty-four children receiving rations, thirty-six endured intemperate parents. But the commissioners were reluctant to judge. Based on their intimate knowledge of the struggle of the poor, they concluded: "In the investigations which we have made on this subject, we have been unable to ascertain the habits of the Individuals previous to the time when necessity drove them to our Institution, we know them now as objects of great poverty and addiction to the indulgence of a vice, which, no doubt contributes to their misfortunes, but we cannot say whether this vice has been the cause of their poverty, or the result of their ruined fortunes."[43]

All one had to do was look at the statistics of poorhouses anywhere in the country to see the overwhelming percentage who languished because of their addiction. During 1850, for example, Richmonders supported about 236 paupers in their almshouse. Of those, 87 percent of the white males and 72 percent of the black males were there because of chronic alcoholism, compared with 49 percent of the white women and 15 percent of the black. Alcoholism cut across class lines. At one point, Charleston housed 105 in the Poor House hospital: The 11 who were diagnosed as intemperate included "a segar maker, overseer, baker, stone cutter, 2 sailors, accountant, spinster, shoe maker, gardener, taylor."[44]

Realistically, by the time directors of city institutions encountered the habitual drunk, there was small hope of reformation through moral suasion. Occasionally when cross-examined by representatives of benevolent societies or municipal agencies, habitual offenders might swear with alcoholic breath that they attended one or another of the temperance schools run by the Cold Water clubs or Total Abstinence societies that abounded in rural and urban communities. There is little to suggest, however, that they took this reform to heart. Tension existed between those temperance and evangelical groups who wanted to pressure sinners into seeing the errors of their ways and the superintendents of public institutions, who accepted alcohol use as part of everyday life and saw little good in punishing those already suffering.

43. Minute book, June 4, 1829, in CPH.
44. Richmond Overseers of the Poor, Annual returns, 1850, in Virginia State Archives, Richmond, Va.

More than any other single cause, intemperance brought men and women in contact with local police. By 1840, mayors in Charleston, Richmond, and Savannah had adopted the practice of spending part of each day "hearing all complaints against notorious or disorderly persons" too disruptive to be ignored and too frivolous for general sessions courts: the feckless drunk collapsed in the city streets, the shrewish fishwife shouting insults at neighbors across tumbledown fences, the unlucky urchins throwing dice or tossing brickbats. Much like rural justices of the peace, their special charge was "suppression of riot and preservation of public order." Since few public officials actually had legal training, they fumbled about, wading through myriads of local ordinances, ultimately relying on "a nice sense of right, of justice, and propriety." The incidence of public drunkenness so pervaded every city (twenty-three charges brought by the Charleston police on just one winter's day in 1855) that those who had to deal with the poor on a regular basis defined alcoholism as part of their benighted condition. In 1856, Charleston's mayor dismissed a man found facedown and drunk in the city market with a two-dollar fine and "some wholesome advice," though thinking that "the hope of reform is remote."[45]

Profound sadness rather than frolic filled the lives of the poor. Anyone who worked with them or could look in their faces understood this. When Emily Burke traveled by steamer from New York City to Savannah, she closely observed a group of Irish workers who had ridden out a hurricane in steerage. They sat dazed and forlorn upon the barrels and chicken coops that crowded the deck. As she studied them, she realized that in their everyday lives they were constantly tossed about and battered as their small boat had been in the angry sea. Many of the women, she predicted, would "soon die of hardships and broken hearts, while the men, to drown thoughts of disappointment in the intoxicating cup, go to drinking whiskey which causes the clime fever to set in from which they seldom recover. Thus ends each year the existence of thousands of these deluded beings."[46]

Officials of poorhouses and insane asylums all over the country noted that newcomers to America frequently suffered from derangement due to "privations on shipboard, the changes incident to arriving in a strange land," and poor nutrition. Their "insanity" was often mild and frequently passed with good care. For those who never regained the ability to function, Charleston's poorhouse housed them in the basement and

---

45. "Mayor's Court," Charleston *Mercury*, January 30, 1856.
46. Emily Burke, *Reminiscences of Georgia* (New York, 1850), 9.

an outbuilding; almost thirty souls, mostly abandoned by friends and family, dwelled there during the 1850s. Twenty-seven-year-old Irishman Terry Moor, "V.D." marked by his name, typified the most serious cases. He indeed proved a "very dangerous" man, particularly to himself. He refused medicine, twice attempted suicide, "bound cords around his scrotum," gashed his body with sharp stones, and, not surprisingly, had "no friends in Charleston."[47]

Charleston doctors often encountered a syndrome similar to one diagnosed by a New York physician involving young immigrant women traumatized by "the combined moral and physical influences of leaving the homes of their childhood, [and] their coming almost destitute to a strange land." Numbers of such women totally overwhelmed by the heartbreaks of their lives resorted to the Charleston Poor House. Many also shared the shock of abandonment. Concerned neighbors carried Sarah Waters to the institution when she slipped into such a deep depression, they feared for her life. A dutiful wife to a rambling man, she had followed her husband from Canada to South Carolina, going from town to town as he sought easy wealth. One night in 1850, he packed up and headed for gold and California, abandoning her to her fate in a strange and foreign place. She collapsed under the weight of her misfortune. Even though the steward and matron, who had seen many cases like hers, reportedly treated her "with kindness and encouraging assurance," Waters' anger raged on and turned inward. The first time attendants turned their back, she tried to hang herself in her cell. Thwarted in this attempt, she spent her days "passing her feces on the floor and then smearing them on the walls of her chamber." She showed no violence toward others "with the exception of kicking at the privates of men."[48]

For several inmates, the basement cell had been home for twenty or thirty years. For one reason or another, often at the request of family members who paid for their care, they remained in Charleston and were not shipped to the state asylum in Columbia. Most were white, but some blacks (decrepit old slaves deemed "uncontrollable" by their masters) lived out their miserable lives there. House physicians experimented on the inmates, testing the latest innovations in "moral treatment," replacing coercion with "the most humane principles" of confinement, and experimenting with drugs on epileptics. Charleston doctors closely followed the work of humanitarian Dorothea Dix, the no-nonsense Yankee

47. Rough minutes, March 7, 1850, in CPH.
48. Governors of the [New York] Almshouse, Sixth and First Annual Reports, quoted in Robert Ernst, *Immigrant Life in New York City, 1825–1865* (New York, 1965), 54–55; Lunatics book, November 18, 1850, in CPH.

schoolteacher who used her small inheritance to finance investigations into the treatment of paupers, convicts, and lunatics in every state east of the Rockies. Although she represented the perfectionist traditions that shoved southerners out of the mainstream of moral reform, Dix played no favorites. She exposed instances of the deranged bound by ball and chain in Vermont cellars with the same fervor that she reported the prisonlike conditions of South Carolina's lunatic asylum. An excellent politician, the thistly New Englander contacted prominent Charlestonians during a trip south in 1859 and left with generous donations for her cause. Following Dix's recommendations, Charleston doctors distributed knitting needles, yarn, sewing needles, and cloth as occupational therapy for the afflicted in their cells. Some patients, like the English soldier suffering "under the idea of vast superiority and unbounded wealth," showed improvement with these methods. Other, more tortured souls who moaned and rocked on brick floors and stabbed at their own hearts with any pointed instruments they could find, obviously needed more heroic methods, like freezing "Shower baths, and Head baths of Emetics." One woman, crazed by grief over the death of her child, was consumed by the belief that "she has the power of raising the dead and that all mankind are her enemies." In addition to restoring her health, doctors tried to "reorder her mind by twice shaving, then blistering, her head." [49] They noted no improvement.

In all facets of life among the poor, women emerge as those most often beaten, battered, and broken by poverty. None of the nineteenth-century ideologies, all geared toward defining the role of free white males, had sufficient flexibility to deal with the growing social problem of white women outside the protective cope of the family, for whom opportunities for success in the meritocratic free market scarcely existed. The overrepresentation of women in the ranks of the poor was as related to their lack of skill and ability to obtain credit as to gender conventions. To compete, women clearly had be empowered with education and equal opportunities for employment. Few endorsed such a radical revolution, though the changing economy clearly demanded it.

The best that city commissioners could do was to try to enforce paternalistic responsibility. City policy attempted to reestablish frayed family ties worn thin under the pressures of poverty and urban life. [50] William

49. Minute book, n.d., in CPH; "Modern Philanthropy and Negro Slavery," *De Bow's Review,* XVI (1854), 263–64; Letter book, February 2, 1853, Lunatics book, February 28, 1853, February 9, 1850, June 6, 1848, all in CPH.

50. Rough minutes, December 16, 1824, in CPH. Charleston's practice contrasts sharply

H. Inglesby, chairman of the commissioners of the poorhouse, took a personal interest in Sarah Spencer, a sixteen-year-old girl too old and worldly for the orphan house but too young for the "Bettering Department" and the company of whores, sailors, and petty criminals. Writing to her stepbrother, Inglesby confessed feelings of "great solicitude for Sarah . . . although she has wandered far from the path of virtue and rectitude." He asserted his conviction that she "may yet, if kindly dealt with, be restored to respectability and at least comparative happiness." Inglesby urged the man to accept his moral duty to take her in "like the Prodigal Son" and receive her "with open arms and a hearty welcome under your paternal roof." As far as the records show, the stepbrother never replied.[51]

Sarah Spencer's youth gave her a claim upon the city that few adult women shared. The "before and after" of Louise Tesky's life makes a mockery of the elaborate professions of patriarchal care. Louise Tesky and her husband were a typical laboring couple. A New York native, she moved to Charleston, where she met Tesky, "a stranger from England." They married in 1842, settled down in a modest neighborhood, and soon had a child. Their prospects looked bright. Tesky worked as a candy-maker in a small shop, where he had a warm relationship with his employer, W. Brookbanks. The Englishman, content in his domestic life, proved also to be "the best work man [Brookbanks] ever had—cleanest, neatest, completant [sic], Industrious." His salary increased steadily over the years from $4.00 a week to $2.50 a day. Tesky and his family were inching toward middle-class comfort when he developed a fatal heart ailment. He struggled to keep working but died in 1853. His son, Robert, was only eight. During the next four years, Louise Tesky's situation changed dramatically. She went from one unsavory job to another, from rented room to rented room—each a little worse than the one before. Robert accompanied her for four years but received so little education and attention that by the time she finally gave up and entered him in the

---

with that of Richmond, where until 1879 anyone pretending to be a relative could simply come to the almshouse and leave with a child. If a parent or relative did show up, there was no record of where the child had gone (Richmond *Daily Dispatch*, September 12, 1856; Richmond Commissioners for Poor Relief, Record Book, 1875–85, entry for March 11, 1879, in Virginia State Archives, Richmond).

51. Rough minutes, April 27, 1845, in CPH. Appointed by the city council, the commissioners of the poorhouse were most frequently professional men (usually doctors) and merchants. According to William and Jane Pease, "42% were of modest or great status; and 50% enjoyed either modest or significant political power" that often derived from the community approbation for their service to the Poor House (Pease and Pease, *The Web of Progress*, 293n39).

orphan house, he could "scarcely speak well." She passed him over to the city just as she sank into certain degradation as a cook in a sailors' boardinghouse on the waterfront. Louise Tesky disappears from public record earning $6.00 a month, half of which the owners of the house kept for her rent.[52]

White women made up almost 13 percent of the white working population in 1848. Except in the capacities of house servant and laborer, more white women engaged in trade and other positions of public contact than did blacks; more women taught school than did men. White women performed 15 percent of the food-service jobs. Clothing work employed the most women; almost one-half of the dry-goods dealers were women. Women also sold milk, fruit, crockery, linens, pastries, and confections. A few broke into the management ranks by running hotels; 4 ran stores; 3 served as clerks; and many (40) kept boardinghouses. Five midwives practiced in Charleston, along with a female "Botanic Practitioner." They monopolized the ranks of laundresses (13), mantua makers (38), milliners (44), seamstresses (87). The largest single occupation was house servant (100), an occupation overwhelmingly filled with slaves (3,384). White women also held the somewhat higher position of housekeeper (13). Many more white women than free blacks (28) worked as house servants. Free women of color dominated the skilled trade of mantua maker (128). This census inevitably undercounts the women who washed clothes or did sewing on the casual labor market, and, of course, prostitutes seldom stepped forward to be counted.[53]

Although the discussion of the economic condition of women seldom went beyond the wringing of hands and the bleeding of hearts, the challenge that hardworking but incredibly poor women presented to traditional thinking about both domesticity and labor introduced gender into the public discourse in ways that the issues of middle-class reform never did. The reality of female poverty ripped through the notion of the sheltered "woman's sphere." Poor women in the city lived on the dark side of the benevolent social conventions that supposedly brought light to the lives of gentlewomen. One minister working among the Charleston poor summed up a poor woman's short and simple life: "Excluded by her position in Society from all active and lucrative occupations—her destiny

52. Commissioner Report, n.d., on Robert Tesky, in COH. Robert Tesky was admitted to the orphan house on December 31, 1857, and apprenticed to a bookseller in July, 1860 (Susan King, *History and Records of the Charleston Orphan House* [Easley, S.C., 1984], 53).

53. There were 491 women among 3,919 Charlestonians listed as belonging to the white productive classes in 1848 (Dawson and DeSaussure, *Census of Charleston, 1848,* 29–45).

linked perhaps to that of a brutal husband, . . . misfortunes and afflictions fall with a heavier blow and with more intense severity" than on any other member of society. He further noted ruefully that when "she ages and falls into poverty, she is little more than a withered flower, . . . unpitied and forlorn," with no alternative but "to retire and die."[54]

Poor women living on their own suffered from an economic and social vulnerability unknown to other whites in the city. Immigrant women, like their laboring fathers, husbands, brothers, and even their children, did the work once reserved for blacks. To get by, they swept and scrubbed, took in laundry, stitched and hemmed, cooked, sold themselves, and begged on the streets. There is ample evidence that at one time of pique or another, many plantation wives compared their lot to that of slaves, but only after knowing the fates of a woman alone can one actually imagine that connection between race and gender.[55] A poor woman, like a slave, owned nothing—not her time, not her property, sometimes not her children. And also like a slave, she knew that hard work did not pay.

Severe deprivation among women of the laboring classes posed such a universal moral dilemma in all industrialized nations, as well as in the urban areas of the North and South, that those who broached the subject often did so with unusual candor. Matthew Carey vividly painted the "harrowing truths" of working women in the slums of Philadelphia.[56] The condition of seamstresses was such familiar horror that the "Shirtmaker," "plying her needle and thread . . . [i]n Poverty, hunger and dirt" had by the 1840s already become associated in the public mind with the shameless exploitation of women by the clothing industry and all who patronized it. Garret rooms in southern cities harbored women living in the pain of harrowing deprivation equal to any of the six thousand Philadelphia seamstresses found by Matthew Carey in 1830. A worse situation could scarcely exist than that of Margaret Ryan, a Charleston widow whose sole livelihood rested upon needlework "when she could get it." Surviving in "great destitution," with "the care of two children and with working late and Early, she could not make over 25¢ to 30¢ a day."[57]

54. McGruder, *Female Domestic Missionary Society*, 8.

55. For one view of the complex dynamic between plantation women and their slaves, see Catherine Clinton, "Caught in the Web of the Big House: Women and Slavery," in *The Web of Southern Social Relations: Women, Family and Education*, ed. Walter J. Fraser, Jr., *et al.* (Athens, Ga., 1985), 19–33.

56. Matthew Carey, "Essays on the Public Charities of Philadelphia," in Carey, *Miscellaneous Essays* (Philadelphia, 1830), 154. A superb account of New York working-class women can be found in Christine Stansell, *City of Women: Sex and Class in New York, 1789–1860* (New York, 1986), especially Chaps. 1 and 2.

57. "Report of the Visiting Committee," January 30, 1856, in COH.

In 1851, an article in *De Bow's Review* proclaimed the opening of Carew and Hopkins' shoe factory in Charleston as a boon to needy women and children. Using the division-of-labor model found so successful in Lynn, Massachusetts, Carew and Hopkins made cheap shoes for slaves by mass-producing the various parts and then hiring out the "closing" to anyone willing to do the final sewing at low cost. The magazine touted this as an ideal opportunity for family members to earn money between household tasks. Poor children especially could benefit from the discipline of this productive work and "acquire habits of industry and application that will be of incalculable use in after life."[58]

The problem with work like that offered by Carew and Hopkins, as everyone who dealt with the poor understood, was that no woman could stitch fast enough or work long enough to gain a proper livelihood from piecework. An article reflecting on this problem in Jacob N. Cardozo's *Evening News* estimated in 1845 that every man's shirt required 20,628 stitches from the sore fingers of some poor woman. During the depressed forties, Charleston women doing the "slop work" on cheap goods received 6¼ cents for homespun shirts and twice that for pants.[59] Even so, competition among the women for this sight-destroying labor was too great and wages, consequently, too small for anyone to make a reasonable living. Factory work, some hoped, would divorce women from their custom of doing self-defeating piecework in their homes, but it also robbed them of the ability to set their own hours and their own pace, and to watch over their children. Instead of proving a boon in the North, the spread of factories had actually deprived women of the more profitable fields of weaving and knitting, leaving only piecework and stitching for seamstresses.

The transition of women working outside their homes hastened the process of family erosion. Short of prostitution or domestic service, women with children had few alternatives. The widowed, the abandoned, and the wives of sailors, without their husbands for months or years at a time, characteristically supplied the labor for retail operations manufacturing cheap men's clothing. Fine goods remained the province of the tailor shop, run almost exclusively by men. Work was seasonal; competition, fierce. Every time a woman picked up a needle to baste or trim a precut garment, she competed not only with similarly situated women but with those on farms and inmates in poorhouses and prisons. With

58. "South Carolina Shoe Factory," *De Bow's Review*, X (January, 1851), 682–83.
59. "A Word for the Poor Seamstress," Charleston *Evening News*, November 2, 1845; "Report from St. Stephen's Chapel, January 1–June 30, 1843," *Gospel Messenger*, XVIII (September, 1843), 168.

the commodification of the clothing industry, manufacturers sought the commercial advantage of lower costs made possible by the wide availability of cheap cloth after 1820 and the cheap labor of women enslaved by necessity. The wards of the Charleston Orphan House spilled over with children of working mothers like Mary Bagley, a young Irish widow with two small boys born ten months apart. "Industrious and anxious to do for herself and her family," she found work as a maid and tried to keep the children with her, but two rowdy five-year-olds proved "an objection to her employers." With no alternatives, she first placed Michael, then Charles, in the orphan house, where they both died.[60]

The unskilled fell into a web of poverty they could not escape. Orphan house commissioners despaired at the fates of some of the girls who had once been in their institution. Typical was a Mrs. Jenkins, orphaned as a child, twice married, twice widowed, so "worn by hardship" at thirty-three that her chances for another marriage appeared slim. She clung to her children "as company and solace" and supported them on "the mere pittance which she forces herself to earn by dragging out a miserable existence in drudgery of different kinds." Intent on finding some security for their children, unsophisticated women married precipitously and often only multiplied their misery. Ann Wilson's second husband was a sailor who could not support her "from poverty" and would not support her children from pride, so she got by taking in sewing "when she could get it" and scrubbing floors even when she was pregnant. Jane Considine, a Belfast native, also had two children when her shoemaker husband died. "Poverty induced her to marry again," this time to a soldier stationed on one of the Sea Islands, south of Charleston. Soon another tragedy struck; she was "duped" by this "villain," who had a wife and eight children at home.[61]

The churchwardens of a Charleston parish intervened in the case of Frances Rychbosch, a widow with four children who "experienced the greatest misery, entirely dependent on the occasional and precarious

60. Commissioners' file, January 16, 1857, in COH; David M. Katzman, *Seven Days a Week: Women and Domestic Service in Industrializing America* (New York, 1978), 176. The story of Charleston's working mothers giving up their children was repeated time and time again, but deaths in the asylum were rare: Child mortality in the orphan house was estimated in 1848 at only about 1.50 percent. This rate, lower than among the population at large, was especially remarkable considering the history of exposure to disease and poor nutrition many suffered before being admitted (Dawson and DeSaussure, *Census of Charleston, 1848*, 45).

61. Application file, March 2, 1863, November 25, 1852, in COH. For a description of similar efforts by English women, see Michael Anderson, *Family Structure in Nineteenth Century Lancashire* (Cambridge, Eng., 1971), 68–78.

bounty of a few charitable and well disposed individuals." She sold off most of her own clothes piece by piece—a jacket, a dress, her shoes—and almost every stick of furniture just to survive, until, according to the warden's report, "overwhelmed with the miseries of her situation, she has become deranged in mind and wholly incapable of affording her children the smallest assistance." After watching the struggles of his neighbor, another widow with four children, a Charleston man concluded: "Tis impossible for a woman left alone in the cold world to sustain herself and her children at the wash tub, thrice within the last two months she has been brought to the borders of the grave through excessive labour striving to work for the bread of her children."[62]

In the course of visiting the poor, the city's "pious and benevolent" were horrified to learn of the pittance afforded to women who did work for the "slop shops." Members of the Charleston Port Society organized the Seamen's Bethel Clothing Store, a cooperative society whose members would meet once a week "to cut out and arrange the work and to give it to industrious females, giving the preference to the wives of destitute families of seamen." The finished clothes would then be sold by volunteers through the store, and all profits, after giving the seamstresses a fair return for their work, would go to replacing their stock of materials and supplying clothing for those sailors who often lost their clothes in shipwrecks and other accidents. The store operated on cash donations from citizens and gifts from local merchants. Most important, in the course of one year, thirty women saw that "a new chance is opening to them from which they may receive the means of earning an honest livelihood."[63]

Women, who most often managed female workers, whether as domestics in homes or seamstresses in shops, found the economics of exploitation as attractive as men did. Women took advantage of one another in numerous ways. For example, when thrifty housewives "bought cheap," they devalued the labor of women performing out-work for clothing manufacturers who cut costs by cheating their laborers. Even those women who expressed their sympathy for poor women in the aggregate through church work or benevolent societies displayed a shocking lack of empathy when dealing with individuals in their own homes. Accustomed to black slaves whose whole existence was submerged in service, city women complained incessantly of the "inexplicable" seething anger and resentment they detected in their white servants. One can only imagine the dynamics between Rebecca Everingham and her maid, Margaret

62. Application file, March 25, 1845, in COH.
63. Charleston *Courier*, March 25, 1848.

Boggs. After fuming about letting her off during visiting hours to see her children at the orphan house, Everingham finally wrote the commissioners asking them to change the rules for her personal convenience, since she "would rather have them come to see the mother" while she continued to work "than spear her to goo there."[64]

During the 1820s, just at the time that popular culture began romanticizing family life, the real status of women and their children declined in all American cities. Economist Thomas Cooper was clearly moved by the widespread and unjust condition of working women. In his collection of lectures given at South Carolina College, he notes in three places the startling fact that most Philadelphia seamstresses working from dawn to dusk scarcely made sixteen dollars annually. Not only pieceworkers but all working women suffered exploitation by the "master dealers, the capitalists," who received twice what they paid their laborers. Cooper blamed the manufacturing system for this situation, which made prostitution more lucrative than honest work. He also probed the deeper cultural reasons for the economic imbalance between men and women and identified several special restrictions and social disabilities under which women labored. The "injudicious" nature of female education, which eschewed the useful and taught girls to be dependent "silly play things" of their husbands, created a situation he identified as destructive to female intelligence and "not necessary for mutual happiness" of a married couple. Lack of training and generally weaker physiology restricted women to low-paying occupations such as upholsterer or bookbinder. Only bias and tradition, he concluded, prevented women from succeeding as watchmakers, perfumers, jewelers, as well as dressmakers.[65]

Free of crippling and arbitrary taxes, Corn Laws, and a rigid class system, Americans enjoyed unprecedented economic freedom, Cooper contended. Only women encountered roadblocks to individual advancement. Like most economists of the time, Cooper recoiled at the idea of special legislation for the poor. The reviled British poor laws only created idleness. As victims of a pervasive and arbitrary exclusion from economic power based on gender rather than ability, women, he suggested, constituted the only class of labor who could still walk and deserve special government assistance. Too often he had observed the tragedy of "female victims of male extravagance" thrown upon their own resources and totally unprotected in person or property by law. Yet (and there was always that *yet*) full endorsement of any program of assistance to women ran

64. Commissioners' file, October 12, 1826, *ibid.*
65. Cooper, *Lectures*, 110–11.

the risk of encouraging either wholesale desertion by husbands or a boom in the pauper population.[66]

Balancing these dangers against the undeniable inequity, Cooper opted for the easy way out. He declared poverty among women as a woman's problem. Ideally, some profitable employments should be reserved exclusively for women, but since this was unlikely, Cooper, who found little to celebrate in the inefficient concept of the lone producer, suggested that women form cooperative societies to avoid lowering wages through excessive competition among themselves. A female tailor's cooperative (that hired a few men to do the immodest job of taking measurements for men's suits) might well succeed if it could produce high fashion at low prices. Rather than wait for male initiative, he urged, women should organize benevolent societies of their own to address the problem of "unfair and inadequate" wages. Cooper's mediation on the plight of women is inconclusive and ultimately disappointing, but it does pinpoint the key to ameliorating suffering of all poor, male and female. Wages had to reflect value added to goods rather than be determined by some abstract level of subsistence. Better wages provided the only meaningful solution to poverty, short of governmental intervention. Acceptance of a labor theory of value flew in the face of the materialistic defense of slavery and planted the seed of conflict between white laborers and slaveholders.[67]

Politicians spoke of ideal possibilities and economists of theory, but those who tried to comfort the hungry, sick, and homeless during the dark night that swept over Charleston in the late 1820s and early 1830s understood the shallowness of prevailing ideology when compared to the depth of suffering. Southern republicanism, with its emphasis upon freedom and race, proved inadequate to address urban realities. For all the sectional differences expressed by politicians at the top echelons of Charleston society, life for those at the bottom closely resembled that of the poor of New York or Boston. Even if the South had split off from the nation during the terrible fight over Nullification in 1832 and 1833, there would be no secession from the world market and its vagaries that threw the unskilled labor into the hell of perpetual insecurity.

What did freedom mean for those poor and white in the South? A minister writing for the Charleston *Gospel Messenger* in 1828 painted a shocking picture for his readers: The laborer without work lives in a present haunted by "ungratified wants, daily disappointments, perpetual

66. *Ibid.*, 306–307.
67. *Ibid.*, 110–11; Conkin, *Prophets of Prosperity*, 147.

mortifications, and increasing anxieties," facing a future "full of terror for himself and his children." This desperate man searches almost in vain for a sense of self-worth as "the rich treat him as a criminal, the poor as a rival, his country as a burden on her prosperity—and the multitude, as an insignificant being, who has no feelings, no rights."[68]

68. *Gospel Messenger*, V (March, 1828), 65.

IV

A PEACEFUL REVOLUTION

He who would love his country had best begin by loving his neighbor.
—William Henry Trescot, 1848

By the 1830s, when so much of America looked optimistically toward the future, Charlestonians feared that their best days were gone. While it may appear from their moss-backed adherence to historic institutions that they believed in the possibility of permanence, of fixing their society at a particular point, keen observation of the events swirling around them never let thinking men and women forget that the true essence of life is change. Evidence that they faced a major transformation in their way of life came from several sources. The "indecreet zeal in favor of universal liberty" threatened their domestic institutions. Transformation of the city's population from a black slave majority to one that was free, white, and increasingly foreign-born challenged traditional social relations. The general and unabated decline of the economy further reduced the state's national political power. Charlestonians confronted their dilemma in different ways. Some struggled to seal their beautiful city in amber against the dynamism of time and block its further decline. Others sought revitalization to catch up with the modern world and shake off their widespread reputation for "Rip Van Winklism."[1]

Charleston's revolutionary generation vicariously felt the relentless and transforming fury of history when they listened to the horrible tales of fugitives escaping to South Carolina from the rebellion and race war in San Domingo in 1793. In one generation, the island went from a slave colony to the world's first black republic. As memories of this cataclysm began to dim for Charlestonians, Denmark Vesey's rebellion in 1822 snapped their attention back to the dangers at their very doorsteps. Like the Stono Rebellion two generations before, the abortive plot masterminded by a free black craftsman crystallized race sentiment in Charleston and reminded all of the potential power of the black majority and the

1. Thomas Pinckney [Achates], *Reflections Occasioned by the Late Disturbances in Charleston* (Charleston, S.C., 1822), 6.

risk of blurring the lines dividing slave and free. Denmark Vesey, a free-man of color, embodied the attributes most feared by southerners. Although black, he possessed all the gifts held for white men. He enjoyed the self-esteem that often characterized slaves born, as he had been, in the West Indies and had traveled widely in his sea journeys with his master. Not only did he have the good luck to win a Charleston lottery and buy his freedom; Vesey could read well and speak with persuasion as he preached his liberating version of the gospel to the local black community. A skilled carpenter, Vesey also epitomized the threat that local craftsmen felt from their free black and slave competition.[2]

For months after Vesey's arrest and execution, fear still hung heavy in the city. The early summer image of would-be assassins of the Charleston elite swinging from hastily built gallows continued to burn in local memory; Thomas Pinckney, whose mother's family had once lived as part of the white minority on Antigua, reflected upon the near catastrophe.[3] His commentary, like most on the Vesey incident, repeated the same caveats propounded for almost a century about the need for white control and the danger of black autonomy. However, Pinckney, diplomat, vice-presidential candidate, and South Carolina's first governor, offered a unique solution to the penultimate question of domestic safety. To enjoy economic progress and sleep soundly in their beds, the aged hero of the American Revolution asserted, Charlestonians must give up their slaves.[4]

Tall and dignified, with a bearing often compared to Washington's, Pinckney encouraged Charlestonians to recognize that their situation on a tightly packed peninsula differed from the rest of the state and much of the South. Of all the circumstances combining to produce the Denmark Vesey rebellion—the legacy of successful rebellion in San Domingo, the ability of slaves to learn to read and write surreptitiously and earn their own wages, the spread of dangerous ideals of liberal democracy so prevalent in the North, the black majority—only the last had a means of resolution. Free laborers must replace the slave. The hard tasks of the city

2. John Lofton, *Denmark Vesey's Revolt: The Slave Plot That Lit a Fuse to Fort Sumter* (Kent, Ohio, 1983), 75–95.

3. Frances Leigh Williams, *A Founding Family: The Pinckneys of South Carolina* (New York, 1978), 10. Born into a prestigious planter family, Pinckney graduated from Christ College, Oxford, read law at the Middle Temple, and practiced in Charleston after returning from the revolution to find his plantation burned. He served as governor from 1787 to 1789, and his strong support for Federalist policies won him the vice-presidential nomination in 1796 (without his consent), appointment as minister to Great Britain, and election to Congress in 1797 (*Dictionary of American Biography* [New York, 1934], VII, 617–19).

4. Pinckney, *Reflections*, 4–5.

and domestic chores should no longer be reserved for resentful slaves who toiled haphazardly with murder in their hearts but should be entrusted to the "brave, industrious, and honest peasantry" from Ireland and other oppressed countries, who would gratefully take them up. Slaveholders would be given sufficient time to sell their slaves, perhaps to the rising gentry of the South Carolina Backcountry, who by virtue of their rural isolation enjoyed safety denied to city dwellers.[5]

Pinckney, a Federalist and member of the Cincinnati, developed two arguments for his plan to transform the labor force of the city suggesting (in contradiction to prevailing republican sentiment) that he believed a greater danger lay in hostile slaves than propertyless men and women. He looked forward to a time when the major barriers to attracting "active, industrious mechanics and labourers"—yellow fever and competition with slaves—would be overcome. Although the source of the epidemics still remained a mystery, he expressed optimism over the city's efforts to clean up the putrid pools and mounds of offal that gave off suspicious miasmas. Pinckney believed in any case that a core of acclimatized foreigners already living in Charleston might provide sufficient encouragement for others to join. But Eden itself, he had to admit, would hold no allure for white workers reduced to the social rank of slaves, as they currently were in Charleston. As it was, Pinckney contended, even high wages could not overcome "the great repugnance felt by a freeman to be placed in any respect on the same footing as the slave." But once the black was eliminated from the city, "a superior class" of workers, and even domestic servants, would flow into the vacuum if offered sufficient incentives. To replace Charleston's 22,432 blacks, he calculated, the city needed only to attract one-half that number, since laborers would bring their wives to work also. Pinckney believed that "the advantages of commerce [were] becoming so extensively beneficial" that all it required to flourish was "a free course," uninhibited by slaves. Confidently explaining the mysteries of the "invisible hand," Pinckney contended that "the supply of all transferable goods is equal to the demand, so that if it be known that Charleston requires any number of mechanics, draymen, &c who will be liberally paid for their services, as many as can be remunerated will find their way thither, provided there be no impediment to their exercising their business with safety and satisfaction to themselves."[6]

Pinckney further outlined the advantages of free labor and advised "Master Mechanics" to choose it over slavery. Using chattel labor was

5. *Ibid.,* 6–10, 16–17.
6. *Ibid.,* 23, 15.

false economy, he argued, since wages constituted only part of the total costs of a slave. "The sick days, the idle days, the doctor's bills, the work-house and guard house fees, which are the results of that intemperance and debauchery so generally prevalent, diminish in extraordinary degree the profits of his labor while it ruins his constitution and morals." And for the slave with no future to contemplate, no family to support, no chance for a life beyond subsistence, where would be "the emulation to excel"? With free labor, "wages are necessarily in proportion to the skill and good conduct of the workman;" by hiring by the job, the employer clearly gained much greater flexibility to adjust labor costs to profits.[7]

Pinckney wanted to see white faces at all stations of the urban economy, as "draymen, porters, fishermen, hucksters, butchers, barbers." He believed "with equal force" that in the interest of domestic safety, whites should also be incorporated into the intimate life of the city as house servants, for among trusted retainers the greatest slave treachery often lay. Under these conditions, domestic service should hold no greater stigma in the South than it did in the North, as long as the wages were high and white servants relieved of intermingling with black slaves. Besides the added safety and more pleasant conditions of living with white people, employers would be liberated from lifetime care of their servants, and that alone would compensate for the relatively high wages they would have to pay a more efficient staff.[8]

The Pinckney proposal underscores the significant difference that commerce and a wage-earning class made in the social and political as well as economic life of the city. That difference, the canny old statesman surmised, threatened to cast Charleston adrift from the moorings of the political culture of the outlying plantation districts. Thomas Jefferson, John Taylor, and other, now-forgotten agrarians of the early Republic had inveighed against the siren song of commercial capitalism and the cities it spawned. Now impotent to seal off their society from the specter of the propertyless (free blacks and poor whites), Charlestonians watched helplessly as they observed the incubus of "faction," predicted by James Madison, that threatened to undermine the harmony and consensus of thought most easily achieved in a society of master and slave.[9]

In 1828, shortly after writing his paean to free labor, Pinckney died and did not live to see the consequences of his only partially fulfilled wish for his native city. In their attempt to revive the waning urban economies,

7. *Ibid.*, 12–13.
8. *Ibid.*, 14, 19.
9. See James Oakes, "From Republicanism to Liberalism: Ideological Change and the Crisis of the Old South," *American Quarterly*, XXXVII (Fall, 1985), 551–55.

local politicians and southern entrepreneurs did struggle to reestablish Charleston's position in the "cotton triangle." Desperate to route commerce through southern cities and promote direct trade with Europe and the western states, even some diehard laissez-faire advocates compromised on the issue of internal improvements. Federally subsidized canals, turnpikes, and railroads promised new markets and new life for "our drooping cities." Charleston investors made plans to bring goods from the cotton-rich interior through improved state roads and a canal system that was already in place by 1817. Not long after the drive for internal improvements began, suggestions that the port should have rail links with inland towns first appeared in the public press. In 1828, the first stock offering was made, and two years later construction started at Line Street. By 1833, the "Best Friend of Charleston" regularly plied the 135-mile track to Hamburg and back, bringing the city fame for having America's first steam locomotive hauling both freight and passengers. But it did little to increase trade. Even though this new economic program failed to transform Charleston into the "Emporium of the South," dreams of tapping into western trade through a Memphis-to-Charleston railroad continued to animate Charlestonians' fantasy and attract their investment dollars.[10]

Efforts to enrich the region through internal improvement projects expanded the laboring class in the South. Since most slaveholders declined to risk their valuable property in dangerous construction projects through malarial swamps, labor contractors energetically recruited northern workers and immigrants, who (as Pinckney predicted) flowed southward to do the dollar-a-day pushing, shoving, hauling, carrying jobs that accompanied the development of the urban commercial economy. Prosperity remained elusive. Cost overruns, delays, broken contracts, and bankruptcies thwarted the efforts of southern entrepreneurs to link their region to external markets. When jobs ran out or they could no longer bear the conditions of gang labor, northern workers threw down their picks and made their way to nearby cities. Although unversed in the customs of slave societies that designated menial jobs for blacks only, they were familiar with the principles of strikes and fair wages, and introduced class tensions and race friction into rather languid urban scenes.[11]

Like Thomas Pinckney, Jacob N. Cardozo, newspaper editor and

10. Richmond *Enquirer*, June 26, 1838, quoted in Russel, *Economic Aspects*, 22.
11. Ulrich B. Phillips, *A History of Transportation in the Eastern Cotton Belt to 1860* (New York, 1913), 150, 152, 260–61; Russel, *Economic Aspects*, 15–32.

economist, understood that the changing demographics of the port city, especially during the mid-1830s, foreshadowed social and political changes in the port city's future. Gazing out across the harbor, he watched with concern as every tide brought in more immigrants, now that modest prosperity had returned to Charleston. From the time packet service commenced in 1822 until 1836, agents sold more than 32,500 one-way tickets from New York City to Charleston.[12] Cardozo noted the ragged clothes and anxious faces and suspected that rather than promoting the urban economy, the newcomers, overwhelmingly Irish Catholic, would become additional burdens on the already strained local relief system. He also feared that this new class of wage worker (a large percentage of whom were between thirty and forty years old and less likely to be married than natives) would transform the economic and social relations of the city in ways Pinckney had not foreseen.[13]

Cardozo's intellectual journey might be said to reflect the evolution of social thought in Charleston during the first decades of the nineteenth century. He moved from Federalist conservatism to the cautious liberalism of the southern Whigs. Born among the Sephardic Jews of the city, he worked his way through the apprenticeship system of the local press establishment, advancing from clerk to become the editor of the *Southern Patriot* in 1817 and an active member of Charleston's literary set. Cardozo would complete his own painstakingly argued economic textbook in 1826, the same year that Thomas Cooper published the first edition of *Lectures on Political Economy.* He used his journal to promote the remnants of Federalist politics and free-trade economic theories. In the interest of unrestricted competition, he cavalierly declared in 1819 (when he was closely reading Malthus and Adam Smith) that all public institutions relieving the poor should be abolished because they rewarded the idle and perpetuated "a race of drones and paupers." His economic thought could not be categorized as uniquely southern, but he did strive in his treatise to discredit the labor theory of value and emphasize the natural harmonies among producing groups. Cardozo believed that Smith's pessimistic class themes applied to Europe but not America, where progress was possible without pain.[14] By 1827, however, the reality of the sick and homeless in his own town challenged Cardozo's confidence. The brutal

12. Christopher Silver, "A New Look at Old South Urbanization: The Irish Worker in Charleston, South Carolina, 1840–1860," *South Atlantic Urban Studies,* III (1979), 149.

13. Cardozo proposed that sea captains who profited from immigrants' fares be made to post bonds for every laborer who disembarked at the port (*Southern Patriot,* July 30, 1836; Dawson and DeSaussure, *Census of Charleston, 1848,* 25).

14. Conkin, *Prophets of Prosperity,* 135–41.

toll of the 1820s on the laborers in Charleston forced him to concede that wages may well fall below the subsistence level in cities, those "certain spots where the population has a tendency to become crowded," of even a relatively new country. If some funds were not available for the poor, the editor knew from experience, "the worst forms of vagrancy must shock the eye and harrow the feelings."[15]

Cardozo found a congenial political home in the Whig party, the political arm of southern commercial interests. Cardozo welcomed the growing economic interdependency accompanying the expansion of capitalism because it "binds all parts of the modern social system in one beautiful and harmonious scheme of general wants." "The poor," he observed in 1818, "are now as necessary to the rich as the rich are to the poor."[16] Since he dismissed the notion of inherent conflict between labor and capital, Cardozo joined a growing number of South Carolinians who saw manufacturing as the solution to the economic woes of the region as well as the private suffering of the poor. At the same time, he remained alert to the social and political dangers accompanying the development of an enfranchised working class.[17]

By 1845, Cardozo predicted that the city had entered an "era that will not bear any large or sudden rupture of social or economic relations" and echoed the Whig position as he cautioned that "true social progress" might only be attained through "Progressive amelioration." At Thanksgiving that year, he expressed his gratitude for numerous aspects of Charleston life, including "a fair distribution of property without inordinate wealth or abject poverty."[18]

To reconcile the inevitable inequality of a commercial economy with democratic expectations, southern liberals departed from the republican shibboleths of virtue and independence and embraced a new creed that reconciled material success and political freedom. Individual agency had long been a staple of southern thought, but its interpretation emerged as one of the major distinctions between the Democrats and the Whigs. Jacksonians construed the idea of a meritocracy in its most egalitarian aspects, but Whigs believed that it confirmed the existing social hierarchy. Consequently, the constraint that Democrats would feel toward gov-

15. *Southern Patriot,* September 16, 1819, December 1, 1827, quoted in Melvin M. Leiman, *Jacob N. Cardozo: Economic Thought in the Antebellum South* (New York, 1966), 206.

16. *Southern Patriot,* August 15, 1818.

17. *Southern Patriot,* quoted in Leiman, *Cardozo,* 213–14; Kaufman, *Republican Values,* 132.

18. Charleston *Evening News,* October 14, 1845.

ernment activism contrasted with the willingness of Whigs to structure public policy to expand individual opportunity. Some years later, when over $12,000 in Charlestonians' taxes went to poor relief, the city council of Nashville, a bastion of Jacksonian individualism, begrudgingly allocated about $500 for all municipal charity and rejected a tax rate increase for indigent health care.[19]

In the thirty years from 1830 to 1860, Charleston (as well as other coastal towns such as Mobile, New Orleans, and Savannah) had to absorb waves of immigrants that would transform the urban labor force in ways no less significant than the later changes in the postemancipation rural South. Charleston began the nineteenth century with a black majority of two thousand, but in the intervening years a stagnating regional economy encouraged many whites to gamble on frontier life in the new, rich lands of Mississippi and Alabama. Similarly pressed by hard times in the North (especially during the depression of 1837), thousands of western Europeans, mostly Irish and Germans, embarked on their second or third migration by boarding the coastwise packets and schooners sailing south. The steady stream of newcomers so altered the lineaments of the urban population by 1840 that a writer for the Charleston *Courier* noted with alarm that "the laboring classes in our city are daily changing, the white laborer is gradually taking the place of the slave."[20] Fears that slavery might be a moribund institution more in danger of withering away rather than being legislated away plagued citizens of southern cities who saw most vividly the population trend.

And this trend would only accelerate. In 1845, the constant stream of foreigners possessing only "their arms and their industry" gained momentum with the potato famine in Ireland and an agricultural depression gripping Germany. Until 1839, South Carolina natives were the largest single group in the poorhouse, and many of those likely came for the medical facilities; after that date, Irish immigrants predominated. By 1845, the Irish not only outnumbered native-born Americans but came close to surpassing all other immigrant groups combined.[21]

The migrations of the early nineteenth century affected all urban areas in the United States, but only in the South did they threaten to erode the racial consensus and alter historic relationships between labor and capital. In what was probably a low estimate, one source suggested that

19. James Oakes, *Slavery and Freedom: An Interpretation of the Old South* (New York, 1990), 121–23; Commissioners of the Poor, Annual Report, 1860, in CPH; Nashville City Council Minute book, July 12, 1859, in Davidson County Hall, Nashville, Tenn.

20. Charleston *Courier*, January 1, 1840.

21. Dawson and DeSaussure, *Census of Charleston, 1848*, 7.

slightly over 12 percent of Charleston's total population held no naturalization papers. Whatever inclinations persisted to use benevolence and charity as social controls upon the northern model were replaced by new incentives to use public and private resources to incorporate newcomers, foreigners, and strangers into the body of the white community. Community leaders sought to elevate them and create what William Henry Trescot described as an "impassable gulf" between the southern hireling and the slave.[22]

The most potent force for the realignment of thought about the white laboring population and their ties to the future of Charleston was the agricultural depression of the 1840s that threatened to depose King Cotton. The economy of the entire region fell into disarray as the price per pound dropped from over twelve cents to about eight. In the depths of the crisis, newspapers carried dismal reports of nickel cotton; some planters realized only a few cents per pound for their product. "Colbert," writing an open letter to Governor William Aiken in 1845, described the depression's ramifications in all aspects of southern life: "the profitless yield of our agriculture, in the languishing life of our commerce; and in the verveless, death-like stillness of all the hands of manufactures and the arts."[23]

Attitudes toward white labor changed as cotton prices dropped in the forties. Some, like Cardozo, looked to the new class of workers as a key to the state's economic future if hoeing cotton gave way to spinning cotton. Prominent Charlestonians who served as trustees of Roper Hospital, where fever-stricken immigrants overflowed the wards, urged the city council to rethink carefully their prejudices against the bumptious foreigners crowding the streets, laughing and talking loudly on Sundays, and carrying hods of bricks. "It might be said," they suggested, "that the spirited enterprises, for which our times stand pre-eminent, have only been brought to a successful termination, by what would seem the indomitable energy of this class of our population."[24]

In the eight years between the federal census of 1840 and a local census, the white population increased by 8.9 percent, and the combined slave and free black population declined by almost a quarter. For the first time since the Revolution, a black majority did not exist in Charleston.

22. *Ibid.*, 9.
23. Russel, *Economic Aspects*, 33–34; Fabian Linden, "Repercussions of Manufacturing in the Ante-bellum South," *North Carolina Historical Review*, XVII (1940), 313; Charleston *Evening News*, October 14, 1845.
24. Charleston *Mercury*, October 10, 1853.

This decrease of 4,000 blacks came on the heels of a decade-long decline; Charleston lost 1,230 of its "colored" population between 1830 and 1840. How could this be explained? Clearly, the white increase in a place as unhealthy as Charleston came from foreign migration and immigration from more salubrious environments, but where had the black population gone?[25] The official explanation argued that most of the 3,000 slaves formerly enumerated in the four wards of the incorporated city now lived on their own, hiring out their time and finding cheap quarters away from their masters on the poorly policed Charleston Neck. Findings of the 1850 federal census support this theory by showing 4,840 slaves in the unincorporated periphery. But despite the change in domicile among slaves, a white majority persisted, as foreigners and newcomers to the city also found that this area close to the small industrial district of the city met their needs.

Population shifts had subtle effects; the perception of the proper roles for the races was one of them. Traditionally, white servants had been so rare in Charleston that in 1822, when young Paul Trapier on his way to study at Harvard was served by white waiters on a stop in New York City, he remembered feeling "so awkwardly that I should have been relieved if I could have asked them to take seats at the table beside me."[26] But when he began his ministry among the urban poor during the 1830s, whites scrubbing floors, driving drays, and even waiting on tables seldom shocked or outraged the white community.

The perennial poverty among the masses of Catholics remained unabated or perhaps even deepened during the 1840s, but the increase in their numbers nevertheless made them a force in the political life of the city. The veneer of religious toleration that characterized the city's early history never fully masked the deep-seated animosity toward Catholics, but local leaders made efforts to bind the divisions in the white community. Desire for social solidarity in the face of mounting external criticism of southern institutions softened resistance to expanding the role of Catholics. The perceived hierarchical and secretive nature of Catholicism continued to conflict with republican ideals, but Bishop England's scriptural defense of slavery and his acceptance of democratic principles had gone a long way toward mending the rift.[27]

25. Dawson and DeSaussure, *Census of Charleston, 1848*, 8, 9.
26. Trapier, *Incidents in My Life*, 9.
27. For his history of the Catholic church's position on slavery, see John England, *Letters of the Late Bishop England to the Honorable John Forsyth on the subject of Domestic Slavery* (Baltimore, 1844).

The deciding factor in Thomas Smith Grimké's unsuccessful bid for mayor in 1832 may well have been his Unionist stance, but the impolitic public comments of this antipapist High Churchman also worked against him. In contrast, his savvy and successful opponent, Henry Laurens Pinckney, delivered a rousing St. Patrick's Day oration to a joint meeting of a Catholic benevolent society and the Irish Volunteers, an annual ritual he repeated throughout his years in office.[28]

When Pinckney spoke to Irish leaders, he did so in the modest wooden chapel dedicated to St. Finbar that had stood since 1821 as the see for Georgia and the Carolinas. As their numbers and political influence expanded, Catholic leaders dared to dream not only of celebrating their faith in a proper cathedral but of making their own powerful architectural statement to assert their new place in the community. In 1846, Ignatius Reynolds, John England's successor, announced his intention to add another church to the city landscape. The proposed brownstone facade conveyed a unique urbanity in feeling, and its monumental size reflected national trends in architecture. When finished in the early 1850s, the Cathedral of St. John and St. Finbar stood as the largest church on the peninsula.[29]

The blurring of the lines between white immigrants and black slaves caused concern throughout Charleston. From the need for white racial uplift above the black, a pragmatic humanitarianism evolved. In response to outraged local sensibilities and the desire for increased distance between the races, a Charleston grand jury moved in 1846 to ban the public whipping of white criminals. Once punished like a slave, a white man, some thought, carried "the stigma of degradation to the grave," and his value as a citizen was lost. Also, the grand jury found that whenever the lash fell on a bare white back, crowds of blacks always gathered to gape at the spectacle, moved to "sorrow for the sufferings of the convicted" or "self-congratulation in the degradation of the white." Black author Henry Bruce recalled that whenever "high toned and high spirited slaves" looked upon sweating and degraded whites, "held, as it were, in a degree

28. William W. Freehling, *Prelude to Civil War: The Nullification Controversy in South Carolina, 1816–1836* (New York, 1965), 181–82; Henry L. Pinckney, Jr., *An Oration Delivered in St. Finbar's Cathedral on the 17th of March 1832 before the St. Patrick's Benevolent Society and Irish Volunteers* (Charleston, S.C., 1832).

29. Severens, *Antebellum Architecture*, 179–82. When Bishop England died in 1842, the city mourned and the bells of Protestant churches tolled in sorrow in a symbol of political, though clearly not theological, harmony. Paul Trapier, then rector of St. Michael's, complained to his vestry that it was highly inappropriate for Episcopalians, spiritual kin "to a long line of martyrs," to display public grief over the passing of any Catholic bishop (Trapier, *Incidents in My Life*, 40–42).

of slavery" by their poverty, they sniffed at the notion that "white blood alone is superior."[30]

In 1838, the poorhouse commissioners proposed redesigning the tread-mill to employ paupers in grinding corn. A committee studied the issue and advised against forcing inmates to tread the mill, the most feared of all punishments in the workhouse, not because the leg-laming device was too severe but "because the long established connection of such an estab-lishment with the Work House has rendered it one of the modes of pun-ishment for slaves and other colored persons." They expressed their re-luctance "to break down any of the distinctions between that class of person and the white population by subjecting them to a common mode of punishment."[31]

Mobility distinguished even the most degraded white laborer from the slave. The majority of the poor were not sniveling malingerers pan-handling nickels on street corners; they were workers and consumers. In some ways, the urban poor on daily cash wages proved the best, most efficient consumers, for while they did not buy much at a time, their needs were predictable: cheap housing, grist and rice, molasses, and dur-ing the best times, a bit of stringy beef or fatty pork. They spent every-thing they got, as soon as they got it, on the intense business of staying alive. Even the institutionalized poor helped churn the market as consum-ers of large quantities of bread, rice, and beef, which were frequently delivered bony, stale, and full of weevils.

Southerners recognized the importance of consumption as well as pro-duction among laborers. When Georgia jurist Joseph Henry Lumpkin wrote his prescription for southern economic independence in 1852, he not only recommended diversification but also cited the need to "increase the class of consumers among ourselves." With slavery already restricting the traditional consumption of the working class, the inability of many poor citizens to purchase basic necessities further burdened the economy. City merchants looked at their ledgers and knew this to be true. A writer in the Charleston *Courier* urged shopkeepers to consider the economic and social interconnectedness of the community rather than their own short-term financial benefit. He singled out "those fools" who happily

30. City of Charleston, Grand Jury Presentment, May term, 1846, quoted in Jack Kenny Williams, *Vogues in Villainy: Crime and Retribution in Antebellum South Carolina* (Co-lumbia, S.C., 1959), 108; Henry Clay Bruce, *The New Man: Twenty-nine Years a Slave, Twenty-nine years a Free Man* (York, Pa., 1895), 38–39.

31. Minutes, January 9, 1839, in CPH. See also the vivid description of the treadmill in George C. Rogers, Jr., *Charleston in the Age of the Pinckneys* (Norman, Okla., 1969), 147–48.

sold to town laborers at inflated prices but preferred to line their shelves with cheap goods ("the fruits of Northern labor") rather than buying locally made products. Preference for northern-made goods sapped the vitality of Charleston's economy and contributed directly to the woes of the southern working class, mostly immigrants with only gossamer ties to the region. Every poor man's dollar quickly found its way into the pocket of a grocer, tavern keeper, or landlord. "How would the merchants feel," queried the *Courier*, "if the poor, who depend upon that very labor for their bread, by way of retaliation, were also to obtain their articles of household consumption from the North?" Just as working men and women at home and abroad understood they had the potential to bend employers to their will by withholding their labor, they could mobilize their collective buying power and boycott uncooperative stores. With the tables thus turned, it would then be "the merchants struggling to pay their rents and feed their families." The *Courier* article closed on an ominous note, cautioning that "if the poorer classes are always thus, they will seek some friendly land and our houses [and goods] will want purchasers"; that is, if "the hospitals and jails do not arrest their footsteps, ere they have taken their departure."[32] For a small price, any laborer could join the large number of immigrants who plied the East Coast on steamers looking for work, taking with them their small satchels, their labor, and their trade.

Since fires regularly purged the city of rickety wooden buildings that offered cheap rents, the lack of affordable housing also discouraged laborers from staying in Charleston for any length of time. The Great Fire of 1839, especially, drove hundreds out of their lodgings as it cut a wide swath across the narrow peninsula. When large numbers of construction workers flowed into the city to work on its reconstruction, the shortages became even more acute. The *Courier* severely criticized "local capitalists" who replaced modest homes with "edifices large and calculated for the dwellings of the rich or for the marts of a stupendous commerce" and predicted that continuing to ignore the needs of the poor in planning "great public enterprises" would inevitably work to "destroy the whole system."[33]

32. Russel, *Economic Aspects,* 107; Charleston *Courier,* September 11, 1847. North Carolinian Hinton Helper raged against such disparities in his appeal to the nonslaveholders of the South: "Instead of keeping our money in circulation at home, by patronizing our own mechanics, manufacturers and laborers, we send it all away to the North and there it remains: it never falls into our hands again" (Hinton Helper, *The Impending Crisis of the South: How to Meet It,* ed. George M. Fredrickson [1857; rpr. New York, 1969], 44–45, 18, 22).

33. Charleston *Courier,* September 11, 1847. In 1857, the Reverend A. Toomer Porter

The need to improve the attractiveness of Charleston to white workers coincided with expanded interest in diversifying the southern economy. Supporters of manufacturing in South Carolina argued that poor whites excluded from agricultural work had a "moral right" to the opportunities of economic and educational improvement offered by wage employment. Since slavery robbed whites of agricultural work and intruded upon opportunities in towns, establishment of factories run exclusively by free white labor seemed the best, perhaps the only, solution to establishing a third economic sphere. The Charleston *Courier* supported manufacturing as a way to bring the poor "into daily contact with the rich and intelligent." Pioneer textile manufacturer William Gregg suggested that his mill and others like it could save "thousands of poor, ignorant, degraded white people among us, who in this land of plenty live in comparative nakedness and starvation." And, Gregg quickly added, whites might well prove even cheaper to hire than free blacks or slaves. In 1845, the Charleston City Council repealed the prohibition against having steam engines within the town limits, believing the public dangers from not developing their manufacturing capacities more treacherous than the threat of fire from the spark-spewing machines.[34]

Other southern states debated manufacturing projects as a means to reinvigorate their sagging economies and occupy languishing poor whites. In 1845, a correspondent for the Richmond *Whig*, a journal that favored further economic diversification, reported his impressions of conditions in northern factories and dismissed all high-flown talk of operatives being "white slaves in wretchedness" as only southern bravado designed to "gull and keep up the spirits of you and your white poor." Manufacturing, he revealed, held the key to political and economic liberation for the South and its masses: "We cannot blind the eyes of our poor people much longer by misrepresenting the laboring population of the North."[35]

---

built two small houses on a donated lot on Gadsden Green with the idea of building "a system of decent houses at low rents for respectable laboring white people," but his plan was interrupted by the Civil War (Rev. A. Toomer Porter, *Forty Years a Rector and Pastor* [Charleston, S.C., 1894], 12).

34. Richard H. Shryock, "The Early Industrial Revolution in the Empire State," *Georgia Historical Quarterly*, I (June, 1927), 118–19; Charleston *Courier*, July 14, 1845; William Gregg, *Essays on Domestic Industry: Or, an Enquiry into the Expediency of Establishing Cotton Manufactures in South Carolina* (Charleston, S.C., 1845), 47, 48. See also T. P. Martin, ed., "The Advent of William Gregg and the Graniteville Company," *Journal of Southern History*, XI (August, 1945), 389–423, and Leonard Stavisky, "Industrialism in Antebellum Charleston," *Journal of Negro History*, XXXVI (July, 1951), 302–22.

35. Russel, *Economic Aspects*, 53; Richmond *Whig*, November 4, 25, 1845, quoted

Virginian John Herbert Claiborne recollected that in the years before the Civil War, opportunities to work in Richmond's cotton mills proved "a God-send" to the poor, especially women. The overseers of Lunenburg County found local farm families reluctant to take female apprentices in their homes, "as they would be required to perform such labour as is generally performed by slaves and would necessarily compel them to labour with the slaves which is somewhat revolting to our natures." Bringing the factories nearer the fields had even the potential to ameliorate economic discrimination of gender; the Richmond *Whig* urged the construction of a cotton factory in the city for the express purpose of providing jobs for the daughters of poor Virginia families, as Lowell did for New England girls.[36]

In Georgia, the Augusta *Chronicle* promised not only a living wage but near riches from mill labor. Assuming that at least four people in a family could "tie a thread," the journal surmised that they could make $16 a week, or $800 a year. If they spent only half of what they earned, their standard of living would greatly exceed those of agricultural workers, and they could then invest $400 in factory stock that paid about 12.5 percent. If all fifty thousand of Georgia's poor whites had done this, the five-year total would exceed $30 million investment for the industry.[37]

De Bow's Review described the rebirth of the household economy, southern-style: "The active industry of a father, the careful housewifery of the mother, and the daily cash earnings of four or five children will very soon enable each family to own a servant; thus increasing the demand for this species of property to an immense extent." Everyone would win. After a brief foray into the cash economy, the hardworking and thrifty could merge into the ranks of the slaveholders. Observing Gregg's experiment at Graniteville, South Carolina, a hopeful commentator writing for *De Bow's* admitted that though none of the three hundred operatives had yet transcended wage labor, they seemed "cheerful and well disposed," despite dawn-to-dusk labor. Supporters of industry as a

---

in Stephen J. Knight, "Discontent, Disunity, and Dissent in the Antebellum South: Virginia as a Test Case, 1844–1846," *Virginia Magazine of History and Biography*, LXXXI (October, 1973), 444.

36. John Herbert Claibourne, *Seventy Five Years in Old Virginia* (New York, 1904), 44–45; Auditor of Public Accounts, "Report of the Poor, Lunenburg County, June 1, 1845," in Virginia State Archives, Richmond; Richmond *Whig*, August 8, 1845, quoted in Knight, "Discontent, Disunity, and Dissent," 444.

37. Shryock, "Early Industrial Revolution," 117. Also helpful is Richard W. Griffin, "The Origins of the Industrial Revolution in Georgia," *Georgia Historical Quarterly*, XLII (December, 1958), 355–75.

remedy for the problem of superfluous white laborers strove "for a synthesis of slave labor in agriculture and white labor in manufacturing and mechanical pursuits, controlled by the cultivated intellect of the South, which would form the basis of prosperity and power." The hoped-for merger of "plow, loom, and anvil" would move the region toward its destiny of wealth and independence. Success depended upon laying aside class differences for mutual advancement and social harmony.[38]

A leading architect of the white supremacy argument and expositor of the Mudsill theory of labor claimed that the foundation of all great civilizations consisted of a lowly and permanent laboring class. James Henry Hammond backed away from his initial contention that only slaves should labor in mills to a position singling out factories as strictly a white preserve. If given their own sphere in the factory, his reasoning went, white workers would not only continue to tolerate slavery but embrace it. Slack economic times had also caused great suffering among the rural poor whites. Various estimates during the 1840s placed their numbers at anywhere from 50,000 to 125,000 in South Carolina alone. *Hunt's Merchant's Magazine* surmised that the cotton states harbored a "mass of unemployed white labor."[39] Joseph H. Lumpkin assured those who feared collecting masses of poor whites together that the role of the southern factory, not unlike the southern plantation, would be to oversee and control the "degraded, half-fed, half-clothed, and ignorant." Wage work would raise their sights and give them a commitment to the community and "an interest in their [own] welfare." Ideological opposition to industry faltered in the face of economic decline. The southern press claimed that the much maligned factory system in the South would be "clean and breezy" to attract the "southern peasantry," in sharp contrast to the hellish "infernos of the Northern capitalists."[40] Factory operatives twisting the cotton threads and guiding the shuttles to make fine cloth or rough duck would become willing lieges in service to King Cotton, grateful participants in the system rather than grumblers and saboteurs. In

38. J. H. Taylor, "Manufactures in South Carolina," *De Bow's Review,* VIII (January, 1850), 26; Chauncey S. Boucher, "The Antebellum Attitude of South Carolina Towards Manufacturing and Agriculture," *Washington University Studies,* III (1916), 257–58; J. H. Lumpkin, "Industrial Regeneration of the South," *De Bow's Review,* X (January, 1852), 49; Taylor, "Manufactures in South Carolina," 25.

39. In 1849, James Henry Hammond estimated there were 50,000 poor whites. Mill owner William Gregg guessed they numbered 125,000, representing one-third of the state (Russel, *Economic Aspects,* 52; *Hunt's Merchants Magazine,* XXII [1851], 649).

40. "Industrial Regeneration of the South," 49; Richard W. Griffin, "Poor White Laborers in Southern Cotton Factories, 1789–1865," *South Carolina Historical Magazine,* LXI (January, 1960), 30.

this way, the poor gained a stake in slavery, the institution that made the cotton industry possible. Reluctant to promote the creation of a permanent white proletariat, architects of the Old South version of the New South creed asserted that for whites, factory work was but a temporary expedient, for in a slave society, every southern male could still dream of masterhood.

In terms foreshadowing the boosterism of twentieth-century textile promoters, Hammond sounded like an auctioneer offering the idle hands of South Carolina's poor to the highest bidder. Not only were southern poor whites numerous, he asserted; they were also used to privation and could be pressed to work harder and longer than the stubborn Yankee farm folk or quarrelsome immigrants. "If driven to that necessity," Hammond insisted, "there is no doubt we can extend our hours of labor beyond any of our rivals."[41] Expecting little more than their traditional diet of cornbread and bacon, inured to the heat, accustomed to rags, these men and women of little hope were seen as uniquely suited to the rigors of mill life in the same way that blacks found their natural place in the field. It is unlikely that any of the sallow-skinned folk of the Georgia hills or Charleston slums who reluctantly signed up to work the looms or sweep the floors ever expected to become planters or southern capitalists. Only pressing necessity drove them to queue up at factory doors to ask for jobs. The work was regimented, wages small, and they were not treated like future masters but like lintheads and foreign minions.

Poor whites excited interest from those who wanted to regiment their labors and those who wanted to control their leisure. Enthusiasm for temperance surged in Charleston during the 1840s as the connections between a sober working class and the progress of the local economy became more closely related. Temperance activity, initially most intense among the cities of the seaboard South, spread over the entire region in two waves. The first lasted from the late 1820s until the mid-1830s, when the dispute over total abstinence and the suspected links with abolition forced southerners to retreat from the national temperance societies. A group of reformed alcoholics in Baltimore started the Washingtonian Society, which focused on alcoholism as a personal rather than social problem and sparked renewed southern interest in temperance. The popular Sons of Temperance and a number of other groups followed suit. By the early 1850s, more than fifty thousand in eight southern states had "taken

41. Hammond even argued that southerners could be pushed beyond the 73½-hour work week of the spoiled northern workers. James H. Hammond, "Progress of Southern Industry: Governor Hammond's Address Before the South Carolina Institute, 1850," *De Bow's Review*, VIII (June, 1850), 519–20.

the pledge." As immigrant populations became increasingly insulated from Protestant reformers by their sheer numbers, temperance workers abandoned earlier hopes for moral suasion in favor of "legal suasion," even before the passage of the Maine Prohibitionary Law of 1850. Temperance reform entered its third phase, going from social transformation to individual rehabilitation to legal restriction.[42]

The male-dominated southern temperance movement provided scant opportunities for leadership among those women passionately devoted to its principles. However, the explorations undertaken by workers such as Thomas Smith Grimké into the effect of alcoholism upon families contributed to the limited debate about "women's issues" in the South. Temperance work brought women together as teams to finance and promote their cause, but in Charleston and other southern cities during the 1840s this interest led many away from gender-oriented concerns to championing the cause of an unlikely hero. Finding an irresistible conflation of moral reform, patriotism, and their traditional nurturing role, numbers of Charleston women threw themselves into domestication of the storm-toughened merchant seaman. Harriet Pinckney, niece of Thomas Pinckney, embraced the sailors' cause so completely that she rented out a portion of her garden to finance the construction of a chapel for homeless seamen that was later named in her honor. Sailors symbolized more than just the supreme moral challenge to the benevolent women of Charleston. Just beginning to understand themselves in the new role of consumer in the mid–nineteenth century, urban women started to see the connection between their economic lives and these sailors (whose stock went up as the depression wore on) because of the crucial role the seamen played in the successful prosecution of trade and commerce.[43]

The typical sailor gave little encouragement to the optimistic women praying for his reform. Washing into the city with every tide and immediately diving into the "vortex of dissipation and drunkeness" once ashore, retching and puking on public streets, giving and receiving unspeakable diseases in the port city's abundant brothels, sailors bore hard-earned reputations as disgusting animals. The moral life of sailors had

42. Jack S. Blocker, Jr., "Temperance Movement," in *The Encyclopedia of Southern History*, 1185–86; Anne C. Loveland, *Southern Evangelicals and the Social Order, 1800–1860* (Baton Rouge, 1980), 151.

43. In 1857, an advocate for the early closings of retail stores believed that the support of local women would assure the success of their campaign. "Although the ladies generally sadly undervalue their influence," a "Reformer" suggested, the choices they made in their daily shopping gave them economic power (Letter to the Editor, Charleston *Courier*, June 6, 1857).

proven such a severe challenge to southern piety that most churches reserved their extra funds for work with pagans in foreign lands rather than this domestic mission impossible. But there was another side to the life of Jack Tar that Charlestonians began to explore. Poorly paid for backbreaking labor, enduring frightful conditions and cruel discipline, never knowing if they would return safely after months at sea, most seamen lived a life far removed from the romantic image of carefree sailor lads happy at work and play. In 1823, during their frenzy of reform activity, Charlestonians founded the second Port Society in the United States.[44] One of its chaplains, William B. Yates, who served from 1836 to 1872, won renown for his passionate sermons enlivened by "unrestrained, frequent and somewhat theatrical gestures." The new chapel on Church Street, bought from the Baptists, was installed with a prow-shaped pulpit decorated in gold lettering *He Taught Them Out of a Boat*. From this unique platform, Yates, an Episcopal priest, threw himself wholeheartedly into his mission and took great pride in bringing tears to the eyes of those thought so unregenerate that even the Methodists had written off as lost.[45]

Charleston women, seizing the opportunity to expand their domestic influence, sponsored boardinghouses that approximated their ideal of female-dominated homes. No-nonsense matrons who managed these sailors' inns gladly took control over the wayward and forbade gambling, card playing, indecent language, cursing, and liquor. These housekeepers eagerly offered to hold the men's pay until they returned safely to the ship and strategically placed tracts such as *A Kind Word from a Sister* where the sailors might find them in a vulnerable moment. A writer for the Charleston *Courier* spoke for many who believed they detected a "moral softening" among hardened mariners exposed to the uplifting effects of gentlewomen. Churchwomen claimed to succeed where jails and police-

---

44. William Harden, *Recollections of a Long and Satisfying Life* (1934; rpr. New York, 1968), 35–36; "Charleston Port Society," Charleston *Mercury*, March 21, 1855; William B. Yates, *An Historical Sketch of the Rise and Progress of Religious and Moral Improvement Among Seamen, in England and the United States, with a History of the Port Society of Charleston* (Charleston, S.C., 1851), 22–23; *Southern Christian Advocate*, September 30, 1853. In 1780, British Bible societies distributed Bibles to sailors but provided no religious instruction. Sympathetic Bostonians founded a short-lived tract society for the religious and moral improvement of sailors in 1812. In 1822, New York's Marine Bible Society became the nation's first.

45. Yates, *History of the Port Society*, 9–10; "A Biographical Sketch of the Reverend W. B. Yates: The Seamen's Friend," in *Temperance Souvenir*, ed. Edwin Heriot (n.p., 1852), 242, 246–47. By 1885, more than fifty thousand sailors had heard sermons on morality and temperance (Thomas, *The Protestant Episcopal Church in South Carolina*, 694).

men had failed by creating "a calm and tranquil haven" and subduing these sinners with "the desirable restraints of religion and morality."[46]

By the 1840s, sailors who truly wished to resist the temptations of seductive port cities could seek out the dove-and-olive-branch ensign that signaled the safe harbor of the seamen's bethels. Directors of the nonsectarian Savannah Port Society, established in 1843, maintained that the sins of sailors were no more heinous than others and insisted that ministers who preached at their chapel address them as citizens and men, "not outcasts from all civil institutions, and irreclaimable in morals, destitute of human feeling, and adverse to religious culture." Although Richmond did not formally sponsor a seaman's association, the press expressed sympathy for these poor strangers. Anxious to have the same sort of facilities as Charleston, one Richmond paper urged benevolent women of their city to turn their powerful organizational talents to the cause of "Old Jack."[47]

No one argued that a sailor's life was exemplary. They were not, interestingly, described as victims of their own sinful nature but compared to wounded soldiers acting in the service of southern merchants. Charged with all aspects of public relief by the city's charter, members of the Charleston City Council voted in 1859 to expand their definition of the poor to include seamen and to support a marine school for boys: "The citizen afloat, as the citizen ashore, are both alike the custodies of the public weal." To share the city's wealth with seamen seemed particularly appropriate, considering the personal risks they assumed in moving the region's products to markets across "the stormy and treacherous ocean." "Sailors," a special committee concluded, "have not had their due share of sympathy."[48]

Interest in sailors and their families brought to light the social and economic costs of poverty. In a fund raising speech for the Seamen's Home in 1848, sophisticated lawyer William Henry Trescot rejected out of hand all mawkish sentimentality about this class. An avid defender of slavery as the ideal relationship between labor and capital, he condemned "the money spirit . . . which counted men and women, but as implements to be used in the mine or the factory, and be thrown aside when broke by diseases or worn out with use." He told a crowd at Temperance Hall that he was not appealing to their sympathy but reminding them of their "social, popular, and patriotic duty." While no one is responsible for the

46. "The Ladies Seamen's Friends Society," Charleston *Courier*, May 21, 1845.
47. Richmond *Daily Dispatch*, July 29, 1859.
48. William Gilliland and W. H. Inglesby, Special Committee on the Marine School, City Council Minutes, June 21, 1859, in Charleston City Council Records.

state of another's soul, he argued, people of a republic must be alert that their custom or economic system "condemns no class of citizens to such labor as . . . drives them into an association with all that is vile and vicious in human nature." In the case of seamen, who risked their lives for pennies bringing wealth to others, the community bore extraordinary responsibility. He directed his comments to the merchants and shipowners in the audience: "Now is not he whom you hire, whose life you purchase for a few pieces of silver, your brother man, and your fellow-citizen? Has he not like affections—like rights and can you believe that your duty to him ends with the payment of his wages?" Even free labor involved the practice of mutual obligations, Trescot insisted. "Do you not feel that though you are higher up, and he is lower down that you are enabled to keep your place, because he keeps his."[49]

Then the Charleston political leader spoke of social equality, though, he was quick to add, not the kind wished for by the misguided advocates of the various "isms." Men might be born equal, but they surely did not stay equal. What he envisioned was a refinement of the southern republic that incorporated all classes of whites:

> where high and low—rich and poor—employer and employed, feel, that each in his own place, they are all members of one body—where the rich modify their wants, and the poor so distribute their labor that the humbler comforts of life shall be within the reach of all—the merchant who owns the vessel and the sailor who navigates it, feel the sympathy of a common nature, and recognize the obligations of a common humanity, by the reciprocal exercise of labour on the one hand, and considerate kindness on the other.

"And it is, I firmly believe," he asserted, "only this principle of mutual responsibility between those who serve and those who are served which can develop and draw out fully the charity of a society constituted as is ours." Just before asking for volunteers to canvass every ward and solicit contributions from local shipsmasters, Trescot reminded his audience: "He who would love his country had best begin by loving his neighbor."[50]

Charlestonians understood the liberal forces in the world beyond their peninsula. They followed especially closely the events of the following

49. Charleston *Courier*, February 8, 1848.

50. *Ibid.* Volunteers formed the Committee of Thirty-Two, to take donations beyond the $3,000 already raised and purchase a suitable building, to be known as the Seamen's Home of Charleston. The list of ward leaders contains many familiar names of men active in local charities, mostly merchants, wealthy from the shipping trade.

year cheering the liberation of Texas in 1848 and the American victory that liberated the rich lands of the Southwest. But many had mixed reactions to the revolutions that were toppling the royal families of Germany, Italy, and France in domino fashion. And no one greeted notices of the formation of the Free Soil party in 1848 or suffrage activity among the women at Seneca Falls, New York, as anything but bad news. Charlestonians began energetically erecting barricades to the erosion of traditional social values. Their own drives for autonomy poisoned by the connection with radical ideals, Charleston women had to fall back and renounce the gains they had made.

In the last months of that portentous year, conservative Episcopalians built a new church in the suburban district of Cannonsboro that pioneered a return to strict observance of ancient canonical practice. Speaking at the dedication, the Reverend Edward Phillips remarked upon the turbulence caused by the European revolutions and asked his equally concerned audience where the conserving forces of society might be found if similar radicalism swept over America. He suggested that they "must look to the schools, to the workshops, to the fields, to the firesides of domestic life, for the elements of virtue and morality, which are to be operated for the conservation of social order, and especially the integrity of the institutions of our Republic." If these safeguards faltered, Phillips warned, "the irresistible tide of immigration" that was already being felt in the city would dash "its waves of European opinions and prejudices upon our shores, [and] where is the rock upon which our Federal Union shall be safely anchored?"[51] Where indeed?

51. Rev. Edward Phillips, "Discourse at the Opening of . . . Church of the Holy Communion, Cannonsborough, November 12, 1848," *Gospel Messenger*, XXV (January, 1849), 295–96. Edward Phillips was first employed by the Domestic Missionary Society and later served as the head of St. Stephen's Free Chapel.

V

CHILDREN OF THE CITY

Farewell, Farewell, necessity, necessity, Death of Death, Lord Thou hast promised to temper the wind to the shorn lambs, have mercy on me, and my brother's poor little orphans.

—David Gavin Diary, 1858

On his American tour in 1828, British naval officer Basil Hall visited one of Charleston's most important landmarks, the large and well-tended orphan house. While watching hundreds of homeless children at play, he suddenly understood what made Americans so unlike Europeans. America was a world in motion. "The whole community is made up of units," he concluded, "amongst which there is little of the principle of cohesion." Americans seem to be "perpetually dropping out of one another's sight, in the wide field over which they are scattered." Among the urban poor especially, "even the connexions of the same family are soon lost sight of—the children glide away from their parents, long before their manhood ripens;—brothers and sisters stream off to the right and left, mutually forgetting one another, and being forgotten by their families." Hall grasped the unhappy truth that whenever breadwinners perished in fevers, drank themselves into uselessness, or simply wandered away, they usually left children "dependent on persons whose connexion and interest in them are so small, that the public eventually is obliged to take care of them, from the impossibility of discovering any one whose duty it is to give them a home."[1]

Alexis de Tocqueville, in America at the time of Jackson's reelection in 1832, also foresaw the dangers of excessive individualism, a potent symptom of the "democratic disease." Social equality and increased mobility, he theorized, usually lead to increased isolation and the misguided belief that the individual controls his own fate. Social cohesion invariably suffered during periods of intense individualism because of the simultaneous abjuration of responsibility toward others. Public virtue, Tocqueville observed, always fell victim to private interest.[2]

1. Hall, *Travels in North America*, III, 165–66.
2. Tocqueville, *Democracy in America*, 506–508; Thomas, "Romantic Reform in America," 657.

Resistant to democratic ideals, benevolent paternalism lingered in Charleston. After more than a century of active benevolence and a well-established elite dedicated to the principles of public service, the political culture of the city continued to link private interests to public acts. Always notoriously quarrelsome about paying taxes, Charlestonians maintained their tradition of voluntary charitable donations; all city institutions benefited from gifts of local citizens. In 1786, the city council first began exploring the possibility of creating an asylum for the orphans of the Revolution and studied the model of Bethesda, the orphanage established by George Whitefield outside Savannah. Within four years, with private donations and public funds, Charlestonians financed the first municipal orphanage in the new Republic. Individuals participated in this great civic enterprise through their generous and often eccentric gifts. Several of Charleston's delegates to the newly created state legislature turned over their annual salary to the orphans' cause; alert beachcombers hauled barrels of butter washed in from a shipwreck to the new asylum; local gamblers donated lottery tickets; confectioners donated ice cream; grocers, watermelons. By 1860, the orphan house enjoyed a unique place among city institutions with a private endowment of over $65,000 to be used for "extras" such as art lessons or advanced education for worthy students.[3]

The Charleston Orphan House (designed as an "institution of national virtue") stood as a celebration of a city beginning its golden age. Local citizens actually regarded their support of the institution, which opened in 1792, as a patriotic act rather than a charitable one. Indeed, throughout its history, the orphan house played an important role in the politics of the town. In 1810, a speaker at the asylum's anniversary celebration in St. Phillip's Church, warning his audience of the transmutability of all things, emphasized the total and unthinkable reversal of fortunes among the slaveowners of San Domingo in the course of less than one generation. No one knew, he warned, what changes lay in store for Charleston, but he understood one thing clearly. Dramatically pointing to the rows of the homeless and abandoned white boys and girls sitting straight in their pews, he urged the assembly to "cherish these children of the public," for they were the key to the city's future. Support of the white nonslaveholding population increased whenever Charleston society felt threatened. In 1831, during the middle of the Nullification debate and at

3. Rev. Thomas Smyth, *Oration Delivered on the 48th Anniversary of the Orphan House in Charleston, South Carolina, October 18, 1837* (Charleston, S.C., 1837), 411–22; Charleston *Mercury*, October 19, 1844; King, *Charleston Orphan House*, 6.

the beginning of aggressive northern criticism of southern institutions, the editors of the *Gospel Messenger* dug through their files and reprinted the 1810 address, believing it held an important message for their discordant times.[4]

The local importance of this institution is shown by the remarkable men who, believing themselves "God's substitutes on earth," accepted benevolence as an incontrovertible part of their roles as Christians and citizens. Service on the board of the orphan house meant much more than civic recognition. It empowered town leaders with direct influence upon the future generations of a class otherwise beyond their reach. As Charleston's elite became increasingly self-conscious about the need to demonstrate their dedication to public stewardship, the orphan house served as a useful tool.[5] Rather than merely warehousing derelict children or leaving that task to religious or private societies, Charlestonians transformed a social problem into a political opportunity. The two thousand white children who passed through the asylum's doors from 1790 to 1860 not only had their basic needs met but also learned about their place in the urban community and their role in a biracial society. The patronage of some of the town's wealthiest and most influential men and women gave the abandoned and homeless a place in a society traditionally based upon the ties of blood, race, and kinship. Although women could play only marginal roles in the operation of the asylum as "Lady Commissioners," many made creative and generous gifts from their own resources. For example, the widowed Mary Christiana Hopton Gregorie, sister of Sarah Hopton Russell, established a trust in her will to finance the education of an orphan-house boy for the ministry in the denomination of his choice. The orphan house served as a workshop where three generations of the urban elite formulated, clarified, honed, and refined their theories of class relations in a patriarchal world.

At midcentury, the Charleston Orphan House was "by far the most imposing edifice" in the port city. The five-story brick structure also symbolized the highest expression of the dream and thought of the community. Built on the site of the old revolutionary barracks just beyond the city line, the asylum was designed by one of the first commissioners, Thomas Bennett, Sr., progenitor of the wealthy and powerful family that dutifully fulfilled its obligations to the community supporting its political and entrepreneurial ambitions. Within its thick walls, the commissioners

4. *Gospel Messenger*, VIII (October, 1831), 292. In 1800, the largest segment of the population comprised children under ten years old (Dawson and DeSaussure, *Census of Charleston, 1848*, 17).

5. Hollinshead, *An Oration Delivered at the Orphan House of Charleston*, 14.

(chosen annually by the city council) tried to reproduce their vision of southern social relations. During the 1850s, the commissioners had it firmly in mind that the asylum must serve as the showpiece of southern democracy. They wanted more than a "Refuge of the friendless outcast." They strove to create an environment where even the sons of beggars or prostitutes might be "fitted for the higher Walks of Life."[6]

To Americans of the 1840s and 1850s who equated fatherhood and patriarchy with power and control, serving as surrogate parents to the poor children of the city had irresistible appeal. The commissioners, who emerged as saints in the civil religion of public service, were honored annually. Every year the city celebrated a feast day in their honor on October 18, the day in 1794 that legend said the whole town assembled to watch the first child received into the newly completed asylum. Hundreds of clergymen, city officials, and small children lined up on Boundary (later Calhoun) Street to form a parade celebrating the founding of the orphan house. They milled about until the city's German band blended its harmonies with the crisp fall air, starting "the joyful and solemn procession." All Charlestonians, Christians and Jews, were encouraged to respond "to the best feelings of our hearts and by the providence of God, to suspend business and amusements, to lay aside private animosities and party feelings, to consecrate our time, thoughts and affections, to the service of the poor."[7]

The anniversary parade presented public theater at its best. All "friends and citizens" were invited to follow behind the prominent men of the city as they led the little children through the town to St. Phillip's Episcopal Church. The commissioners of the orphan house headed the parade, followed by the mayor and city officials. In their annual display of unity, clergy of all denominations walked together, reluctant Catholics alongside Lutherans, flowing Episcopal robes contrasting sharply with the plain clothes of the Baptists. Orphan house nurses and staff kept the city's children moving in straight lines. Most tradesmen and mechanics granted a holiday to their apprentices raised in the institution, who cheered as their family passed. To the citizens watching from the curb, as well as the children trying to keep step, the intended message as the commissioners progressed through their city's streets was the same: "Behold in us your father."[8]

6. James Stirling, *Letters from the Slave States* (London, 1857), 252; Minutes, November 8, 1855, in COH.
7. Charleston *Mercury*, October 19, 1844; "Address of the 55th Anniversary of the Orphan House," *Gospel Messenger*, XXI (January, 1845), 300.
8. Charleston *Mercury*, October 19, 1844; Smyth, *Oration*, 412.

The parade wound through the main thoroughfares: down King, over to Meeting, turning at Cumberland until reaching its destination at St. Phillip's on Church Street. Once in St. Phillip's Church, a carefully tutored inmate read the traditional "Orphans' Address," praising a father's love as "holy, true, unselfish, heavenly." The ritual reading continued, expressing appreciation to the city for rescuing its children from "the poison of evil example and desperate necessity," and to the commissioners: "You have been to us as Fathers and with what delight and gratitude do we acknowledge the ties that bind us to you."[9]

Bound to community service and to one another in a fashion reminiscent of the ancient English frankpledge, the commissioners spoke during their weekly meetings around the long mahogany table in their meeting room at the orphan house of the problems of the poor as problems of the entire community. They made most of their decisions in an atmosphere of agreement and demonstrated the consensus for which the city and the state had long been famous. Chancellor Henry W. DeSaussure, a commissioner before moving to the state capital, Columbia, wrote to Commissioner Daniel Stevens offering assistance to any former inmates in the state capital "from our Beloved Institution, which I cherish very affectionately in my heart." DeSaussure expressed particular delight in Stevens' "account of the harmony of the Board, so long continued." In sending his regards to the commissioners, he added, "I honor their Labour and love their virtues."[10]

Harmony prevailed among the commissioners, even as the public men of the city rotated in and out of office. Extended terms assured continuity. From 1840 to 1860, forty individuals served on the ten-man board with an average tenure of eight years. Henry Alexander DeSaussure, the chancellor's cousin and chairman of the commissioners from 1838 to 1865, left an indelible mark upon the philosophy of the orphan house. Always an advocate of the child, whom he usually considered more "sinned against than sinning," DeSaussure preferred counseling to corporal punishment. He won the affection of hundreds of boys, who wrote for advice (and money) addressing him as "father." He so endeared himself to the girls that many asked him to walk them down the aisle when they returned to be married in the orphan house chapel. Upon his death, the children wore the black crepe armbands of deep mourning. In DeSaussure's will, he passed on to his eldest son the symbols that had defined his

9. Martin Hurlburt, "The Orphan's Address," Miscellaneous file, in COH; King, *Charleston Orphan House,* 106.
10. Commissioners' file, November 14, 1837, in COH.

life: his eagle from the Society of the Cincinnati, the family Bible, the gold sleeve buttons from his father, and a pair of silver pitchers presented by his fellow commissioners of the Charleston Orphan House.[11]

Other names important to the history of the city reappear in the story of the orphan house. Christopher Gadsden donated wharfage for all the building materials; Gabriel Manigault probably designed the chapel. Active supporters included Charles C. Pinckney, Nathaniel Russell, Elias Horry, Langdon Cheves, and Thomas Smith Grimké. No Charleston family was more closely associated with the asylum than the Bennetts—builders, politicians, philanthropists, planters, mill owners. Thomas Bennett, Sr., designed the original orphan house; his heirs were its future architects over three generations. Not only did they lend their time, money, and name to the projects, but they practiced personal stewardship by regularly taking children from the asylum into their homes. The tradition actually began with the senior Bennett's wife, Anna, who personally assumed the indentures for two girls to learn domestic work.[12]

Anna's son Thomas Bennett, Jr., South Carolina's governor from 1820 to 1822, continued the family tradition by serving six years as commissioner and also brought an exceptional eleven-year-old German boy from the asylum to raise with his own children. By the time that young Christopher G. Memminger met Thomas Bennett's gaze, the boy's gray-blue eyes already held their great power, an almost "magnetic force." Orphaned at four and left in the Charleston asylum in 1807 by his immigrant grandparents on their way to Philadelphia, the future treasurer of the Confederacy already showed extraordinary skill in mathematics at nine. While at the orphan asylum, Memminger sat in the same classroom with boys who would never make more than two dollars a day. The memory of his asylum experience and the knowledge of how different his life might have been had fate not intervened gave him an overpowering sense of responsibility to be worthy of his blessings.[13]

The deep and lasting friendship between Memminger and the governor's son W. Jefferson Bennett proved a fortunate alliance for all the children of the city. They both served long terms as commissioners of the orphan house and provided the impetus behind renovation of the free

11. King, *Charleston Orphan House*, 2–5; Wills of Charleston County, South Carolina, Vol. LXII, 1862–68, p. 528, WPA Typescript in Charleston Public Library, Charleston, S.C.

12. Anna Bennett took Catherine Shafer in 1802 and Janet Stewart in 1807 (King, *Charleston Orphan House*, 6, 32, 50).

13. Henry D. Capers, *The Life and Times of C. G. Memminger* (Richmond, 1893), 15–19.

school system. Bennett's cousin Celia Campbell felt an equal commitment to the poor youth of the city. Upon her return from a grand tour, she (like the Grimké sisters) renounced "the hollow, purposeless butterfly-life" of southern debutantes and found her own way—first by teaching Sunday school to poor children, then by personally raising funds for a convalescent home to provide poor women with an alternative to the charity ward. In the benevolent community, Celia Campbell enjoyed the reputation as the "Florence Nightingale of Charleston," and Bennett held the informal title "Second Founder of the Charleston Orphan House."[14]

As American society changed, the role of the orphan house changed. At the same time that Basil Hall made his observations about the disconnectedness of American society, moral reformers began focusing upon the family as the key to social order. Speaking in modulated tones from their parlors and sitting rooms where thick walls muted the sounds of angry confrontation, the nineteenth-century middle class generally referred to families of the poor as having a special pathology remote from the feelings of affection and loyalty that characterized their own domestic lives. When the idea became more widely accepted that good citizens were not created spontaneously by religious conversion but developed day by day in controlled home environments, urban reformers began taking long hard looks at the family life of the poor. They did not like what they saw. The city's children, it seemed, were being raised by parents who for the most part outraged "even common decency by their gross immoralities, and low degrading sensualities."[15]

In response to the increasing number of dependent children supported by local communities during the 1820s, Thomas Cooper argued in his *Lectures on the Elements of Political Economy* that the state should sanction no marriage without proof of the couple's ability to provide for and educate their children. "Marriage," Cooper contended, "is not a contract between a man and woman for their mutual pleasure; there is a third and a far more important party to the contract; viz: the public," which had a direct interest in the children that might be produced. Projection of the government as parent evolved from the medieval English

14. "Celia Campbell," in *Yearbook of the City of Charleston, 1881* (Charleston, S.C., 1882), 253–60. W. Jefferson Bennett also took a likely Scot boy as an apprentice into his milling business. An apt pupil, Andrew Buist Murray married Bennett's daughter and gained control of the business from Bennett's own sons. Serving as a commissioner of both the poorhouse and the orphan house, Murray further repaid his debt by leaving over a million dollars to the city upon his death (Fort Sumter Memorial Association, *An Account of the Fort Sumter Memorial* [Charleston, S.C., 1933], 3–4).

15. Commissioners' file, June 14, 1855, in COH.

doctrine of *parens patriae* giving the king certain rights of interposition in family affairs. By the mid–nineteenth century, Americans had translated this ancient doctrine as making the state the "superparent" of all minors.[16]

In Charleston, the orphan house commissioners represented the interests of children in family conflicts. They assumed roles in the life of the poor most closely resembling some amalgam of magistrate and secular priest. They even took turns holding Sunday-evening services at the orphan house and teaching in the Sunday school. Their statutory control over the city's children provided a mighty lever over the personal morality of poor parents. As nineteenth-century Solomons, they served as mediators in family disputes, took away children from the abusive, and returned them to the penitent. In the course of their duties, they walked the narrow steps up to third-floor rented rooms, sat in the January cold of unheated chambers, and most important, looked into the eyes of poor women imploring the city to save their children.

Such interviews severely tested both parties, the men in frock coats and the women in rags. One of the commissioners described his visit to the rented room that Margaret Ryan shared with her four-year-old and an infant of only a few months. "Her destitute situation" shocked him. He asked "about her mode of getting her living" and discovered that her husband had died after a long chronic illness. She explained how she sewed morning until night but could earn less than a quarter a day; keeping both her children proved impossible. After their talk, the commissioner concluded, "I found her [a] poor woman and from the references she gave me, they spoke well of her, . . . she gives up her child reluctantly."[17]

Before accepting any child, the commissioners insisted that parents renounce all legal claims, to prevent their putting children in and taking them out at their convenience. Both parties signed an indenture making the child "an apprentice to education" with the commissioners as their "masters." If a parent did decide to retrieve a child, another investigation took place to monitor improvement. Commissioners imposed strict guidelines: no heavy drinking, steady work, school for the child, and if a woman remarried, the new husband must be a suitable father and a good provider. But they did not operate without exceptions.[18] In 1855, the

16. Cooper, *Lectures,* 348; Jamil S. Zainaldin, "The Emergence of a Modern American Family Law: Child Custody, Adoption, and the Courts, 1796–1851," *Northwestern University Law Review,* LXXIII (1979), 1054–61.

17. Commissioners' file, January 30, 1856, in COH.

18. *Bylaws of the Orphan House of Charleston* (Charleston, S.C., 1861).

mother of an orphan house girl wanted to regain custody of her daughter. George Coffin, the visiting commissioner that week, paid her a visit and made his report: "I called upon the mother of Sarah Ann Mills, who seems entirely dependent upon her needle for support, but extremely anxious to have her daughter as a companion. She appears to be a very uneducated person, but correct. It is one of those cases that I feel reluctant for the girls sake to grant the application, but feel sorry for the parent."[19]

The commissioners had the authority to remove children forcibly from unfit or dangerous parents. Despite the power and standing of city officials, some women often furiously defended the sanctity of their homes. In 1827, Margaret Boggs, well known by the night patrol for her frequent drunk and rowdy conduct, returned home from another night in jail to find that the steward of the orphan house had entered her rooms and taken her children. She discovered that neighbors, noticing her chronic drinking and frequent absences, had secretly reported her to the city authorities. She fell into a rage at the news but collected herself enough to write to the commissioners of the orphan house. Boggs began her letter with the ritualistic humility, promising "an entire change and reformation." As she wrote, though, her anger gained control. The Irish mother concluded with an indictment of the town fathers: "What was at the time by you considered as a duty (though my children were taken off from me by surprise) . . . may be deemed oppression now that I can prove my ability to keep my children free from encumbrance to the public." An excellent seamstress when sober and well able to support the children, she denied the commissioners had any right to intervene in family matters or judge her. The relationship between mother and child, she argued, superseded any claim of the city: "My children, Gentlemen, are my own and I am their mother. They are the only link which binds me to this world: judge then of my lacerated feeling to live separated from them both."[20]

Used to the short-lived promises and emotional pleading of alcoholics, the commissioners refused to reunite the family until Boggs found some respectable person to vouch for her sincere love for the children and her intention to reform. A sympathetic neighbor swore that for the three months since she lost custody she had been faithful to her oath of abstinence made "before God and the townspeople" and had promised to send her children to the local free school. The commissioners had an

19. Fifteen-year-old Sarah went home, and two years later the commissioners gave her a fifty-dollar dowry when she married (Minutes, November 22, 1855, February 19, 1857, in COH).

20. Indenture file, April 17, 28, 1827, in COH.

obligation, Boggs's supporter pointed out, to fulfill their part of the compact since this Irishwoman had met as closely as she could "the requisite conditions prescribed to her, by your wisdom; having thus fulfilled your demands of her Duty towards you, she requires you, Gentlemen, to fulfill yours towards her by restoring to her bosom what only makes life dear to her." And they did.[21]

The evidence of their own words suggests that the poor possessed a strong sense of the difference between the public's responsibility and their private prerogatives, though inconsistencies abounded. Even those who resisted compulsory education welcomed, and expected, assistance in controlling unruly children. One Charleston woman turned responsibility for her son over to the men of the Hebrew Orphan Society: "I give the Society full control of my son, Sam, as I won't have anything to do with him in any shape or manner. I hope you make a man of him." The abandoned wife of Nickolas Ferenbacher, unemployed watchmaker from Baden and father of six, also pressed her claims upon the town. Mary Ann Ferenbacher assumed control of the family finances, became the disciplinarian for her six children, and borrowed money from relatives to open a small dry-goods shop. She put food on the table through "rigid economy and ceaseless industry," but her sons ran riot, totally beyond her control. The young Ferenbachers spent their days absorbed in side-street amusements and petty crimes with ragtag gangs of street urchins. Frequent absences expressed their contempt for the tedium of the "paupers' school." When the town fathers agreed to receive only one son, Ferenbacher, pressed by a "burden she could not bear," reminded the city officials of the implications of the southern patriarchal tradition: "My children are yours. They are natives, they are Southerners, and though their Father has forgotten himself, and deserted them, this is their country. And though poor and friendless, shall my son not be heard because a Mother's tongue alone urges his claim. . . . Oh, save him from being a curse to the soil that gave him birth, and spare the Mother from the anguish which this Mother must endure at the mere debasement of her child." So it was that Johann Himrik Richard Ferenbacher, the southern boy with the German name, was brought under the mantle of Charleston's elite.[22]

The fragility of their family structure set the urban poor apart from mainstream southern culture. The surest indicator of class differences resides in the effects of poverty upon an institution usually considered the

21. *Ibid.*
22. Tobias, *The Hebrew Orphan Society of Charleston, S.C.,* 15; Application file [*ca.* November, 1844], in COH.

bedrock of social stability. For men and women with only their labor to sell, market forces released a furious centrifugal force that tore at the very fabric of domestic relations—forcing mothers to give up their own children to nurture the offspring of others, pushing fathers into peripatetic searches for work or alcoholic escapes, and robbing children of childhood. The commissioners of the Charleston Orphan House rescued a sixteen-year-old girl struggling to care for three siblings and a drunkard father with the pennies she made from stitching pantaloons and vests. Her life had devolved into a living hell for the seven months since her mother's death, the commissioners learned, because "the Father beats her and the other children and is very crass to them all."[23]

The temporary nature of most wage work—until a railroad was built, a canal dug, a building finished—made life for a laboring family particularly precarious. Moving from job to job, workers sometimes traveled hundreds of miles for the chance to make an extra twenty-five cents a day. Many found it easier to travel light. Tensions between family cohesion and making a living wage intruded upon immigrant families with particular severity, but Irish workers, at least, more frequently than not traveled with their wives and children. The *Irish American* newspaper summed up the apparent sentiment of many: "If this world is worth living for it is because we enjoy the relations of the family," and without it "there is no propriety, there can be no order." In 1850, 80 percent of the Irish in Charleston had children with different birthplaces. As Hall observed, theirs was a world in motion; 70 percent of the Irish families in Charleston in 1850 had moved on by the next census.[24]

In the workaday world of the poor, the family operated as a fragile economic unit that bound men, women, and children in mutual dependency. Everyone worked; necessity dissolved bourgeois notions of "spheres." Any disruption in their economic equilibrium—the birth of another child, death, illness, unemployment—dramatically affected every family member. Their mutual need often first drew men and women together; their mutual dependency then forced them apart. Poverty clearly worked a fearsome calculus upon families. Early marriage and ineffectual birth

23. Application file, n.d., in COH.
24. The *Irish American,* quoted in Ernst, *Immigrant Life,* 179; Christopher Silver, "Immigration and the Antebellum Southern City: Irish Working Class Mobility in Charleston, South Carolina, 1840–1860" (M.A. thesis, University of North Carolina, 1975), 42. Over half the children in Silver's study were born outside of South Carolina, and at least 10 percent list New York City as their birthplace. Among the three hundred families that came to Charleston from 1850 to 1860, only 26 percent of the children were born outside of South Carolina.

control doomed the married poor to excessive numbers of children. Irish-woman Catherine Hartnette, to cite an extreme example, had twelve by age thirty-four. The impossibility of raising large families on low and irregular wages pressed heavily on both men and women. In the heat of an argument over money, John Andrew Buckheister, a native of Ham-burg, Germany, and city constable with a reputation for violence toward his prisoners, beat his wife Frances nearly to death in front of their chil-dren. According to one city missionary who visited the haunts of the laboring classes, husbands and wives, parents and children, lovers and friends, filled the air with "quarrels and cursing and blaspheming, 'til the blood runs cold to hear it." In 1853, eleven-year-old Mary Ann Croghan fled from a home where her parents engaged in a nightmarish whirl of fighting and drinking to beg for sanctuary in the poorhouse. Seeing the scars of physical cruelty, the steward took her into the institution where "she was protected by the Commissioners who refused to deliver her to her parents," sending her to the orphans' asylum instead.[25]

Domestic violence ravaged the poor families documented in the rec-ords of city institutions. "Renegotiation" of the obligations of husbands and wives accompanied the disruptive and often painful transition from the rural productive household economy to the family wage economy of the city and caused deep conflicts between men and women. Not only were women and children empowered by their ability to earn cash, but they also had other masters. Wives had always been expected to labor, and labor hard, but as servants they cooked meals and scrubbed floors in the homes of other men. One Charleston minister who operated a sewing school and helped poor women find repair work they could do at home complained that husbands, enraged over outside interference in their homes, posed the greatest obstacle in the success of his enterprise. Angry and often drunk, they burst in upon their wives, snatched garments from callused hands, and tossed them in the fire.[26] Children, once under paren-tal control until they had children of their own, could find an apprentice-ship to another master at age fourteen.

The interactions of the commissioners, parents, and children show the family as a political as well as a private institution. Supremacy of the interests of the public over those of individual parents was adopted in northern cities as in Charleston. The Boston School Committee declared

25. Roper Hospital Casebook No. 2, April 12, 1860, March 3, 1858; Wallace, "Re-ports of Charleston City Missions," *Southern Episcopalian*, II (August, 1855), 490–91; Minute book, December 15, 1853, in COH.
26. Stansell, *City of Women*, 80–81; Rev. A. Toomer Porter, *Led On! Step By Step* (1896; rpr. New York, 1967), 98–100.

in 1853 that compulsory school attendance regardless of parents' wishes was in the best interests of the community, since "the parent is not the absolute owner of the child."[27] Some years before, Thomas Smith Grimké had reached the same conclusion but framed his justification in terms of God's will rather than the growing authority of government agencies over private lives. Since "family Government [is] the foundation of Society," Grimké wrote to the orphan house commissioners trying to persuade them to establish a Sunday school, "every child belongs first to God, next to his Country, and lastly to his Parents," who in truth "are merely Trustees in the Order of Nature of Society."[28]

The commissioners dedicated themselves to reproducing in the orphan house a close approximation of ideal family life. Henry A. DeSaussure, a father with six children of his own, personally believed that the asylum should serve as a substitute for the "mother's knee, the father's countenance, the hearth, the social board, the conventional rule." Harsh discipline had no place in his scheme; the children did not eat, sleep, work, and pray by the whistles and bells that regulated northern institutions. Instead, the patriarchs set out and enforced a policy of "kindness and gentleness" to create an atmosphere "of cheerful and ready subordination, or active and voluntary industry, and of physical, mental, and moral improvement." As with their own children, they sought to direct and control by winning affection and establishing dependency.[29]

The commissioners hoped to elevate poor white children by training them to follow the proper path rather than breaking their will. The staff received very specific guidelines. The commissioners trusted the matron to nurture the "Spiritual life of the house" and "instill into the youthful minds around her, feelings of reverence and gratitude to their Heavenly Father and to impress upon them a sense of their moral responsibilities, and the lessons of virtue and piety." Daily prayers and weekly chapel set the rhythm of life in the house. The duties of the nurses included "granting all favors, allowing all indulgences, and practicing all forbearance . . . to make their orphan home a happy one." Contrary to the unhappy experience of Oliver Twist, punished when asking for "more," the staff encouraged the children of the city "to make their needs known" at mealtime. The commissioners expected the steward to promote "generosity, gentleness, honesty, truth and cleanliness" through example. To avoid the brutalizing and degrading effects of corporal punishment, they urged him

27. Stanley K. Schultz, *The Culture Factory: Boston Public Schools, 1789–1860* (New York, 1973), 306.
28. Commissioners' file, April 1825, in COH.
29. Minutes, June 25, 1857, *ibid.*

to "repress, by all the moral influences of the establishment, all selfishness, cruelty, falsehood, and impurity." Training included an emphasis upon self-discipline often lacking in the education of other young southerners. The annual report for 1859 praised the good behavior of the older boys at a public event and observed that "this self-control and elevated sense of propriety is a most important development and achievement in the education of the young, particularly in this class of children." [30]

A unique blend of Christian charity and southern liberalism combined with the precepts of racial supremacy to form the ideological matrix for the orphan house. It stood as a showplace where travelers and skeptics could witness the true philanthropy that animated southern hearts. Few who watched healthy children dashing around among the statuary that dotted an expansive lawn could doubt the munificence of this community. Local leaders hoped that the sight of rescued youngsters at play and prayer would give the lie to all the vicious insinuations about the misanthropy of southerners and the perniciously brutalizing effects of their society. And often it did. One visitor left the institution after watching the children go through their academic exercises of recitations, singing, and calisthenics convinced that he had seen southern democracy in its purest form. [31]

Only the vitriolic and skeptical British journalist James Stirling accused the commissioners of "bathos" in creating such an artificially lovely setting. Poor children accustomed to Sunday frocks and great kindness, he charged, would only find the world all the more heartbreaking when they faced the grim and lonely reality of the nineteenth-century city as poor adults. But even worse and more socially irresponsible, in Stirling's view, was that through the establishment of an attractive haven for the "progeny of the reckless and sinful," the city held "out a premium on prostitution." Their best intentions, then, only went to encourage immorality. [32]

Stirling misunderstood the asylum's mission and especially misjudged the motives of its directors. Although their rhetoric often reflected the prevailing romantic vision of childhood, the patriarchs of Charleston knew what they were about. By the time of Stirling's visit in 1854, their interest in the asylum transcended personal desire for "vulgar applause" or attempts to buy "golden opinions" for themselves. The orphan house had evolved as an important vehicle not only for their own self-justification

30. *Bylaws of the Orphan House of Charleston*, 22; Minutes, September 1, 1859, in COH.
31. S. S. to Charlie and "Doc," April 5, 1861, in Willis Grandy Briggs Papers, Southern Historical Collection, University of North Carolina, Chapel Hill.
32. Stirling, *Letters from the Slave States*, 253.

but for the vindication of their social class and the system. Only days before the outbreak of violence over Fort Sumter, a North Carolina visitor expressed amazement and delight that the leaders of the old slave capital had created an environment where "the son of a beggar, if he be active, persevering, honest and studious may fill the highest places in the gifts of their friends and country."[33]

Orphan house officials defended their liberal policies by arguing that immoral parents do not necessarily breed immoral children. They insisted that each generation was autonomous and free of the past. This seems a curious position for Charleston patriarchs to adopt, given the importance they put upon tradition and maintaining continuity with the blood of their blood through naming and inheritance patterns.[34] However, reluctance to visit the sins of the fathers upon the sons and mothers and daughters served as an important defense mechanism for the ruling class of slaveholders, as illustrated by the position of Commissioner DeSaussure. His insistence in 1855 that "children are not participants in parental errors" reflects a familiar southern contention that being born into the slaveholding world was an evil "like the gout, one of inheritance" for which there was no remedy. In the opinion of the commissioners, bastardy and prostitution unhappily existed as an inevitable part of the fallen world. Charleston's slaveholding elite declined to pass judgment upon the children of the sinful. DeSaussure made a stoic appeal for accepting the ways of the world by arguing that "the mental suffering of erring humanity can best be ameliorated by the soothing hand of time and the charities of oblivion."[35]

Driven by the multiple imperatives of good works, political strategy, and tradition, the commissioners kept the importance of their mission constantly before the city council. They faced opposition from elements of the city government who thought that they operated the asylum as their own fiefdom. Others thought the cast-off children of the poor did not need such grand accommodations. Certain "jealousies" persisted over the "Private Fund" of public donations over which the city had no

33. S. S. to Charlie and Doe, April 5, 1861, in Briggs Papers.

34. For insightful discussions of generational dynamics among slaveholding families, see Michael P. Johnson, "Planters and Patriarchy: Charleston, 1800–1860," *Journal of Southern History*, XLVI (February, 1980), 45–72, and Bertram Wyatt-Brown, *Southern Honor: Ethics and Behavior in the Old South* (New York, 1982), especially 117–48.

35. "South Carolina," *New England Magazine*, I (September–October, 1831), in Eugene Schwab, *Travels in the Old South* (Lexington, Ky., 1973), I, 20; Henry A. DeSaussure, in *The Proceedings on the Sixty-Sixth Anniversary of the Charleston Orphan House* (Charleston, S.C., 1855), 48; William S. Jenkins, *Proslavery Thought in the Old South* (Chapel Hill, 1935), 52.

control. Every quarter or so, the council asked the commissioners to find some method of retrenchment in recognition of the city's waning fortunes, and every quarter or so, they successfully defended the orphan house budget through a combination of logic, their personal prestige, and the general sympathy of the council with their cause. In 1855, when reformist William Porcher Miles became mayor, he faced the unenviable task of reconciling his supporters' demands for reforms and local improvements with "an impoverished treasury" and an electorate restive under heavy taxation.[36] The orphan house not only continued to enjoy municipal support during the city's time of trouble but received increased appropriations.

DeSaussure congratulated the elected officials on their difficult decision to expand and renovate the asylum to meet the increased needs imposed by immigration and deaths from epidemics. He assured them of the lasting benefits of their action, for "public charities are not long burdens upon communities—the investments for them return in a thousand blessings." The handsome building, he added, also stood as a "lasting memorial of the wisdom and judgment of the Council who fearlessly incurred the expense." Support for such a popular cause only proved their political skill. As DeSaussure, not a bad politician himself, assured the aldermen that "their constituents, a frank and manly people, will never withhold a generous confidence from those who faithfully and independently subserve their true interests and the city's welfare."[37]

The city's welfare, most agreed, depended upon the preservation of local institutions, of which slavery loomed as a central feature. Before assuming their roles as white men and women, the abandoned, derelict, and orphaned children first had to learn the lessons of race. The opportunities for intermingling and empathy among the lowest classes, black and white, greatly disturbed the town's leaders. Persuasive evidence exists that competition for employment divided the laboring classes along racial lines. Less is understood about the social dynamics among the groups that shared alleyways, raucous nights in tippling houses, and poverty.[38] And nothing is known about the interaction among children. Poor white women working as domestics, especially immigrants, who infrequently

36. Charleston *Mercury,* November 10, 1855.
37. DeSaussure, in *Sixty-Sixth Anniversary of the Charleston Orphan House,* 46–47.
38. For the best general study of free blacks in the South, see Ira Berlin, *Slaves Without Masters: The Free Negro in the Antebellum South* (New York, 1974). For an excellent inquiry into the racial dynamics of free blacks, slaves, and whites, with a special emphasis on Charleston, see Michael P. Johnson and James L. Roark, *Black Masters: A Free Family of Color in the Old South* (New York, 1984).

had no family members to help with child care, tended to board their children with other mothers. Sometimes those mothers were black. No one thought twice about white children in black arms or children of both races playing together until age and station divided them. However, incursions across the color line, without the barriers of caste, proved intolerable. Citizens alerted orphan house officials whenever they caught sight of white children boarded with free blacks. Nurses scrutinized all children that entered the asylum to certify their white blood.

Knowing that from birth children grope for clues to their identity, the commissioners always took certain and speedy action when facing a situation such as that of Laura and John Moore. Their parents, Eliza and Malcolm Moore, belonged to the city's large Irish immigrant population. Before John was six, Malcolm abandoned family responsibilities for alcoholic reveries. Like so many other deserted women, Eliza resorted to scullery work in a home where her children were not welcome. Unable to secure any other child care on her monthly salary of seven dollars, this illiterate Irishwoman lodged her little children in the home of free blacks. In southern cities, where porches allowed good vantage points, the population kept a rather close eye on neighborhood comings and goings. One vigilant neighbor reported seeing the Moore children in the company of blacks and urged a prominent local man to investigate. Commissioner Frederick Ford visited Eliza Moore and learned she needed to place her children with the city but had not yet met the asylum's twelve-month residence requirement. He successfully pleaded her case before the other commissioners. She agonized over "having been compelled to turn over her children to the protection of Negroes," Ford contended, "but it was the best she could do." The commissioners agreed that the Moores proved an extraordinary case and represented the very scenario that the institution tried to prevent. They waived the rules and accepted two more little Irish children into the asylum community.[39]

From its founding, the Charleston Orphan House stood as a vehicle for racial uplift. Among the first donations were a pair of slave women to serve Charleston's poorest white children. The institution's later policies deliberately accentuated distinctions between the children of the city and the servants of the house. Although the children's household duties varied over the years, slaves who lived on the grounds relieved them of many of the onerous housekeeping chores performed by orphans in other places. Blacks did the demeaning work, the scrubbing and hauling and lifting and digging, and they did that only. The commissioners insisted

39. Application file, September 22, 1853, in COH.

that blacks must never serve as instructors in the carpentry, weaving, or sewing classes. They reserved the position of nurse for the many white women needing a job.

As the commissioners reviewed the careers of boys they had guided through the orphanage, they noted jurists, doctors, and ministers among the lists of carpenters and steamfitters. One stands out from the others as clearly embodying the southern dream. To protect his privacy, the records identified him only as a former member of the Georgia legislature. He returned to the asylum about 1855 to walk once again through the gardens, "a middle aged gentleman" remembering his youth. He came upon Commissioner DeSaussure and told his saga, the typical American success story of luck, pluck, and marrying well: "Yes, thank God that I was protected in this blessed institution." After finishing his basic education, the commissioners apprenticed him to a country merchant. He explained that while working out his time, "I acquired my master's confidence, became his copartner, married his daughter, and upon his death, continued the business for our common benefit; and having accumulated property for the family and myself, sold out and we all removed together to Georgia, and vested our property in lands and negroes, as planters."[40] Could the old patriarchs have had a better vindication of their labors?

Defining poor children's role in society required delicacy and a sense of balance. On one hand, an important purpose of the asylum was to educate the offspring of the destitute and encourage their identification with the values of the white community, but on the other, they were objects of charity, and that relationship had its own important dynamics. Even the commissioners lacked a uniformity of opinions. One controversy over the proper dress of the girls simmered in board meetings for more than three years during the 1840s. This minor issue drew its larger importance from what it revealed about the divided southern mind on the issue of elevation and shaming. A few days after the October anniversary parade in 1845, a local benefactor, noticing the drab and faded uniforms, offered to give all the little girls calico dresses to wear on Sundays and to public events. It seemed simple enough: Who would not prefer cheerful calico to coarse homespun? But when the time came to vote on accepting the gift, the famed harmony of the board receded, exposing two very different interpretations of what the public image of the children should be. When pressed, a number confessed that they regarded the inmates as different from most children. The commissioners who wanted to thank the patron but decline the offer feared that brightly colored

40. DeSaussure, in *Sixty-Sixth Anniversary of the Charleston Orphan House*, 47.

frocks could encourage the vanity that the institution worked so hard to suppress. Come Monday morning, a once-docile child might well resent changing back into the faded stripes of the house uniforms. Worse still, insight into the advantages enjoyed by other children might make them restive and even question "the condition [in] which a benignant God has placed them."[41]

The dissenting commissioners also understood the need to capitalize upon "the sympathy of those who come in contact with these little unfortunates." If dressed up and looking pretty, the little girls might start to "feel important"; "their manner will drive away sympathy and no one will care for the orphan who is so well cared for." Daniel C. Webb expressed the need for the community to recognize the objects of its charity. A uniform, he contended, would assure "that our little charges be known abroad, be recognized everywhere, as the children of the public; . . . not as creatures of disgrace, but as the little ones whom it has pleased the city to bestow its protection upon. . . . It is a guard to them, they know that they are known to others and if found in vice or wickedness abroad, that every citizen is a father to them, every citizen will notice their vices, every citizen will stand up for them, will protect them."[42]

Attorney Henry D. Lesesne led the "Committee on Calico Dresses" in their deliberations. They discussed with intensity and seriousness the implications for the self-image of the child and the public image of the institution. The humbling effect of the faded uniform, the majority agreed, did not outweigh the unfair stigma it imposed upon the children and their parents. To walk hand in hand down the street on Saturday visits with their child in a patched orphan house dress only added public embarrassment to the pain of separation. The commissioners well knew that clever mothers often brought other clothes in a bag and as soon as they rounded the corner out of sight of the asylum, made a quick change from the city's child to their child.

Other factors also guided their decision. Most agreed that the shabby old dresses caused as much pain to the community observing them as to the girls wearing them. Besides, all classes, even slaves, had some nice clothes for Sundays and holidays. The winning argument that freed the girls from the rough-made sacques and placed them in calico (at least on Sundays) surrounded the issue of race and status. Opposition to new clothes dissolved when the argument was made that "homespun is very much confined to our servants when engaged in the most menial offices.

41. Minutes, October 30, 1845, in COH.
42. *Ibid.*, October 30, 1845, March 2, 1848.

With white persons in our cities, it is unusual and peculiar and the wearer knows that she is an object of remark wherever she goes, if not made to feel in a way that is more mortifying."[43]

In light of the true nature of the orphan house population, fear of pridefulness and excessive vanity seem rather farfetched. One little girl came to the asylum directly from her mother's deathbed at a local brothel. A young boy had watched his father beat his mother to death in an insane rage. Some had been starved, tortured, abused, abandoned, locked in closets, and shuffled from one household to another. Others regularly woke up screaming from the nightmare memory of losing their whole family to disease. Because the precommittal experiences of the children varied so wildly, their abilities and behavior also ran the spectrum. Some children inevitably proved beyond the salutary influence of the asylum.

But with confidence in their system and themselves, the commissioners claimed that the machinery of their asylum could transform Charleston's outcast children into useful "ornaments to society" and "implant a new nature in them." These businessmen and lawyers eschewed romantic idealizations of childhood but believed wholeheartedly in the powers of systematic ethical training. In 1855, the Reverend Charles C. Pinckney, Memminger's son-in-law, described the process of salvaging the city's little original sinners: "We see the fatherless running to ruin in our streets; we take them by the hand; we lead them to their designated home; care for their souls; educate their minds; inculcate moral and religious principles. . . . We strive to rescue them from the temptations of vice and pollution of the world, and to 'train them up in the way they should go,' trusting that they will not depart therefrom."[44]

If children did depart from acceptable behavior, the commissioners promptly cut them off from the town's charity and their concern. William Nunan, already "a wanderer among the persons of deprivation which infest this city at twelve years old," tried to burn down the asylum in 1861. One of the horrified commissioners quickly arranged to place the angry twelve-year-old on a ship bound for foreign ports with the firm stipulation to the captain that he "never be brought back to the city of Charleston." Silas Bunch acted so perversely when relatives took him home during an illness that they returned him to the orphan house as

43. *Ibid.*, March 2, 1848.
44. S. S. to Charlie and "Doc," in Briggs Papers; Minutes, June 25, 1857, in COH; Steven L. Schossman, *Love and the American Delinquent: The Theory and Practice of "Progressive" Juvenile Justice, 1825–1920* (Chicago, 1977), 50–51; Rev. Charles C. Pinckney, in *Sixty-Sixth Anniversary of the Charleston Orphan House*, 24–25.

soon as possible. The commissioners in turn passed him along to the poorhouse: "That boy's misconduct has been so unpardonable, so immoral, and ungrateful to the Institution in return for all the care and attention bestowed on him . . . that he shall be allowed to remain in our house no longer." In contrast to many institutions, the most severe threat the commissioners wielded was expulsion; they placed wire screens on the bottom-floor windows to keep intruders out rather than children in.[45]

The commissioners indulged in no delusions about the odds against these children, "a class of being which for special reasons need a continual watchfulness over their welfare." They knew that they could not countenance in them the same idleness enjoyed by their own children. Exhibiting their unflagging optimism about the possibility of mobility through hard work, the commissioners focused on education as the key to success. As one commissioner observed, unless the children received "an education comparable to that of the others they will have to compete with, we cast upon life's ocean without chart or compass, the immortality committed to our guidance." No good intentions, however, could compensate for the fact that the children of the city, in the asylum or out, received little formal education. Interest in the orphan school roughly paralleled the fluctuating enthusiasm for free schools. After erratic advances during the 1820s, both systems declined steadily. In 1850, an orphan house committee investigated the operation of the school and in masterful understatement concluded that "things might be better than they are." Under the direction of only one teacher, noise and confusion reigned as seventy-three students tried to recite in unison in the "stentorian voice" used by scholars of that day. Profanity covered the walls, and, with the ultimate disrespect for good order, "the corners of the room [were] abandoned to the vulgar necessities of life." The children behaved so riotously when assembled all together that the overwhelmed and outnumbered superintendents abandoned evening prayer.[46]

With few good teachers willing to endure such conditions, "geography and arithmetic were taught by guessing, and spelling by intuition" in the first few years of the 1850s. Students read only haltingly, and mathematical skill seldom went beyond computations on ten fingers. Of the 188 children in the orphan house, 152 attended classes, and 61 percent of those struggled with the mysteries of the alphabet. Learning was strictly by rote. Students in the girls' school behaved well in general, but

45. Minutes, March 26, 1863, January 1, 1861, in COH; Commissioners' file, January 1, 1862, *ibid.*; Indenture file, April 5, 1846, *ibid.*

46. Commissioners' file, n.d., *ibid.*; Minutes, June 25, 1857, *ibid.*; Charleston *Mercury,* January 23, 1854; Minutes, October 17, 1850, June 25, 1857, April 12, 1866, in COH.

the boys abused their desks and presented a "disorderly" and "slovenly appearance." Clearly these conditions demanded improvement.[47]

From 1853 to 1855, when the fortunes of the city seemed on the rise once again, the city council approved a dramatic renovation of the orphan house. The commissioners brought the building up to the most modern standards and cast out the vermin-infested wooden cots in favor of iron beds. The changes transcended the superficial appearance of the asylum, for during these years, the tireless efforts of W. Jefferson Bennett and Christopher G. Memminger brought new confidence and sense of direction to the institution. In 1854, they encouraged the other commissioners to hire New Yorker Agnes Irving, who specialized in the latest progressive method of classifying students according to their abilities instead of their ages and allowing them to advance at their own rate. Using the tutorial system, the school could employ only six teachers for the entire house. Each of the three grades in the grammar school required its own teacher, but two of the five primary classes were remedial, demanding only monitors among the advanced girls to help younger students master the fundamentals. By 1857, 253 children attended classes in the asylum school, and only nine "abcdarians" still struggled with the alphabet. Parents even tried to enroll their children as day students. To the city council's delight, greater efficiency reduced the average annual cost per pupil to $9.50. Not only was this new system "novel and interesting," exuded Henry DeSaussure, but truly "bids fair to explode and supersede the ancient formula of education."[48]

By 1855, the commissioners had learned from mistakes of the past sixty-five years and studied the institutional policies of other cities. One example of their success, Mikell Covert, an inmate for fifteen years, had graduated from medical school that spring. The commissioners undoubtedly rocked back in their chairs with pride when they read his letter saying he was "joyful with gratitude for your fostering care and liberal charity and the more than Parental guidance of your venerable Chairman." He described his early life, separated from his mother when she entered the poorhouse: "Thrown upon the charity of a cold, unfeeling world, I

47. Minute Book, February 5, November 23, 1856, in Papers of the Commissioners of the Free Schools, City of Charleston Archives, Charleston, S.C.; Minutes, June 25, 1857, October 17, 1850, in COH.

48. Minutes, March 25, June 2, 1852, June 25, 1857, in COH; Charleston *Mercury*, January 23, 1854. For comparison, the Bethesda Orphan School of Savannah educated forty boys that same year. Of those, thirty-two had mastered spelling and reading, sixteen could "cipher," six could write compositions ([Savannah] Union Society, *Proceedings, 1858* [Savannah, 1859], 16).

soon found with that abstract iciness, there gushed many a warm-spring of human sympathy, welling up from hearts of love and pity for the poor Orphan." For Covert, the most extraordinary part of his experience occurred when, after he was "nurtured in common" with the other boys, the commissioners bestowed upon him "the peculiar benefits" of their bounty through "the Education of the Rich Man's Son." If they had any question about the value of their efforts, Covert's parting words surely convinced these fathers of orphans that they followed the true course: "And, now, Gentlemen; in bidding you farewell, in no spirit of boasting, let me assure you, that by energy and rectitude, I will never put to blush, the fair and benign countenance of my Alma Mater."[49]

At last Charlestonians had worked out the highest example of "refined philanthropy." By acting the part of father, "good Samaritan and Christian friend" and reforming the individual rather than society, the commissioners believed, they held the formula to encourage the best and the brightest and cope with the dull and intractable. They enjoyed applause from all over the South for their enlightened programs "rewarding and advancing the worthy" as they set out to create from this raw clay "industrious, capable men" and "honest, faithful women."[50]

In 1811, the state legislature had pioneered efforts to give children born on the margins of society the opportunity to overcome their fate. Along with a bill establishing a free school system, the assembly created a scholarship for one orphan house boy to attend South Carolina College annually. The state offered this opportunity so that "the child of Charity may one day be hailed as the Historian, the Legislator, or the Saviour of his Country." What a wonderful experiment to rescue derelict children and "train them up in the way they should go," then test them in the rigors of a classical education with the most advantaged boys of the state. This would be not only a true vindication of the aristocracy of talent but also a testimony to the wisdom of the city's patriarchs. They were particularly clear that for the experiment to succeed, the children needed protection from "evil associations and vicious associates who despise wisdom and outrage virtue." In other words, their parents. Part of the reforms of 1855 included reducing parental visits to Wednesdays only and allowing inmates to go to their parents only in an emergency.[51]

49. Commissioners' file, March 13, 1855, in COH.

50. Minutes, June 25, 1857, *ibid.*; DeSaussure, in *Sixty-Sixth Anniversary of the Charleston Orphan House*, 32; Richmond *Daily Dispatch*, April 30, 1857; Charleston *Courier*, July 28, 1859.

51. *Bylaws of the Orphan House of Charleston*, 32; City council file, July 15, 1815, in

Inevitably, the boys with the cleanest faces, neatest handwriting, and best manners captured favorable attention. Their lives, even in the institution, differed markedly from those who struggled with the alphabet, broke windows, and cursed the matron. The city authorized the commissioners to single out those boys who "exhibit superior talents, united with approved moral qualities" to attend the High School of Charleston. If successful in this program, they would be eligible to attend the College of Charleston, the nation's first municipal college. Other opportunities also benefited Charleston's orphans. In the 1840s, adventuresome boys with a mastery of ciphers could apply to the United States Naval Academy School. After 1859, those preferring to serve their state could attend classes on the city's merchant marine training brig *Lodestar* and wear a dashing uniform with the traditional belt and sheathed knife. The South Carolina military schools began tapping a likely source of recruits in 1854 by offering two scholarships each year to orphan house boys.[52]

Once the asylum started tracking the brightest boys early, the relationship among the boys changed. Teachers watched closely to sift out those capable of mastering a classical education from those who would have to struggle to learn bare-bones educational basics before apprenticeship to a local tradesman. Although officially a boy's fate was not determined until he was fourteen, the annual awards for achievement and merit, along with the naming of class leaders, made the distinction between future lawyers and future blacksmiths apparent much earlier. Intending to teach the lessons of the superiority of race, the institution reflected a social reality and reinforced the stigma of class.

A variety of light industries operated on the city's periphery, offering opportunities for boys to learn the principles of carriage making, construction of windows and sashes, or pipefitting. The ancient system of apprenticeship flourished in southern cities that offered little else in public education. At the outbreak of the Civil War, Charleston workshops retained a degree of intimacy between worker and employer that had nearly disappeared in the North. Innovations in mass production and infusions of cheap foreign labor made apprenticeship almost obsolete. Craft unions also attacked the system, which allowed employers to use underpaid boys instead of hiring family men. Decline of the apprentice

---

COH; Pinckney, in *Sixty-Sixth Anniversary of the Charleston Orphan House*, 24–25; Minutes, June 14, 1855, in COH.

52. Charleston *News and Courier*, May 29, 1941; Charleston *Courier*, August 21, 1859.

system closed off entrees to the professions among the poor in northern cities. According to the Charleston Orphan House registers from 1820 to 1860, sixty-six boys (almost 5 percent) found apprenticeships with printers, seventy-five with merchants.[53]

In a slave society, other dangers accompanied the indenture system of labor. Where the relationship between master and apprentice was not always well defined, the commissioners feared that the distinctions of race might blur and a temporary expedient become permanent bondage. Most potential masters understood the social taboos. When an Upcountry printer who had trained several orphan house boys during the 1850s applied for two more apprentices, he assured the commissioners that he understood his relationship with the boys to be paternal and promised "to supply them with food and clothing, as well as attend to their moral training as I would my own children." Reflecting the shared community concern, he added: "I wish not to make slaves of my own race."[54]

Whether the relationship between master and apprentice resembled that of father and son or employer and laborer, it was usually laced with some degree of tension and resentment. Some who took on the orphaned children wanted only cheap labor; for their part, the children, institutionalized most of their lives, wanted only freedom. The publisher of a South Carolina newspaper summed up the experience of many who tried to remove the impressionable children from the evils of the city: "I have had two boys from the [Charleston] Orphan House, but the little chaps grew tired of country life, as they said, and runaway."[55]

Proving the combined healing powers of love and work, boys and girls from the most unpromising and despairing backgrounds often developed into productive citizens during the course of their apprenticeships. In 1859, J. C. H. Claussen, a prosperous and apparently patient Charleston baker, took on several orphan house boys from troubled backgrounds.

53. The Charleston Typographical Union passed a resolution in June, 1860, that no member "shall work in any office where boys are put on by the piece or on time," but the Civil War eclipsed debate on the issue (Charleston Typographical Union, No. 43, Southern Typographical Union, No. 1, Minutes, 1859–1862, in South Caroliniana Library). For a dated, but useful, description of early labor agitation see Yates Snowden, *Notes on Labor Organizations in South Carolina, 1742–1861* (Columbia, S.C., 1914). See also Ulrich B. Phillips, "The Slave Labor Problem in the Charleston District," in *Plantation, Town, and County: Essays on the Local History of American Slave Society,* ed. Elinor Miller and Eugene D. Genovese (Urbana, Ill., 1974), 7–28.

54. Charles Hancock to Commissioners of the Charleston Orphan House [*ca.* 1850], in Indenture files, COH.

55. [Savannah] Union Society, *Minutes of the Union Society, 1790–1858* (Savannah, 1860), 155; Indenture file, July 10, 1866, in COH.

When he was three, William Christian Buckheister's mother placed him in the orphan house with his three older brothers. His father, fired from the city guard for his "violent and tyrannical conduct to a poor female debtor," later beat Buckheister's mother senseless. James Cook had been in and out of the orphanage several times as his family fortunes waxed and waned. Yet at fourteen, both boys proved satisfactory workers. Claussen found Buckheister "quick and lively, sometimes rather wild and playful, but with strict and definite orders easily managed, his conduct generally good . . . is very kind and of a sociable and generous disposition." Cook, according to the master baker, showed promise as a good worker with improved behavior, "a steady and sober disposition . . . though his disposition is not so kind."[56]

What we know about the miserable situations that befell even a well-supervised child can only suggest the horror experienced by those with no one to intervene on their behalf. John Henry had been in the Charleston home only about a year when apprenticed at age fourteen to William Peronneau, a miller and lumberman from a distinguished Lowcountry family. He labored with other boys for almost eight years, and just as John Henry's twenty-first birthday approached, Peronneau reneged on his contract, claiming he did not have the funds to meet his obligations, and refused to give him any of the standard "necessities" or money at the end of his tenure. Young Henry wrote the commissioners describing his desperate condition, with "not a shirt to my back." He expressed his disillusionment at his shameful treatment at the hands of "a Gentleman of his Standing" and implored the commissioners to see that "an Orphan has his Wrights."[57]

The commissioners sent children away from Charleston reluctantly. Concerned for the feelings of parents, they also wanted to monitor the apprentices' conditions. In 1859, they faced a dilemma and had to invoke Solomon-like wisdom to decide which version of the following scenario to believe. Putting aside their prejudice against farming as an unworthy career, they had apprenticed a boy, John (sometimes called Caesar) Hays, to a North Carolina farmer in 1859. In his six-month report, the boy's master, J. S. Charles Moore, expressed general pleasure with the arrangement, noting that John "has not had a day's sickness since he came to us, has proved quite tractable, and seems industriously disposed." Although the boy labored in the fields, Moore assured the Charlestonians that his status was not compromised: "I have had him working with other hired

---

56. Commissioners' file, October 18, 1859, in COH.
57. *Ibid.*, October 8, 1829.

laborers (white men) on my farm and at times assisting in my smith shop, his improvement in business, I am pleased to say is satisfactory. He is willing and anxious to learn. His present situation gives him every opportunity of qualifying himself to overlook, or attend to a farm of his own. I hope in time to give him oversight of mine. He can acquire if he shows a turn for trade a knowledge of the Blacksmith's." Understanding that his obligation to John included academic as well as practical education, Moore expressed his "regret . . . that he is so little desirous of improving his mind. I have to use a great deal of perseverance to make him attend to his books. In his spare Moments, especially on Sabbath mornings and evenings when not at Church, he has also been trying to improve in writing." Moore hoped "he will grow more fond of his books" and planned to use the long winter nights to accelerate his progress.[58]

John "Caesar" Hayes told another story. After working for Moore for two years, he wrote a letter, suggesting either a gift for hyperbole or a decline in the North Carolinian's fortunes, to the matron of the orphan house, likely more sympathetic than her husband. Clearly Hayes benefited little from his studies:

> Dear Friend
>   i now tuk the pleasure off righting to you. that you ar all well and [k]no[w] i St[a]rt to tell that they Do Beat me with the Cowhide . . . [make me] work on Sunday and Dont haf feed us and Cloath w[ith] one peare off Shoes in the winter and nun in the Sumer and if you ples to Right them. if you Dond, i will lev them and go A way to sun place els[e] and stay wear i Can git Somthing to eat and som to Wear and [not be] Beat and tell the Boys to take cear not [to] com to such a place lik i have and this is All i have to Say. this is not very good—one pear of Brices in the winter and All old Cloth[es]. Work both night and Day. i am Well; time is hard—with All Corn Bread All tim.[59]

While their friends ate the cornmeal of a laborer's table, those boys chosen to attend the high school continued to enjoy the comforts of the orphan house, which by the mid-1850s included steam heat and modern plumbing. Enthusiasm for supporting orphan scholars was renewed with every college graduate produced by the charity home. Upon his graduation from the College of Charleston, one young man who later became a school principal thanked the commissioners ("My Kind and Generous Friends") for the many years of "undeserved—perhaps unrequited kindness" and especially for the "delight" they so clearly took in fostering

58. Stewards' file, October 18, 1859, *ibid.* (punctuation added).
59. Indenture file, March 31, 1862, *ibid.*

intellectual talents "even when found in an Orphan." His appreciation for the utter "disinterestedness" of their benevolence transcended gratitude or duty, he wrote, but instead excited in his "mind—a higher—a holier feeling."[60]

Truly delighting in molding the futures of promising young men, the commissioners allocated more money for their care than for the others. Good clothes, they agreed, made the boy as well as the man. One of the first schoolmasters wrote to the board that "it would please me, I confess, to let those boys who are destined to the professions [be] a little distinguished from the rest in those respects that youth take a pride in." He expected that the promise of these rewards might serve a greater encouragement to perseverance "than the best penal code." By 1855, the steward of the house explained that there were two classes of boys—those bound for the professions, who had to be provided with the "expensive clothing necessary for a similar appearance with their classmates," and those in gray homespun, receiving a "plain English education."[61]

In the fall of 1855, six of the most promising had set out for the High School of Charleston dressed in their new clothes; only two ever finished. Instead of striving for improvement and expressing gratitude, the advantaged boys grew increasingly dissatisfied with life in the asylum and resisted the benevolent despotism of the commissioners. By 1857, the older boys were feared out of hand. They pushed the rules to the limit, refused to obey the staff, began disappearing during chapel services, and dared to leave the grounds without permission. High school officials suspended two for misconduct. Some weeks later, another treated the matron in such an "insubordinate and disrespectful manner" that the commissioners dispatched him to the cellar "prison." After a few days in solitary confinement on bread and water, he grudgingly agreed to apologize to the woman in a "humble manner." In sum, they acted like adolescents chafing under paternal authority, anxious for affirmation from their peers. The reaction of the commissioners, still very much the kind fathers, was to impose a lenient demerit system, one demerit for each infraction. After committing a hundred infractions, an inmate faced immediate indenture and the end of childhood.[62] One day the offender would be called to the commissioners' room and meet his new master as he started a new life in the rough clothes of a tradesman's apprentice in the city.

60. Severens, *Antebellum Architecture*, 184; Commissioners' file, February 26, 1842, in COH; King, *Charleston Orphan House*, 103.

61. Inmates' file [*ca.* 1815], in COH; Stewards' file, January 25, 1855, *ibid.*

62. Minutes, September 3, 1857, June 24, 1858, December 17, 1857, January 7, 1858, all in COH.

At the same time that the high school boys were experiencing difficulties, the young men chosen for college began falling from grace. Benjamin Lloyd, for example, decided he would rather be a country merchant than a scholar at the College of Charleston, and he was obliged with an apprenticeship. William Green left the South Carolina Military Academy under the cloud of academic failure. Soon the commissioners heard the news that the asylum's first cadet at Columbia's Arsenal Hill Military Academy had been expelled for "neglect and general inability and indifference."[63]

"Question authority" would have been an appropriate slogan for college students during the 1850s. Like the generation over a century later that actually did coin that phrase, restlessness and animus toward parents and all restriction coalesced on college campuses. Able for the first time to exercise their sense of entitlement without the disapproval of the strong father, students in southern colleges often reveled in the excesses of their class—drinking, dueling, gambling, bullying—unrestrained by the sense of responsibility that theoretically tempered such practices. For orphan house boys, such freedom must have been exceptionally heady.

Scarcely attempting to crush the spirit of the advanced boys, the commissioners fell into the eternal parental dilemma of fostering independence of spirit and mind while maintaining a salutary control. In 1855, Thomas L. Deveaux presented the commissioners with a situation that tested their principles as much as his. Deveaux came to the asylum from Charleston Neck when he was ten. He maintained an excellent academic record until his senior year at the College of Charleston when he sided with his classmates by signing a petition criticizing a faculty member in a dispute over a disciplinary action. A college official immediately warned Commissioner DeSaussure that this action severely jeopardized the charity boy's standing at the school. DeSaussure used reason and persuasion first, requesting Deveaux to "recede from the position assumed by the class" if he could do so "without compromising his honor." Loving honor more, Deveaux refused to abandon his schoolmates. He remained in the asylum, where he had lived throughout his college years. One evening the commissioners confronted him, explained that his first responsibility was to his "family," reminded him of his obligations to the asylum, and ordered him to finish his education. Deveaux refused to blink. The commissioners turned him out of the house.[64]

A few years later, as the commissioners increasingly doubted the wis-

63. Ibid., March 25, 1847, December 10, 1857; King, Charleston Orphan House, 120.
64. Minutes, April 26, 1855, in COH.

dom of their policies, they received another letter about one of their charges, this time from South Carolina College, about a young German immigrant, Frederick Gustavus Behre. Few could remember a young man with such promise—a top scholar and class leader, much like the young Christopher G. Memminger. He annually garnered all the school prizes. He aspired not just to practice law but to be a professor of law. Behre, it seemed, could do no wrong—that is, until the riot. When the soft-spoken Augustus B. Longstreet assumed the presidency of the college, the restless students on the Columbia campus vowed to test his will. They presented him with a demand for a holiday to commemorate John C. Calhoun's birthday. Predictably, Longstreet refused. In retaliation, some students tarred all the benches and stopped classes. Longstreet moved swiftly and decisively by suspending half the student body for six months. Even then, reinstatement depended upon successful completion of strenuous exams. An uncontrite Behre, found guilty along with the other pranksters of "resisting the authority of the Faculty," returned to the asylum.[65]

The commissioners, more fortunate than most fathers because they could consult one another, debated his future and chose leniency. They were so lenient, in fact, that instead of punishment they voted to reinstate his former clothing allowance "with the view of relieving Mr. Behre from embarrassment resulting from his suspension" and urged him to study diligently for the readmission exams. The next month, upon hearing that the college had begun the process of readmitting some of the suspended students, they summoned Behre and enthusiastically offered to send him immediately to Columbia to plead his case. Behre refused to go. At this point, the commissioners understood the meaning of Behre's actions. His challenge was not to Longstreet but to them. The model boy had tired of trying to please; the scholarship student was tired of being grateful. This time they wasted little time in debate. They forthwith suspended Behre from all privileges of the asylum "for rebellion against the authorities of the institutions which fostered him." Pleading that he was not rebellious, only unprepared, Behre stayed on until December when he left his fathers' house for a teaching position at Walterborough Academy. He left the commissioners on a positive note, praying that they receive all the

65. Jon L. Wakelyn, "Antebellum College Life and the Relations Between Fathers and Sons," in *The Web of Southern Social Relations: Women, Family and Education*, ed. Walter J. Fraser, Jr., R. Frank Saunders, Jr., and Jon L. Wakelyn (Athens, Ga., 1985), 107–22; Kett, *Rites of Passage*, 53–56; Minutes, January 22, 1852, April 8, 1858, May 20, 21, 1958, in COH. See also Steven M. Stowe, *Intimacy and Power in the Old South* (Baltimore, 1987), 142–53.

"blessings which an Orphan's God alone can bestow." Yet they were bitterly disappointed.[66]

The commissioners transferred their hopes to other students. Henry Gray also enjoyed an elevated status in the asylum. Entering at age four, he remained through high school and while a student at the College of Charleston. A model student, he served as librarian of the book collection. The commissioners had great hope for his future until one evening in 1856. During a routine visit in the older boys' quarters, Commissioners W. Jefferson Bennett and William Enston, two of the wealthiest men in the city, stopped by Gray's room. In the course of the conversation, the commissioners asked him to explain why he had appropriated some of the dining-hall chairs for his own use. Gray replied, with some surprise that they should even ask. On those occasions when friends stopped by for a visit, he retorted, "I would not like them to sit upon the floor." Gray continued in his account of the incident that Bennett, the master of over seventy slaves, "then ordered me in language only used towards menials" to "carry those chairs downstairs." In the haughty manner of the young gentry rather than an orphan house boy, Gray retorted, "I'll have them carried down, but will not carry them myself." At this, Bennett turned to Enston and complained, "That's raising up boys for good manners." As they swung around to leave the room, each man snatched up a chair. Gray fired off the last word to their backs, that he "was very much obliged" to them. Shortly after this interchange, the commissioners called Gray in to hear his account and probably did little more than give a stern reprimand.[67]

The commissioners convened in June, 1858, and asked themselves the question asked by parents and social reformers from time immemorial: "Where did we go wrong?" They had tried to be conscientious, devoting time, thought, and energy to their charges. Every year the city, with a shaky financial outlook, had dug deeper and deeper into its slim reserves to maintain the children and improve their situation. The commissioners had promised that their investment would accrue tremendous human dividends. Now what did they have to show? In fatherly fashion, the commissioners concluded they had spoiled the boys. Trying to ameliorate their unhappy circumstances, they had overcompensated. All indulgent

66. Minutes, May 20, 21, June 24, 1858, in COH; Inmates' file, May 26, December 30, 1858, *ibid.*

67. Minutes, October 8, 1857, *ibid.* Gray never finished college. Not long after his saucy words to Bennett, he fell ill and the commissioners sent him to New York for treatment, where he "ended his collegiate career with his earthly career and sleeps on the banks of the Hudson" (Minutes, January 7, 1858, *ibid.*).

fathers, they agreed, suffered the ingratitude of sons from time to time.

Underlying much of the superfluous talk, however, was the constant doubt that perhaps nurture could never supersede nature. Preconceptions about the invincibility of blood overcame liberal assertions. By 1858, the ideal that formed "so beautiful a part in perfecting our unrivaled institution," elevating poor children from mongrel backgrounds into gentlemen, receded into the category of "a hazardous experiment."[68]

In 1858, Dr. Benjamin Huger replaced W. Jefferson Bennett as the head of the asylum's school committee, and a new era began. Reason rather than wishes, he determined, would now inform their decisions. Past idealism about the transforming power of education fell away. Considering the expense—and, as it had turned out, the seeming inappropriateness of professional training for orphans—the school committee concluded that "education, especially when spoken of in relation to the class of persons admitted to this house, does not consist entirely of the knowledge obtained from books." Even a high school education should be reserved for young men of "decided genius or unusual intellect with high moral tone and physical development and promise." Most important, the inmates should be more self-sufficient. What poor children really needed was "the ability to perform the duties of Life, which will in all probability devolve upon . . . [them] when they leave this institution." The inmates now had the responsibility to wash their own clothes. Saturday play was cut short by chores in the laundry, sewing room, and garden. Admitting that the sudden change from their former indulgence might be shocking and even "somewhat laborious," the commissioners concluded that some physical labor might well "add zest to the exercises of the school."[69]

In some ways, class probably explains the failure of many of these young men, but not in the way the commissioners imagined. The immersion into the world outside the asylum inevitably challenged the boys' sense of themselves. It was one thing to be top boy in orphan school and quite another to be forced to recite with students who had tutors or had attended the best preparatory academies. Even lack of ability or preparation does not explain the failure of the college boys in the 1850s. They faltered because they lacked the clear sense of place and mission that those with honored names enjoyed. College for the planter class merely put a bit of polish upon well-faceted stones; by their last year, they had places reading law in the offices of family friends, sitting behind desks of cotton brokerages, or living the life of a plantation master. There was

68. *Ibid.*, June 27, 1858.
69. *Ibid.*, June 25, 1857, April 27, 1854, July 11, 1872.

little certainty for a son of the city. Not surprisingly for orphan scholars, failure frequently came during their senior year.

Scholarship boys inherited no patrimony; some did not even know their fathers' names. When asked about family, the opening line in all southern conversations, what could they say? Did Frederick Behre, for example, sit at the dinner table with the family of a friend and explain that he had been born in Hamburg, Germany, and was given up by his mother at age nine when she went into the poorhouse? Or when asked the second question, "Where are you from?" did Thomas Deveaux willingly admit that he was born on Charleston Neck, the haven of pickpockets and prostitutes?[70] While at college, or even the High School of Charleston, a preparatory school of the first order, feelings of difference and even inadequacy were bound to arise. Some doubtless felt like impostors and wondered about the relevance of Greek texts while their mothers stitched shirt collars, their brothers worked as machinists, or their sisters as domestics.

Compounding the pain of what one sociologist has identified as the "hidden injuries of class," the boys also labored under the burden of great expectations. Orphan house children heard of great deeds every day at chapel service, in every Sunday sermon, and especially at the ritual annual anniversary ceremonies. At no time was the message to the children any more direct than at the anniversary in 1855, a high point of optimism. The Reverend Charles Coatsworth Pinckney concluded his sermon with a daunting charge: "And to the children and beneficiaries of this paternal institution, let me briefly say, that I hope they will always so conduct themselves that their advocates may never be ashamed. Remember that the public have a deep stake in your characters; that if you fail to improve your opportunities of becoming useful citizens, you not only injure yourselves in time and eternity, but defraud those by whose care you are protected and blessed."[71]

In no uncertain terms did the commissioners remind their wards that along with their startling elevation to scholars and gentlemen they bore grave responsibilities. Other boys, boys who had eaten at the same tables and studied at the same desks, had become not only hardworking and good, but heroes. Lacking the social security of the young men from great old families, the orphan house children bore the same burden of posterity. They endured equally with boys named Heyward or Manigault the nearly insuperable burden, as Bertram Wyatt-Brown has gracefully

70. King, *Charleston Orphan House*, 116, 119.
71. Pinckney, in Charleston Orphan House, *Anniversary Addresses*, 26.

phrased it, of "almost mythological heroes from the families past."[72] The list was impressive. Former orphan house boys sat in legislatures and on high courts, and stood in pulpits across the United States.

For those uninspired by scholarly achievement, the story of Thomas Holdrup held great allure. Removed from the poorhouse to the orphan house at eight, he served his apprenticeship as midshipman aboard the brig *Hornet*. Commissioned an officer while still in his teens, he served with Commodore Perry during the War of 1812. And, rumor had it, he actually overheard Perry's immortal words during the battle on Lake Erie, which so inspired him that he was decorated for his own "intrepidity." Holdrup ended his career as commodore of the naval station in Washington, D.C. Thomas Gedney also left the house for naval service. He had a distinguished career and is chiefly remembered for discovering a new channel into New York harbor, having a Coast Guard cutter named in his honor, and claiming the mutinied slave ship *Amistad* as salvage.[73]

But then there was Edward Appleford Love. One of the first selected to go to South Carolina College, he left for Columbia with great fanfare. The transition to the freedom of college life apparently overwhelmed him after being institutionalized since age six. After a short time, a school official wrote to the commissioners of Love's total "aversion to staying at the College." Wanting more explanation, they conducted an investigation among his associates, who reported that he had lost money gambling. Burdened by guilt and shame at his dishonorable behavior, the commissioners concluded, Love had fallen into "deep melancholy" and suffered "mental derangement."[74]

No one at the commissioners' table could better have understood the particular poignancy of being admitted into the sacred circle of the educated, but never actually being a part of it, than Christopher G. Memminger. Just as he claimed always to remember that "I was once a poor boy myself," he must have recollected his experience at South Carolina College, where he was known as "the Charleston boy," the protégé of Thomas Bennett. Only twelve when he began college, the childish "round about" jacket he wore accentuated his youth and slight build, so that he was frequently mistaken for some town boy who had wandered onto the grounds. But no one meeting his intense eyes, set off by jet black hair and

72. Richard Sennett, *The Hidden Injuries of Class* (New York, 1972), 269; Wyatt-Brown, *Southern Honor,* 118.

73. King, *Charleston Orphan House,* 42, 17, 61; Howard Jones, *Mutiny on the Amistad: The Saga of a Slave Revolt and Its Impact on American Abolition, Law, and Diplomacy* (New York, 1987), 3, 47.

74. Inmates' file, February 18, 1817, in COH.

a sharp nose, could misunderstand the complexity of the young man. Every feature suggested his great seriousness of purpose; even his lips "were so much compressed that his mouth [was] but as a line." Remembered by his classmates for his studiousness and strict devotion to the rules, Memminger conveyed the overall impression "of care, of serious deliberation," and frequently sadness, even as a youth.[75]

Intensely religious, he felt guided by divine destiny. So by the 1850s, when this German boy had become a Charleston patriarch with eight children and an expensive pew in Grace Episcopal Church, he was the least patient with the failings of poor boys who floundered. Dismayed by their ingratitude and shocked at their performance, he agreed that education for the dependent poor be practical and in a meaningful gesture ordered the school committee to donate the "philosophical apparatus" to the new community Model School upon which he redirected his attention.[76]

What of the girls of "particular cleverness" in Charleston's Orphan House? The contrast between the fate of girls of ordinary abilities, apprenticed as milliners or even housekeepers, did not seem so stark against that of their male counterparts who went out to fit pipes or bake bread, but for the talented young woman approaching fourteen who easily mastered what the girls' school offered and craving more, realized there was no more, disappointment ran deep. While their cohorts among the boys donned waistcoats and looked into a boundless future, they patched their old dresses and saw only a life of toil before them. To make their situation even worse, enhanced opportunities for the boys brought a corresponding decline in the quality of the girls' education. There was still work to be done in the asylum. Although the commissioners expressed periodic concern for the girls' intellectual development, the pressures of household economy forced them to increase their responsibilities as the institution grew. In addition to washing and ironing, the more mature girls had to dress the younger children and mend their clothes. They rushed through all their chores, then attended class. Missed lessons were expected to be studied at night; teachers were encouraged find some time to hear recitations outside class hours. Since the girls labored under such tight schedules, school instructors recommended that girls study the shorter story of the United States rather than the more demanding world history. The committee on discipline concurred and agreed to dispense with

75. Capers, *Memminger*, 18.
76. Minutes, June 15, 1857, April 27, 1854, in COH.

formal training in grammar. If interested, the girls could study geography "in their leisure time." With these changes, made in 1855, the commissioners raised the girls' sewing-room time to six or seven hours daily. Ever interested in advanced education, the commissioners also decided to fill the free hours on Saturday with instruction in starching clothes and fine handwork from "some white person." To encourage hard work in the laundry, the "Lady Commissioners" conducted weekly contests among the girls. Each neatly folded her week's work, placed a card with her name on top, and hoped to win praise—perhaps a small prize. At the end of each term, girls won prizes of books and little reticules for sewing achievements. Boys received pens and watches for their work in Greek.[77]

Although there is no reason to believe that the commissioners held any but the gender conventions of their day, they still deplored the lack of opportunity for the girls of the institution. Their letters and official records clearly reveal their wish that poor women had access to profitable employments, that hardworking widows could keep their children, and that they had alternatives to drudgery for promising girls. They fully understood the ironic condition of bright girls, who caused "no trouble, expense, or disappointment," in comparison with the ungrateful behavior of the privileged male inmates.[78] By offering a fifty-dollar dowry and a wedding outfit, they hoped to increase the girls' chances of marrying an honest mechanic and made it clear that they could always turn to the commissioners in desperate times. Many did. The commissioners made loans in times of trouble, wrote letters of recommendation, and provided legal assistance. They celebrated when young women started families of their own and were there to receive their children if life turned sour. The commissioners, who ruled their institution like oriental despots, also created within the walls of the Charleston Orphan House a world of women when few orphan societies even admitted girls. Except for the boys' schoolmasters and steward, who along with his wife oversaw the physical plant and general operation, white women held all the employments in the institution. They made it a place where women with no family support could make a respectable life for themselves.[79]

77. Discipline committee file [*ca.* 1855], *ibid.*

78. Minutes, June 24, 1858, *ibid.* As part of the free-school reforms engineered by Bennett and Memminger, the city opened in 1859 a normal school for girls who wanted to continue their education and receive teacher training.

79. King, *Charleston Orphan House,* 9. Richmond had no public orphanage for either boys or girls until the Civil War made such institutions a matter of patriotism rather than charity. A few local women organized the Female Humane Association in 1841 to teach the

The commissioners frequently hired mothers of inmates and gave them a safe haven, proximity to their children, and a wage comparable to what they might find elsewhere. One of these women, Mary Claybrook Manno, became the sewing mistress and held that position for fifty years. Obedient, skilled in household duties, pious, she embodied during her long life of service a becoming domesticity. It was Mary Manno, rather than one of the "Lady Commissioners" (usually wives or female relatives of prominent men), whom the orphan house officials held up to the girls as a model. Unlike the boys, who were all told they could rise to wealth and power with wit and hard work, girls, everyone understood, achieved worldly comfort only through inheritance or matrimony. For the girls of the city, possessing wit but lacking patrimony or prospects, only hard work appeared in their future.[80]

Mary Manno's story shows the positive impact of the institution upon the lives of three generations of women. In 1810, the churchwardens of her parish placed her (at age seven) in the orphan house, where she stayed for eight years before going to live with an uncle. Hers was the familiar story of marriage, childbirth, widowhood, and destitution. At twenty-four, finding herself alone with an infant, she successfully appealed to the commissioners for a position in her old home and a place for her child. Appointed sewing mistress in 1835, she trained and advised hundreds of girls over the course of her fifty years. When she became too infirm to work, the commissioners invited her to remain in the house at half pay in recognition of her service as an "upright and faithful officer, whose life is worthy of imitation and whose memory should long be cherished." When her daughter (also raised in the orphan house) died, Manno's son-in-law placed their child with her to grow up in the institution. Manno had the pleasure to see her granddaughter, Mary L. Lequeux, become a teacher in the orphans' school but died without knowing she would replace Agnes Irving, the formidable superintendent who in 1854 started

---

homeless, but high aspirations fell to small budgets; continuation of the institution was a month-to-month affair. In Savannah, Bethesda Orphanage remained strictly for boys. Women of the Savannah Female Society found not only disinterest but "prejudice" and hostility. In the late 1850s, the Inferior Court, which had jurisdiction over Savannah's orphans, faulted the society for foolishly emphasizing formal education rather than teaching the "domestic duties of Housekeeping" (*Constitution and Bylaws of the Female Humane Association of the City of Richmond, adopted 1833* [Richmond, 1843], 3–4; M. M. Wilmans to William Duncan, September 19, 1860, in William Duncan Papers, Georgia Historical Society, Savannah, Georgia).

80. Sewing mistress file, February 18, 1892, in COH; King, *Charleston Orphan House,* 12, 15, 52.

the program to keep the brightest girls as instructors in the asylum.[81]

In their quiet way, the small percentage of girls remaining to work at the orphan asylum represented the institution's greatest success story. Raised in the most imposing building in the city, sitting quietly in starched dresses during long Sunday services in the chapel, knowing in their hearts that the promises of a bright future intoned by the commissioners at the elaborate anniversary celebrations did not apply to them, they nevertheless continued conscientious studies in the classroom and industrious labors in the laundry. These young women (whose names are lost except as entries in crumbling record books) were sometimes little more than servants in the house, but they were vital to the continuity of the institution. They became substitute mothers to the other children of the poor. The values and attitudes they developed in the orphan house (their only inheritance) would thus be inculcated in future generations of the children of the city.

Desiring to move beyond the Charleston Orphan House and do more for all the children of the city, including the girls, C. G. Memminger directed his attention to the larger questions surrounding public education. He replaced the well-meaning but not very effective Rev. Charles Hanckel as head of the free school committee. After his work with the homeless and orphaned, he burned with another idea. South Carolina, he believed, though mercilessly criticized in the North for the depth of poverty among its poor, could be transformed, "like the army of Prussia," to a state "in which no man could be found who was not able to read his Bible or write his own name." Because of the initial hostility of the agricultural Upcountry to financing an educational program that would largely benefit the towns, Memminger began his revolution in Charleston. There, growing concern over the potential political power of uneducated laborers in 1849 made citizens more willing to accept a 5 percent increase in property taxes with the first glimmerings of a return to cotton prosperity.[82] Over the next decade, Charlestonians would undergo a remarkable change in sentiment toward the concept of universal education.

81. Sewing mistress file, February 18, 1892, in COH; King, *Charleston Orphan House*, 15.

82. In 1853 the state legislature increased its allocation for common schools from $37,000 to $74,400—the first increase since 1811. Funding remained at this level only to the outbreak of the Civil War (J. Perrin Anderson, "Public Education in Ante-Bellum South Carolina," South Carolina Historical Association *Proceedings* [1933], 4–5; Nita Katherine Pyburn, "The Public School System of Charleston Before 1860," *South Carolina Historical Magazine*, LXI [April, 1960], 90–91).

Memminger and his fellow commissioners announced their bold plans for a new educational system on the Fourth of July, 1856, and linked the project with the principles of 1776: "the obliteration of caste and class, the general welfare, the greatest good for the greatest number."[83] The task of restructuring Charleston's archaic school system involved a delicate mix of Memminger's three interests—finance, education, and politics. He persuaded his dear friend and adoptive brother, W. Jefferson Bennett, to join his crusade in 1854 and gave Bennett the assignment of creating the best school possible. Inspired by educational leader Henry Barnard's visit to the state in 1855 (the committee tried to recruit him as a superintendent), Memminger and Bennett ignored the growing local antipathy toward northern institutions and personally led a delegation to New York, Boston, and Philadelphia to bring back teachers trained in the most up-to-date methods.[84] In two years, Bennett completed his mission. Charleston's coeducational Model School, proof of the ability of a slaveholding society to provide for all its classes of white citizens, opened in 1858. The free school committee, which had tried diligently to break through the reluctance of the poor to attend the stigmatized "pauper academies" of the past, was shocked and delighted when twice as many students showed up as expected. An enormously proud Memminger stood before a crowd of excited townspeople and introduced them to six hundred well-scrubbed scholars, including some of his eight children: "Before you now stand an assembly of children whose good manners and attainments have already cast to the wind all doubts about the intermixture of class—all theories as to the peculiarities of our people—all uncertainty as to the value of the common school education."[85] By the fall of 1859, parents pressed to register 2,786 children in the eleven new schools that had been built and staffed during South Carolina's crucial decade.[86]

One of the schools that opened in 1859 was the first school for girls in South Carolina ever built with public funds. From his exhaustive study

83. "Speech of C. G. Memminger, esq., on the occasion of inaugurating the Common School System at Charleston, S.C., July 4, 1856," quoted in *American Journal of Education,* II (1855), 556; Capers, *Memminger,* 112–13.

84. The legislature recruited a number of orphan house commissioners to direct the free schools: George Buist, William C. Bee, Dr. S. H. Dickson, in addition to Bennett and Memminger (Pyburn, "Public School System," 92–93).

85. *Report of the Board of Commissioners of Free Schools to the Citizens of Charleston* (Charleston, S.C., 1857); Mattie Crouch Kneece, *The Contributions of C. G. Memminger to the Cause of Education* (Columbia, S.C., 1926), 14.

86. David D. Wallace, *South Carolina: A Short History, 1520–1948* (Columbia, S.C., 1966), 464. Charleston had about four thousand school-age children (Charleston *Mercury,* June 24, 1856).

of the topic, Memminger had concluded, "It is evident that the best interests of society demand for the one sex an education corresponding in all respects to the education of the other." The building, constructed in the popular Italianate style, towered over St. Phillip Street. Classrooms and other educational spaces such as a library occupied the first three floors. In a remarkable use of architecture to make a political statement, the commissioners located their meeting room on the fourth level under a dome that dominated the entire structure.[87]

The Female High and Normal School (later named for Memminger), where "the rich and poor meet on the platform of Common Humanity," helped close the gap between education for boys and for girls. Female high school students underwent a "complete English education," including training in French and voice. The Normal School offered college-level courses and prepared its graduates to teach in the elementary grades. Explaining the rationale for this educational innovation, Memminger insisted a woman needed to develop more than her "maternal instinct." She should have the opportunity to achieve educational excellence, not just to influence her children but to promote "her own internal happiness." Over the portal of the school was *Educate Your Daughters and You Educate the State*.[88]

School reform, like support for the orphan house, aimed to soften the class lines that undermined Charleston society in the same way the thirteen tidal creeks crisscrossing the peninsula steadily eroded all efforts to fill them up and convert them to solid ground. An issue of intense national debate throughout the nineteenth century, the question of free education forced Charlestonians to define and expand their concepts of the public realm and social democracy. By offering a larger share of the city's resources to the white working class, Charleston's progressive leaders tried to position themselves to remain in control during social changes they believed would sweep the town. But like earlier efforts to bring liberal reforms to Charleston, Memminger's efforts would be blown away in a storm of reaction.[89]

87. Christopher G. Memminger, in *Report of the Board of Commissioners of Free Schools to the Citizens of Charleston* (Charleston, S.C., 1858), 7; Severens, *Antebellum Architecture*, 243.

88. Christopher G. Memminger, "Address of the Female High and Normal School in Charleston, S.C.," Charleston *Courier*, May 24, 1859.

89. Charlestonian Stephen Elliott pushed a bill through the state legislature in 1811 guaranteeing each district three hundred dollars annual support upon completion of a schoolhouse and granted modest tuition supplements for students to attend private academies. Massachusetts, first among New England states, did not organize its basic education until 1837.

VI

THE END OF AMBIGUITY

Poor people can see things as well as rich people.
—George Fitzhugh, 1854

The return of prosperity to Charleston in the 1850s transformed the gloom of the preceding years into cautious optimism. Throughout the decade, one economic record after another fell, until the price of cotton approached its highest point in history with the crop of 1860. Yet the rebounded cotton market did not translate into an improved standard of living for the city's wage earners. During these flush times for planters, a Charleston seamstress explained that she could not even feed her children: "From the straightness of the times and the cheapness of labor, I can scarcely earn an individual support." James Buckingham noted that the South had more people in need than the North, despite the prevalence of higher wages, because "there are not so many resources of employment," especially for foreign immigrants. On his journey through the South, Frederick Law Olmsted was surprised to find "as much close packing, filth, and squalor, in certain blocks inhabited by laboring whites, in Charleston, as I have witnessed in any northern town of its size." [1]

Extremes of wealth essentially defined nineteenth-century urban life. Charleston proved no exception. The editors of the city's 1848 census admitted, "Pauperism is the inevitable accompaniment of cities." Southern slaveholders as a class held more property than the richest tier of northern society, but there was not much difference in the well-being of the poor in the regions. According to one recent study, perhaps as many as one-third of all American men included in the 1850 and 1860 censuses had little more than the clothes on their back and small change in their pockets. Of those with estates less than $100, two-thirds lived in cities and one-half were foreign-born. From the late 1830s through the 1850s, perhaps one-third of New York's work force suffered unemployment. In

---

1. Commissioners' file, October 4, 1855, in COH; James S. Buckingham, *The Slave States of America* (London, 1843), I, 51; Frederick Law Olmsted, *A Journey in the Seaboard Slave States in the Years 1853–1854* (New York, 1856), 404.

1860, 56 percent of Charleston's free population owned nothing. At that time, 3 percent of the free white men controlled the aristocratic old city's wealth, the most fortunate 20 percent holding 93 percent of the economic resources.[2]

One of the intangible results of the widening discrepancy between the white classes was a decline in the sense of belonging among the poor. Despite its aristocratic reputation, Charleston had always been a city where even the most humble natives could find a cool breeze along the harbor, enjoy sunsets that flooded the Ashley River with pink and gold, observe the comings and goings of downtown businessmen, and imagine life in elegant mansions. The city lost its intimate nature during the 1850s with northward expansion and the creation of various zones of manufacturing. Railroad yards and warehouses dominated open spaces. Charleston lost the qualities of the pedestrian city that bestowed a certain equality upon all citizens who shared an ability to walk to jobs, parks, or shops. With no effective or efficient system of public transportation, the laboring classes clustered in areas that offered the greatest possibilities of employment, leaving the more beautiful parts of the old city to those with their own carriages, who showed open resentment toward intruders in their neighborhoods.

Not only did the laboring poor who pounded the streets looking for day work suffer from the growing divisions in the city; even the middling classes of clerks and bookkeepers felt a loss of status. When the Charleston City Council, in its never-ending search for revenue, considered selling to a private concern Moreland's Wharf, adjacent White Point Gardens and one of the last "public pleasure grounds" overlooking the harbor, they met with passionate and quite unexpected resistance from those "without a country place" or a "coach and pair." In a letter to the editor, "A Few Young Americans" complained that though "it may be a matter of indifference to the wealthy, to those not so highly favored in this world's goods, it is a matter of consequence that they have some place where they may resort with their families and enjoy the gambolings and rollicks of their little ones."[3]

2. Dawson and DeSaussure, *Census of Charleston, 1848*, 46; James Oakes, *The Ruling Race: A History of American Slaveholders* (New York, 1982), 39; Leo Soltow, *Men and Wealth in the United States* (New Haven, 1975), 25, 36, 101; Michael P. Johnson, "Wealth and Class in Charleston in 1860," in *From the Old South to the New: Essays on the Transitional South*, ed. Walter J. Fraser, Jr., and Winfred B. Moore, Jr. (Westport, Conn., 1981), 66.

3. Randall M. Miller, "The Enemy Within: Some Effects of Foreign Immigrants on Antebellum Southern Cities," *Southern Studies*, XXIV (Spring, 1985), 40–43; Charleston

The increase in the propertyless white laboring class so transformed the social ecology and the politics of Charleston that the pretension of the old city as the idealized patriarchal republic was one sustained by only the most guileful. By 1850, the white population of Charleston surpassed that of slaves and free blacks by ten thousand. All southern coastal cities tried futilely to stabilize their populations to balance out-migrations to the Southwest. South Carolinians became particularly defensive when the census of 1850 revealed that its natives had fairly flowed out of the state during the past thirty years; the number who had chosen to live in another state equaled about two-thirds the number that stayed behind.[4] Charleston continued to lose its native population throughout the 1850s, at the same time that the number of slaves also declined as increased cotton production now warranted their return to the plantation districts instead of hiring out their time in the city. The next census would show that the number of foreign-born whites equaled about 16 percent of the entire population, but when compared with natives, the percentage rises to about 30 percent. Charleston, therefore, had the same percentage of European-born as many northern states.[5] While the total population of the city remained constant at about 42,000 (with the taxpaying population probably a third of that), the need for public charity climbed. As immigrants poured into the city with new force in the 1850s, tax rates

---

Mercury, July 4, March 30, 1860. A similar response occurred in Savannah in 1852 when the city sold off much of Springfield plantation, next to the city, in large parcels. A letter to a local newspaper complained that "the rich monopolize the lands about the city, and the poor have no hope, unless those lands under control of the city shall be parcelled out in smaller lots" (Savannah *Evening Journal,* March 1, 1852).

4. Tommy Rogers, "The Great Population Exodus from South Carolina, 1850–1860," *South Carolina Historical Magazine,* LXVIII (January, 1967), 16; *Southern Quarterly Review,* VII (1853), 142–43; Joseph J. Spangler, "Population Theory in the Antebellum South," *Journal of Southern History,* II (August, 1936), 360–89.

5. According to Charleston's 1848 census, 58 percent of the population was Charleston-born and 21.2 percent foreign-born, whereas Boston's population, as recorded in the 1840 United States Census, had 35 percent native to Boston and 24 percent foreign-born (Dawson and DeSaussure, *Census of Charleston, 1848,* 9). In 1860, the percentage of foreign-born among the entire white male population in the ten largest southern cities surpassed that of nearly every northern city (Silver, "A New Look at Old South Urbanization," 141–72; Ira Berlin and Herbert G. Gutman, "Natives and Immigrants, Free Men and Slaves: Urban Workingmen in the Antebellum American South," *American Historical Review,* LXXXVIII [December, 1983], 1181–82; Miller, "The Enemy Within," 33; Rev. Oscar Hugh Lipscomb, "The Administration of Michael Portier, Vicar Apostolic of Alabama and the Floridas, 1825–1829, and the first Bishop of Mobile, 1829–1859" [Ph.D. dissertation, Catholic University of America, 1863], 289–90; Ella Lonn, *Foreigners in the Confederacy* [1940; rpr. Gloucester, Mass., 1965], 26).

also rose in response to demands for the institutional assistance this population required. In 1856, the priest at St. Stephen's Mission ordered Bibles in English, German, Spanish, French, Italian, Danish, Welsh, and Norwegian. A pattern emerged, alarmists warned, indicating that "the submissive, acclimated, non-voting Negro" was being replaced with "the turbulent, feverish, naturalized foreigner," so crippled by hard times in the North that "death by pestilence [was] not more fearful than by famine." Many wondered where it all might end.[6]

When renewed profitability of plantation agriculture punctured many of the sputtering efforts at bringing industry southward, the hope of finding profitable work for the urban poor also died. Writing from the rural solitude of Port Royal, George Fitzhugh represented those opponents of the misbegotten effort to ape New England, with its "little truck patches, the filthy, crowded licentious factories, [and] the mercenary shop keeping, slavish commerce," but neither he nor any of the others who resisted manufacturing had any proposal about what to do with the unskilled who swelled southern cities annually.[7] When the prospect of large-scale factory work for the poor passed, Charlestonians resigned themselves to enlarging their welfare institutions.

In 1848, the last great local initiative, the Charleston Cotton Manufacturing Company, opened in a large Columbus Street building overlooking the Cooper River on the "most charming spot in the city." Committed to hiring whites only, the owners had expected to draw their operatives from the large concentration of poor in the nearby Hampstead area of Charleston Neck, but local workers resisted regimented labor in the noisy racket of the smoke-spewing mill. Labor problems compounded the pressing difficulties of undercapitalization until after sputtering along for four years, this symbol of the city's futile attempt to diversify its economy collapsed in ironic finale. Rather than eliminating the need for a poorhouse, the factory *became* the poorhouse in 1852. One local observer saw in the closing of the factory the symbolic end of the city's antebellum aspirations: "The buzzing wheel and humming loom give place to pallet and cot, the bell no longer calls the young and active to their work, but bids the old and feeble sick seek their rest; . . . over the portals where we read 'Industria,' we now read 'Charity.'"[8]

6. Thomas, *The Protestant Episcopal Church in South Carolina*, 264; *Southern Quarterly Review*, VII (1853), 142–43.

7. Russel, *Economic Aspects*, 199; "Wealth of the North and the South," *De Bow's Review*, XXIII (December, 1857), 587.

8. Minute book, June 20, 1855, in CPH; Henry P. Archer, *Local Reminiscences, De-*

After decades of mending and patching the crumbling Queen Street building, the commissioners of the poor voted to abandon its filthy cistern and leaking privies and move the town's paupers to the upper wards on the Neck, into the structure vacated by the luckless manufacturing company; they renamed it the more euphemistic almshouse. The old asylum reverted to use by indigent free blacks, who had been living in some rooms of the workhouse fitted out for them in 1842. Taxpayers also dug deep into their pockets to subsidize Roper Hospital, built near the Medical College on Queen Street to serve the sick poor. They spent over $200,000 on renovations for their favorite institution, the Charleston Orphan House, which stood in 1855 as a splendid mix of mansard roof, Italianate portico, and Corinthian columns, higher than any other building except the churches.[9]

A cluster of urban services, once on the town's periphery and now in the center of a residential section, incorporated institutions of humanitarianism and control, including the workhouse, the district jail, the Marine Hospital, and the house of correction. Also renovated at great expense during the same decade, they were distinguished from one another by their architectural forms. Those providing care mostly followed the classical style. Those inflicting punishment incorporated castellated details in their design similar to those found on The Arsenal and The Citadel, South Carolina's military academy. Dual motivations fired excitement for these renovations. Undeniably, Charlestonians felt a moral obligation (as they had historically) to provide basic services for the growing class of immigrants that made demands on public charity. This wave of reconstruction also suggests that most citizens still viewed the city in a national context and imagined that even if their factories ground to a halt and their trade once again grew stagnant, somehow this outward and visible sign of their own progressivism might yet secure them a place among the nation's great cities. The *Courier* issued an optimistic note in 1856 when the house of correction was updated in brownstone. It predicted that when all the planned work was completed, "Charleston [will] soon compete successfully in point of the number, cost, and finish of her public buildings, with any city of her size." The subtext of this expansion in social services was that for all the claims of southern distinctiveness, Charleston really was just like any city of her size, subject to the problems of unemployment, domestic violence, poverty, alcoholism,

---

livered before the Mutual Aid Association, No. 1 of Charleston, S.C., June 6, 1889 (Charleston, S.C., 1893), 18.
    9. Minute book, June 20, 1855, in CPH.

crime, and disease. What slavery as an institution did for the urban environment was to make it potentially more volatile.[10]

The concept of the social worker as professional began to evolve in the
North during this time, but Charleston's elite continued to oversee all
aspects of urban life such as education, unwed mothers, orphans, medical
services, and poor relief, even though the role of the public man was
already becoming somewhat anachronistic as the poor of the city became
increasingly foreign and so numerous as to be beyond their control. Ac-
knowledging demographic realities, politicos from established families
continued the Charleston tradition of strategic inclusion by inviting out-
siders with Irish or German surnames to run on their tickets. Since benevolence continued to be seen as an important aspect of local gover-
nance, they clung to their seats on municipal boards and commissions
throughout the nineteenth century. In 1854, a young woman who threw
over the traces of southern gentility for the bohemian life in New York
City recognized familiar characters in the latest bestseller, *Hard Times,*
a "satire on some of the most glaring evils of the present day." Rather
than describing the self-satisfied philanthropists of London, she quipped,
Charles Dickens may well have been revealing the inner motivations of
"some of the good people of Charleston, that lovely centre of all that
is good and virtuous," who "'Compound for sins that they're inclined
to / By damning those they have no mind to.'"[11]

The liberal ethos that underlay the growing emphasis upon the atomistic individual as the center of social organization pushed relentlessly
through the rhetoric of an organic community, and nowhere does it
appear so clearly as in public discussion about the poor. Throughout
Charleston, the benevolent army experienced extreme battle fatigue. Energies waned among those who started relief work in the heady years of
early 1820s or during the period of grim necessity during the 1840s. Disillusionment plagued men like William Gilliland, who had worked hard
as a city alderman for many years and been active with his wife in dispensing aid to the needy around town. He penned terse entries in his
account book in 1860 that showed his growing annoyance at seeing the
same conniving faces year after year. After bailing a Mrs. O'Neal out of
the city lockup and sending her off with two dollars, Gilliland confided
to his journal that "she makes poor mouth and I don't believe much in

10. Severens, *Antebellum Architecture,* 184, 162–66; Charleston *Courier,* March 19,
1856.
11. Ada A. McElhenney to Julian E. M. Mitchell, September 25, 1854, in Nelson
Mitchell Papers, Mitchell-Pringle Collection, South Carolina Historical Society, Charleston,
South Carolina.

her." Eliza Bingin tracked him down to relate her tale of woe. She told the familiar story of a sad life with a drunkard husband, but failed to move Gilliland, who had heard it all many times before. He dismissed her with a dollar: "I think she drinks. She is Irish, has been here for 20 years. . . . I don't like her looks or talk." The 1860 annual report of the increasingly tough-minded Sisters of Charity of St. Michael's Episcopal Church railed against those paupers who enjoyed the city's benevolence so thoroughly that they chose not to work. "Almost every dollar given at our door is a bounty on pauperism and an endorsement of vagrancy," the report warned, and went on to complain that this was probably true of all money "bestowed without the requirement of some work in return." [12]

The image of the poor as Christ's surrogates faded and was replaced by an unsympathetic rendering of a class lacking the self-control and motivation needed for success in the modern competitive atmosphere. In 1851, a Charleston journal sponsored by the Episcopal church complained about the common attitude of its readers: "We cast our eyes over the poor as a class in society, a wretched herd, very many of them as bad as they are wretched, and because we cannot by any well devised scheme of political economy help them all, we care effectually to help none." [13]

One of the most significant factors in the changing face of Charleston charities was the receding of women from roles of influence as the male-dominated public institutions assumed greater responsibility for the poor of the city. Many small independent women's groups fell victim to the depression of 1840. The Ladies Garment Society of St. Phillip's Church, for example, went into debt during that time and had to make desperate calls for funds through the press, not simply because the demand was greater than in past years (which it was) but because members increasingly neglected to pay their annual dues of about fifty cents. [14] Even interest in the estimable Ladies Benevolent Society waned from its peak of activity during Mary Grimké's day. Apparently others besides Sarah and Angelina resisted joining the family tradition of visiting the poor. One annual report wistfully commented, "Pleasant, indeed, would it be to see the fair daughters of our land deeming it a sacred duty, as well as privi-

12. William H. Gilliland, Account Book, September 26, 1860, November 15, 1860, in Perkins Library, Duke University; "The Sisters of Charity of St. Michael's Church," *Southern Episcopalian,* VI (February, 1860), 586.

13. James Warley Miles, "First Annual Address Before the Church Home," *Gospel Messenger,* XXVII (July, 1851), 113; "Plea for a Church Hospital," 476.

14. *Gospel Messenger,* XV (December, 1843), 265–66.

lege to carry on the work in which a pious mother had begun, continued and even ended her career."[15]

As it was, surviving society members frequently had to dip into their own pockets to support the patients, who usually averaged about two hundred a year. Some of the financial problems no doubt stemmed from the depreciation of stocks in the society's endowment; membership also suffered from the growing perception of the limits of piety in solving the problems of the city. Twenty years after the great flourishing of the benevolent societies, even the most dedicated volunteers had to admit that poverty would persist despite their most fervent efforts. The 1847 annual report of the Ladies Benevolent Society ruefully noted, "The theme which tells of human suffering is seldom varied, and the round of duties in which your visitors tread, month after month, and year after year seems never ending."[16] In 1855, the superintendent resigned from that society, and no one would step forward to serve in her place. Northerners who struggled with the same hopeless reality often took a path closed to southerners by turning to antislavery work, a reform that unlike temperance or work among the poor, possessed a solution.

During the 1850s, the pathways through which women struggled to expand their realms narrowed in Charleston. Local women went on record as specifically denying their interest in movements for greater equality. Louisa McCord's attack on the campaign for enfranchisement among northern women stands out as the most notable, but at all levels women retreated from activities that in any way challenged the idealized patterns of social organization. After many years of effective work in the city, Charleston's Episcopal Prayer Book and Tract Society assured readers of the *Gospel Messenger* that they claimed "no *independent* organization, [but] desire to consider themselves simply as *instruments* in the work of proclaiming the 'truth as it is in Jesus,' within the assigned limits of their labors and influence."[17]

In 1850, some "wise and prudent Christian men" embarked on a project modeled after those often found "in Protestant countries of the old world" to redefine the "virtuous woman" in response to the pressures of the modern age. Although replicating many of the services offered by the

15. In 1847, thirteen members died and nine resigned, while only six were added (Charleston *Courier*, June 23, January 23, 1847).
16. "Annual Report of the Ladies Benevolent Society," Charleston *Courier*, January 23, 1847; Middleton, "Ladies Benevolent Society," 232.
17. Louisa Susannah McCord, "Enfranchisement of Women," *Southern Quarterly Review*, n.s., V (April, 1852), 322–41; *Gospel Messenger*, XXV (August, 1848), 143.

city, the proposed Episcopal Church Home had a unique three-tiered mission of providing a home and work for abandoned women, a school and practical training for orphaned girls, and a program to encourage those women "sufficiently disengaged from the more urgent claims of natural and social duty" to practice Christian charity by visiting the poor "without the dangerous entanglement of vows or irrevocable engagement." The Church Home represented just one step, an Episcopal priest asserted, in the struggle to demonstrate that once "sectarianism and individualism" had run its course, only the church, not the "vagaries of liberalism or the semi-infidel theories of 'inalienable rights,'" offered any genuine hope of social unity. The role of women in church work had to be reexamined to prevent their exodus out of the sanctuary and into the lecture hall, as they were doing in the North.[18]

During its first years, the home came under constant assault because Charlestonians imagined reactionary Episcopalians establishing a new type of "Romish conventual system." In 1852, still trying to defend the home from these charges, the Reverend Charles H. Hall told his congregation in St. Michael's Church that the issue of redefining social roles for women belonged to a worldwide movement that threatened to change all established institutions: "We cannot much longer avoid regarding this subject, as we have done, by citing such texts as . . . 'Let your women keep silence in the Churches' as if that settled the whole question. It has nothing to do with it." "In politics may we never change her lot," he vowed, but added that to maintain its authenticity in the age of expanding spheres, the church did have the obligation to "reverence" the work women performed in feeding and clothing thousands of the poor. Clearly they proved themselves entitled to "better work and a higher sphere in the Church, than the needle and scissors afford." He defended women from the charge that in doing their "imperfect and inconsistent" charity work they were "venturing" too far into the world by recognizing that acts outside their homes were not necessarily "unnatural." "Female piety," proclaimed Hall, was not limited to the family circle alone. "It belongs to the Church."[19]

Through the Church Home, leaders of Charleston's Episcopal church experimented with redefining the sphere of women's religious activities beyond teaching Sunday school and joining charitable societies. It was Hall's hope (and the hope of all who supported this initiative) that the

18. Charles H. Hall, "A Sermon, Preached at St. Michael's Church, Charleston, in behalf of the Church Home, . . . 11th June, 1852," *Gospel Messenger*, XXIX (October, 1852), 193–94; Miles, "First Annual Address," 115–16.
19. Hall, "Church Home," 194, 200.

home would serve as a model by which women could participate more fully in the ecclesiastical life. A woman could make the church her family without the "paraphrenalia of vows and scapularies." To reconnect women, piety, and benevolence, Hall proposed they be incorporated in a renewed apostolic crusade to redirect their considerable but diffused energies from "individual and occasional charity" to "that organized system of good works, which shows that the Church as a *Church* is alive." [20]

The fundamental concept of creating a family atmosphere by bringing the elderly to live with the orphan proved flawed. Many of the girls resisted the hard labors they were expected to perform. The old women, hardened by lives of toil, embittered about the unfairness of their circumstances, fought and quarreled among themselves and with the impertinent youngsters. After only three years, the officers tried to restore harmony by buying another building and separating these women at opposite ends of their lives. [21]

The Church Home experience actually only proved how out of touch with the modern age the Episcopal church had become. After eight years of struggle to keep solvent, the officers (all men), hoping that the institution could hold on until some of the wealthy citizens who had promised bequests (mostly women) might have their wills in probate, finally abandoned their original objectives because of a dearth of "a higher degree of self-denying charity" in the community. The idea of developing a cadre of women to devote themselves selflessly to the church attracted little interest during the 1850s; those who did participate were mostly, like Sarah Russell Dehon (who died in 1857), legatees from another age. [22]

The growing antipathy toward the poor derived in part from their ethnicity and was fueled by fear. Crime posed a perennial problem, but evidence mounted annually that pointed to the great unwashed as somehow responsible for the epidemics that crippled all southern cities from time to time. Before medicine formally accepted the germ theory or identified the *aedes aegypti* mosquito as the source of contagion, two schools of thought dominated the debate over the source of yellow fever. Some believed it stemmed from indigenous causes. Others argued that the fever

20. *Ibid.,* 200–201.
21. Church Home of the Diocese of South Carolina, *The Sermon and Reports at the Third Anniversary Celebration of the Church Home, June 11, 1853* (Charleston, S.C., 1853), 8. At this time, there were six "Lady Associates" and fourteen orphans.
22. Church Home of the Diocese of South Carolina, *The Reports at the 8th Anniversary Celebration of the Church Home, June 24, 1858* (Charleston, S.C., 1858), 3. Sarah Dehon Trapier, who might have been supportive of the Church Home, suffered from curvature of the spine and was very restricted in her activities (Trapier, *Incidents in My Life,* 27).

stowed away, as it were, sailing into the city on the same ships that brought strangers and left with cotton. Robert Mills contended, in his statistical analysis of the state in 1826, that draining the swampy areas was more critical to the city's well-being than either improved care for the poor or free education. Only by thus altering the "climate of the country," he predicted, would "incalculable blessings" flow to the city and its residents in the form of improved "health, population, wealth, and political strength." Despite the advantages of a semitropical climate to the city's exotic charm and nurture of Lowcountry staple crops, geography worked against Charleston's rise as an important commercial center. Besides suffering through intense summer heat and dusty, suffocating streets, Charlestonians were "visited season after season with a mortality which weighs with depressing sadness and discouraging influences on the public mind." The city suffered "under a species of absenteeism, disastrous to social enjoyment and injurious to the accumulation of wealth among us as people who leave the city to escape the awful conditions take their money with them." "If we would have our city populous and wealthy," the city council concluded in 1856, "we must make it healthy." "In vain," a special committee on public health declared, "will we build Rail Roads and remove the barriers of the ocean, unless we can invite strangers to come among us with an assurance of health. Without this great blessing, wealth itself will lose its attraction. And it will therefore be better for us first to spend money in getting the former, unless we can make up our minds to see all that lost which we have been lavishing to secure the latter."[23]

The development of public health and the improved understanding of the way disease spreads challenged the long-standing belief that city dwellers were all susceptible to yellow fever or smallpox, which seemed to fly on the winds. Disease, it had been thought, worked with a deadly democracy, wafting through the tall shuttered windows of mansions with the same determination that it wedged its way through cracks in the loose boards of ramshackle shanties. During past epidemics, the ties between citizens seemed strengthened by mutual suffering. However, as the city expanded, with the poor and newly arrived immigrants increasingly segregated in the lowest and least desirable parts of the city, distinct patterns of infection emerged. The Charleston Board of Health and private aid societies kept detailed reports in an attempt to scientifically pinpoint the

23. Mills, *Statistics of South Carolina*, 463–64; Charleston *Mercury*, April 2, 1857; Clipping file, February 5, 1856, in Charleston City Council Records.

origin of yellow fever. They found a very low incidence among South Carolina natives. The highest was among "strangers." During the 1858 epidemic, for example, 172 fell victim to yellow fever; of these, 73 were Irish and 50 German.[24]

In the search for the source of epidemics, all evidence pointed to the neighborhoods where immigrants huddled. The fevers almost invariably struck first those living on the crowded side streets near the docks, in the low places flooded after a rain, beside public dumps, and along alleys thick with garbage. In the winter of 1856, a special committee of the Charleston City Council found much circumstantial evidence linking the dumping of offal scraped from the streets with the incidence of disease. Although not able to claim cause and effect, they did observe "that as the savage shark follows the Cooley ship . . . or the hungry wolf scouts the marching armies, so disease attended on filth, putrefaction and decomposition." The committee argued forcefully that the city end its practice of using urban waste as landfill in its relentless battle with the sea. The council needed little scientific knowledge to imagine the effects of the almost tropical southern heat on the accumulated "remnants of the butcher's meat—the parings of vegetables, the pluckings of poultry, the washing of culinary and domestic utensils, the decayed fruit, the spoiled fish, the bones, feathers, scales and other refuse parts of cooked and uncooked animals, the sour remnants of the table and kitchen, the greasy and fetid water in which these remnants have been fermenting."[25]

Scientific advances altered the nature of discourse about disease. Increasingly vivid and credible descriptions about its environmental origins painted the sick poor as the source of epidemics rather than the victims. An earlier report by Charleston mayor Henry L. Pinckney complained about "the frequent collection of numerous persons in the same houses, and the consequent filthiness of the houses and impurity of the atmosphere about them, which not only cooperated with intemperance in predisposing to disease, but contributed largely of themselves to create and diffuse the infection." After one foray to see the victims of the epidemic of 1852, a writer for the *Southern Quarterly Review* reported to sheltered readers that whole families lived in disgusting lodgings where "a burning sun sends down its almost perpendicular rays upon the chambers, ten feet square, closed between walls, with but one window and one

24. *Report of the Committee of the City Council of Charleston upon the Epidemic Yellow Fever of 1858* (Charleston, S.C., 1859), 68.
25. Clipping file, February 5, 1856, in Charleston City Council Records.

door for air and light." They breathed stagnant air and cooked their food amid the noxious fumes of "accumulating filth and offal of tens and scores of bodies."[26]

Seeing other whites in this scarcely human condition left visitors impressed by the differences between classes rather than by their shared humanity. Some southerners imagined that by doing the work of slaves, foreigners had violated a law of nature and that their susceptibility to yellow fever (from which blacks were theoretically immune) was their punishment. The Charleston *Mercury* succinctly summarized the divisive impact of disease in the political climate of the 1850s: "Sanitarily considered, there are in all cities, but two classes of people: the very ignorant, who are commonly very filthy, and very poor, and the better informed who are commonly not very filthy and not very poor."[27] Continuing research on this subject suggested that the wallows of immigrants, in particular, created breeding places for disease. According to a member of the Charleston Health Department, the northeast portion of Ward 3, dominated by Irish workers, presented a sanitary nightmare: "The lots . . . are almost always in a slough, and in warm weather, emit the most disgusting and offensive odors; upon these are crowded small, ill-ventilated, filthy, dilapidated hovels, the basement floors of many of which I have seen floating or submerged by the rains or tides for weeks at a time."[28]

Seasonal epidemics that stalked cities in the South every summer and fall proved the equivalent of war, with its heroes, victims, and occasional abridgments of civil liberties. Citizens spent most of their energies dodging death, staying in their houses, and bolting their windows lest tainted night air wedge its way into their fortresses. Their fears were well founded; epidemics surely killed more Charlestonians than did rebellious slaves. Newspapers agreed to censor reports of the raging fevers and the casualties they wrought, and continued to proclaim the health of the city in order to prevent the quarantine of the port and the decline of trade. From New Orleans to Richmond, public men formed Howard associations to tend the sick poor not only in their own cities but wherever epidemics struck, and awarded medals and citations to those who "dis-

26. *Annual Report of the Health Register for the Year Ending December 31, 1867,* as quoted in Silver, "A New Look at Old South Urbanization," 64; Henry L. Pinckney, *A Report Relative to the Proceedings of the Relief of the Sick Poor* (Charleston, S.C., 1838), 17; *Southern Quarterly Review,* VII (1853), 144.

27. Jo Ann Carrigan, "Privilege, Prejudice, and the Strangers' Disease," *Journal of Southern History,* XXXVI (November, 1970), 568–78; Charleston *Mercury,* September 16, 1852.

28. Quoted in Silver, "Irish in Charleston," 151.

played a heroism unknown in the battlefield." Seeking out the sick poor in the black night of the epidemics often meant pulling on thick boots to walk through stinking mire, breaking down cellar doors to find the un-mourned bodies of whole families covered by their own black vomit, carrying an extra kerchief to subdue the foul odors that lingered in nar-row streets, and bracing for what was often the harrowing experience of a lifetime—a totally different experience from the genteel calls of prayer societies. Cranmore Wallace, a Christian urban missionary, cautioned a comfortable Episcopal congregation in the wake of the 1854 epidemic that "within a square [block] of your own homes, are purlieus of misery and vice, from entering which you would shrug back in horror."[29]

Rather than shrinking back, earnest Charlestonians formed ward in-spection groups in 1852 to search, not for the suffering poor, but for standing water, stagnant pools, and old neglected cisterns. A letter to the *Mercury* urged delicacy on the part of those well-attired men who would appear at their neighbors' doors and ask to see the privy. This sudden interest on the part of the gentry, the writer warned, might well stun the "poor knave who has no other claim to our notice than that which the possibility of his contaminating the atmosphere he breathes in common with us gives him." The *Mercury* advised courtesy toward those on the peripheries of these disease-breeding stews. In all dealings with this class, the writer concluded, they should take care "to throw a bone to a dog" since "it is safer to be rude to our equals than our inferiors."[30]

Generally cynical about the city's social reformers, the *Mercury* par-ticularly enjoyed caricaturing the sanitary committees, "some hundreds of men whose business it isn't to visit some others whose business it is," who inspected the poor sections in search of hazards to the public health. Beyond the obvious presumption of poking into other people's private business, the mission was futile. As an educational task force only, their authority was limited to suggesting, "in the gentlest manner possible, the occasional and moderate use of some antiseptic or disinfecting agents." And even if epidemics did emanate from these "inaccessible and disgust-ing locations," this critic deduced, all their carefully printed regulations for clean living meant nothing to ignorant and illiterate offenders.[31]

29. Charleston *Courier*, September 1, 1853; Pease and Pease, *The Web of Progress*, 191; Wallace, "Reports of Charleston City Missions," *Southern Episcopalian*, II (August, 1855), 490.
30. Charleston *Mercury*, September 17, 1852.
31. *Ibid.*, September 16, 1852. On the first of September, the city council resolved that two citizens from each block of every ward must visit every lot and report all unsanitary conditions to the mayor.

Even though meant as a political jibe at Whiggish meddlers, the *Mercury's* commentary correctly questioned the limits of old-fashioned voluntary efforts in the face of modern problems. Rather than fund appropriate public health systems with trained professionals, Charleston's benevolent tradition continued to subtly coerce conscientious citizens into exposing themselves to filth and disease as part of their civic duty, "to make his election between an onerous unpaid Scavenger service and unpopularity."[32]

William Porcher Miles bridged the gap between the old patricians and modern politicians. His ascent from college professor to reformist mayor of Charleston confirmed the significance that urban communities attached to public service. In 1855, Miles had joined sixty-four other Charlestonians who volunteered to help their "sister communities" in Virginia suffering from yellow fever epidemics. A false report of his death focused attention upon the professor's sacrifice and fulfillment of the "noblest impulse of humanity." Much to his surprise, Miles returned home from Virginia a local hero. The press carried stories of his selfless performance and public proclamations of "All honor to Professor William Porcher Miles." In recognition of his "heroic conduct" and taking advantage of the publicity, Whigs of the city had nominated him for mayor before he boarded the train home. Miles, nonplussed at his celebrity, received a gold medal from a benevolent society. He handily won the election against an anti-immigrant Know-Nothing candidate and instituted a reform administration.[33] Motivated by the need to give a more up-to-date appearance to the city and to eliminate the graft and nepotism of the old regime, he replaced the antiquated night watch (charged with enforcing slave curfews) with a full-time uniformed police force trained to regulate poor whites. Savannah, a city with an even larger immigrant population than Charleston's, had introduced a more efficient police into the South and provided the model for "Paddy Miles' Bull Dogs." Miles also turned his efforts to restoration of public credit; the value of the city's bonds issued to underwrite the railroad projects had suffered discounts of 15 percent in 1856. Understanding the connection between improving

32. *Ibid.*

33. Charleston *Courier,* August 25, August 31, September 14, September 20, 1855; *Dictionary of American Biography,* VI, 1617; *Harper's Weekly,* February 10, 1860. Miles acted contrary to the advice of his old friend William Gilmore Simms, who advised him to avoid being "too virtuous," as it would shock the Charleston people so accustomed to political corruption and "expand nothing on projects of any sort" (William G. Simms to William Porcher Miles, January 5, 1856, in *The Letters of William Gilmore Simms,* ed. Mary C. Simms Oliphant *et al.* (Columbia, S.C., 1954), III, 417–18).

the health of the city and its future prosperity, he introduced a new system of storm drains to sweep rotting filth from the streets. Inequities in state tax laws further cut city revenues. Charlestonians staggered under nearly 25 percent of the whole state burden as Miles's ambitious administration sent the annual budget climbing from $507,000 to $565,000.[34]

While the first blush of success clung to his mayoralty and the promise of reform held the city's imagination, Miles successfully stood for a seat in Congress in 1856. Soon, however, the price of progress and the decline in business caused by his stringent quarantine measures for incoming vessels thrust voters into a somber mood. The mayoral election of 1857 reflected dark changes in the local temperament as F. D. Richardson, a Know-Nothing sympathizer, came very close to defeating reform candidate Charles MacBeth by preaching against "the horrors of Catholicism, Germanism, Irishism, Policeism, Drainage and Quarantine, and all the rest of the thirteen deadly sins" that had made the city itself "a sick man."[35]

William Gilmore Simms diagnosed the source of the Port City's internal disease: "There are two very distinct cities in Charleston—the old and the new—representing rival communities."[36] And they were always at war. The future-oriented sentiments of the city supported efforts to extend the benefits of citizenship to foreigners, struggled to maintain a national identity in the face of growing sectional alienation, and tried to find a middle ground for the expanding white laboring class. Conservatives resisted accommodation to changes in the city and desperately sought to institute policies to block Charleston's slide into a world that challenged them to live up to their long-held values of liberty and democracy. They turned their heads to social realities and sang paeans to the homogeneous South that still resound in historical scholarship today.

Confronted with a changing world, Charleston's writers and thinkers, such as Simms and Jacob Cardozo, joined other southern intellectuals in expending their considerable mental energies not in merely defending slavery but in portraying the peculiar institution as a positive force for good. Reflecting this change of sentiment, the city council went from a short-lived, embarrassed attempt in 1841 to limit all slave sales to a secluded place behind the workhouse to the decision during the 1850s to flagrantly sell and trade slaves in an open market next to the venerable Exchange Building at the head of Broad Street, the most public place in

34. Clarence M. Smith, Jr., "William Porcher Miles, Progressive Mayor of Charleston, 1855–1857," in South Carolina Historical Association *Proceedings* (1942), 30–39.
35. Charleston *Mercury,* November 3, 1857.
36. Quoted in Severens, *Antebellum Architecture,* 255–56.

town.[37] Since the city was now clearly not going to join the new industrial age, its citizens glorified the old ways. Falling behind the rest of the nation, Charlestonians began to make more of regional distinctions than really existed. Thwarted in every attempt to provide a livelihood for poor whites and suffering from higher taxes related to various attempts to modernize the city, conservatives, who never fully resolved the issue of wealth distribution in a republic, became increasingly restive over the burden of misfits out of place in the southern democracy.

The competing forces at work in the evolving vision of the city may be clarified by tracing the change in classical analogies through which Charlestonians attempted to understand and explain their experience. Southerners had from the time of the Revolution sought connections between their history and those of the ancient slaveholding republics. In the first glow of liberation from British mercantilism, Americans strove for a political economy that protected the property of the individual and guaranteed to workers the fruits of their labor. For their historical model, they drew upon an idealized "Christian Sparta," a simple city-state dedicated to the common good and immune from the selfishness and striving for personal gain connected with commerce and luxury.[38]

The Jeffersonian vision receded as Charleston's commercial star began its ascent. During the 1820s, Charlestonians compared themselves to Romans during the days of the Caesars, uncorrupted citizens of a center of learning and political virtue made possible by the labors of slaves. During the next twenty years, the unreliability of the agricultural economy pushed the city into more aggressive pursuit of manufacturing and commercial advantages to achieve economic parity with the North. The divisive Nullification crisis of 1832, along with the subsequent changes in the city's political economy a few years later, capped off the Augustan Age of Charleston.

With subsequent changes in the economy and society, Charlestonians sought new models to fit the changes they experienced. Accepting that social inequality and dependency would forever be a fact of life among some segments of the population (as would greed and avarice among others), claims of republican virtue receded among those who accepted the inevitable intrusion of the modern urban world. Catholic bishop John England, speaking to the Hibernian Society, pointed out that while Philadelphia and Boston both vied for the title Athens of America, Charleston was destined to emerge as the "new Tyre," the proud and independent

37. *Ibid.*, 157–58.
38. McCoy, *Elusive Republic*, 49, 71.

Phoenician center of trade and shipping known for the skill of its sailors and the talent of its poets.[39] The selection of Tyre as a model suggests that the individualistic model of social relations had begun pushing aside patriarchal concepts.

Decisions regarding which groups qualified for public charity reflected the community's desire to draw more clearly the distinctions of color, caste, and class. Definitions of "the poor" represented a political challenge to those interested in social welfare. In 1847, John Adger, speaking to his congregation at the Second Presbyterian Church, identified the poor of the city as "a class separated from ourselves by their color, their position in society, their relation to our families, their national origin, and their moral, intellectual, and physical condition. . . . They belong to us. We belong to them." Even as he spoke, the comforting days of social symmetry had passed, if indeed they had ever existed. Politicians also moved to clarify the halfway status of the free black. After the fateful Denmark Vesey conspiracy in 1822, punitive legislation fell upon the free black rather than the slave, as it had after the colonial Stono Rebellion. South Carolina and other states began efforts to enumerate and track all free persons of color within their borders through a capitation tax, an annual registration fee of two dollars first set in 1792. In 1841, the state legislature strengthened the laws against manumission of slaves (first passed in 1820 and frequently observed in the breach) to eliminate the common practice of placing a favored servant in trust to another master who essentially agreed that the slave live as a free person. Throughout the 1840s, the courts worked under the assumption that any white person had the power to discipline, correct, or punish a free black.[40]

Also during the 1840s, the relationship of free blacks to the city relief system had undergone close scrutiny. Richard Yeadon, a commissioner of the poor, particularly wanted to clarify the question of what claims free blacks had on the charity of the city. A wealthy Charleston lawyer, Yeadon epitomized the quintessential public man of the nineteenth century. With a lucrative law practice, he had the means to indulge in "disinterested" liberality. Childless, he had the time; a Whig, the inclination. A commissioner of the poor for eleven years, Yeadon held the presidency of many Charleston benevolent societies and served as a trustee of several public institutions. Although a moody and often difficult man, he won a

39. Quoted in Severens, *Antebellum Architecture*, 96. Throughout its history, Tyre suffered several conquests but managed to stage remarkable revivals until its final devastation by the Arabs (*The Interpreter's Dictionary of the Bible* [New York, 1962], IV, 721–23).
40. John Adger, *My Life and Times* (Richmond, 1899), 166–67; Johnson and Roark, *Black Masters*, 42–50.

reputation as a friend to the poor, a protector of the weak, and an exemplary citizen.[41]

Yeadon found that the relationship of the slave to the city was murky. The supposed lifetime bond between master and slave broke down most frequently in the cities. Masters who hired out their slaves lost track, lost interest. On those occasions when either negligent or insolvent masters "freed" their ailing slaves, city officials faced the additional burden of fitting these blacks into a system designed to elevate the white pauper.[42] The managers of Savannah's poorhouse and hospital declined any responsibility for blacks, since the institution was technically a private corporation. Richmond harbored sick and superannuated slaves in dank basement rooms of the city poorhouse at their masters' expense. Charleston's poorhouse theoretically received blacks only if insane or otherwise a threat to society. But records show that the commissioners judged every petition upon its merit and admitted slaves of very advanced age or severe disability strictly on the basis of need. For a yearly fee from her owner, they agreed to keep Agnes, a young slave horribly burned by a fire whose "unsightly appearance" and "unpleasantness" offended the lady of the house. In 1820, the commissioners overcame the most strongly held objection to including blacks by hiring black nurses to relieve the white staff of the impossible situation of ministering to blacks. The finances of the city during the 1830s doomed a plan for a separate medical facility for blacks. Mayor Henry L. Pinckney agreed to let some destitute or deranged blacks into the sick wards of the Poor House, even though he thought it "contrary to the true spirit of our policy" and "repugnant to my feelings."[43]

Of particular appeal to Yeadon's legal mind during the early 1840s was the thorny question of sorting out the public's obligation to those blacks who had spent a lifetime as free men and women, contributing to

41. Minute book, June 29, 1870, in CPH; John Calhoun Ellen, "The Public Life of Richard Yeadon" (M.A. thesis, University of South Carolina, 1953). During the course of his life, Yeadon belonged to the following associations: Charleston Bible Society, Fellowship Society (president, 1838–70), South Carolina Society, Charleston Free Schools Commission, Charleston Poor House Commission, Shirras [Free] Dispensary Commission, Board of Trustees of the College of Charleston, Free Masons, Charleston Bar Association, Charleston Port Society, Board of Trustees of the Sailors' Home, Board of Trustees of the Confederate Widows' Home, and the South Carolina Historical Society.

42. See Richard Wade, *Slavery in the Cities: The South, 1820–1860* (New York, 1964), and Claudia Goldin, *Urban Slavery in the American South, 1820–1860: A Quantitative History* (Chicago, 1976).

43. Minute book, September 18, 1850, March 6, 1820, in CPH; Henry L. Pinckney, *Review of the Preceding Year, 1838* (Charleston, S.C., 1839), 40.

the community through their labor and their taxes. In cities where free blacks congregated, they posed a threat to the fundamental assumptions of the southern system by proving their ability to live on their own and representing to slaves a possibility besides bondage. Excluded by law and custom from many of the skilled jobs, intense and profound poverty defined the lives of most free blacks. According to one account, one-third of those in South Carolina reported no cash income at all. Chief Justice Joseph Henry Lumpkin of Georgia described the hopeless position of a free black in his state: "He resides with us and yet is a stranger. A native even and not a citizen. Though not a slave, yet he is not free. Protected by law, yet enjoying none of the immunities of freedom. Though not in a condition of chattlehood, yet constantly exposed to it. . . . His fancied freedom is all a delusion."[44]

In 1842, Yeadon decided to tidy up the loose ends of the relief system and make a definitive statement about the relationship of caste and color to entitlements from the community. That year, Cupid Jones, an elderly free black and veteran of the state militia, applied to the commissioners of the poor for "out-relief" from the city, which would permit him to receive rations of third-rate beef and dry bread three times a week from vendors at the city market. Yeadon and fellow commissioners George Buist and Edward Elfe formed a "Committee of Three" to determine the city's responsibilities and powers relating to the free black. The long and complicated deliberation that resulted in Cupid Jones's ultimately receiving one weekly ration at the taxpayers' expense suggests the serious implications that the commissioners believed public benevolence held for the social order.[45] The arguments that unanimously carried the day are worth considering in some detail to understand better the criteria for public responsibility.

The Committee of Three (lawyers all) commenced its investigation, naturally enough, with a painstaking search of all the relevant state and local statutes since the 1712 ordinance charging the various parishes with "prevention of the perishing of any of the poor, whether young or old." The members wended their way through the intricacies of archaic legal language, paying special attention to any restrictions on those eligible for public charity. For over a century, legislators had used the most inclusive terms: "all and every poor," "any person," "all impotent, lame or otherwise infirm persons," "any pauper," "strolling beggars," "sojourners,"

44. Joseph Henry Lumpkin, quoted in Ralph Flanders, "The Free Negro in Antebellum Georgia," *North Carolina Historical Review*, IX (1932), 268.

45. [Richard Yeadon, George Buist, and Edward Elfe], *Duties and Powers of the Board in Relation to the Free Colored Poor of the City* (Charleston, S.C., 1842), 4.

and "servants." The language of the law, the committee reasoned, encouraged the mantle of public charity to be as broad and "wide as humanity counsels." Not only white citizens and residents of Charleston qualified for merciful treatment by the city but aliens, immigrants, transients, and persons of every color and hue, whether Indians, mulattoes, mestizos, or blacks.[46]

Impressed, but reluctant to accept the implications of the literary evidence, the committee dissected the funding history of the existing poor-relief system. City institutions, particularly the orphan house, had received voluntary gifts from both blacks and whites. The municipal government imposed fines and assessed fees for licenses from all city dwellers, black and white. Free blacks of working age labored under a "discriminating capitation tax" that hindered their ability to establish cash reserves for emergencies. They also paid taxes on their real and personal property. Thus, the committee concluded, "as a matter of right and justice, as well as of logic and law, their own poor are entitled to relief out of a fund to which they contribute 'equally' with the more privileged classes of the community."[47]

As it unraveled the situation, logic forced the committee to concede that color served as a very poor guide to entitlement. Its investigation revealed that officials had granted aid to deserving individuals from the free black community and had supported slaves willed to the town from time to time. For years, the commissioners of the poor for suburban Charleston Neck had been granting rations and medical treatment to the families of all free men or women who had at any time paid taxes. If it was the "original intention" that color should be the criterion for relief, why, the lawyers queried, was the Indian, who was "in many particulars of an inferior caste," considered a fit recipient of poor relief and not the free blacks, "who stand still lower in the scale of civil right and privilege, but not lower in the scale of humanity?" As a result of this enquiry, the city remodeled the old workhouse for indigent blacks, reserving the poor-house as strictly a haven for whites. One of the few public comments on this decision came from William Gilmore Simms's magazine, praising Yeadon's report as "conclusive and manly" in holding up the "policy and humanity of our people" and expressing surprise that the question was even raised in "a Christian community."[48]

Simms and Yeadon fairly represented the spirit of community feeling

46. *Ibid.*
47. *Ibid.*, 8.
48. *Ibid.*; *The Magnolia: or Southern Appalachian*, n.s., II (January, 1843), 139.

on the question of providing some comfort to the sick and ailing in the black population more or less equivalent to that extended to the whites. When the question became equal competition between the able-bodied white man and the hearty free black, however, sentiment hardened. Across the South, in the state legislatures of North Carolina and Virginia, arguments rang out for tighter restrictions of this intermediate class—black but not slave, free but not white. But in 1852, the Charleston *Mercury,* a journal not usually known as the voice of moderation, cautioned against squeezing this class out of the South to the North or Liberia. The *Mercury* outlined the scenario most feared by Charlestonians. With only two classes—black and slave, free and white—"no Society is safe where the links are disunited thus." However, with "the intervention of a third or connecting class between, by birth and caste affiliated with the latter, and by interest and partially by position connected with the former, there is both security and advantage . . . and the dangers of collision, open or secret, between the two are greatly abriated." If this link between the races and the classes broke, "that great law of gradation that runs through the universe, will be violated in our social organization." If "the free negro [was] to the slave state what the lightening rod is to the building," as the *Mercury* contended, then the free white laborer might be the fiery bolt that would inflame and destroy the divisions between slavery and freedom upon which southern society uneasily rested.[49]

Throughout the 1850s, Charlestonians saw the solidification of a new class of wage earners sliding into the interstices of the urban economy, competing for the same jobs that slaves held, and blurring the distinctions between race and poverty. The cisatlantic reputation of the Irish for brawling and resisting regimentation followed them south. As a matter of principled practicality, many Charlestonians hired them only when black labor was unavailable or too expensive. Compared with the faithful old slave retainers who still moved noiselessly about the best old homes in Charleston, Irish maids seemed crass and insolent. Northern-owned southern hotels that hired Irish waiters with their cocky manner and indecipherable brogue irritated southerners still uncomfortable with white servants.[50]

Tales of the horrors experienced by white planters on San Domingo passed from generation to generation of Charlestonians and persisted in the public memory. An incident in 1855 illustrated their anxiety about the possibility of a race war, not the type where slaves slit the throats of

49. Charleston *Mercury,* October 12, 1854.
50. Lonn, *Foreigners in the Confederacy,* 26–27.

masters, which kept an earlier generation awake in the night, but an all-out conflict between foreign labor and black slaves. In early spring of that year, about thirty enraged Irishmen (brought south by labor contractors to build a branch of the Northeastern Railroad) began agitating over their shoddy treatment. Just north of the Charleston line, this core group pressured others to stop work in protest over violation of their contract. Their agreement with the railroad set wages at $1.25 a day, but on payday they found the company had reduced their wages to $1.00, claiming a decline in profits. The leaders among the workers harangued, argued, and pleaded with their cohorts to walk out and refuse to compromise. But most had families to feed, so they grabbed any cash they could get. The frustrated organizers then resorted to more radical measures. According to the Charleston judge who tried to reconstruct the events of that day, the more agitated Irishmen, urged on by an "arch seducer," "banded together, flourished bludgeons, paraded the line of the road in formidable numbers, displayed a hat upon a pole as [a] flag, ordered contracted laborers to quit and in default of acquiescence, threatened with violent words and demonstrations to find a speedy means to enforce the mandate."[51]

At first, only the sheriff and a small posse rode out to the site. A few recent disturbances among railroad workers within the city had been easily quelled. The ringleader rejected all their earnest efforts to "expostulate and persuade," and declared "he would never be taken alive." Horrified at the venom and resolution of the strikers, the sheriff sent for a detail of the local voluntary militia. Prominent citizens such as Wilmot Gibbes DeSaussure, captain of the Washington Artillery, quickly slipped on their uniforms and boarded train cars for combat. The Charleston Light Dragoons were bathed in their dust as all four units converged upon Seven Mile Pump, where the renegades were hiding.[52] By this time, the rabble-rouser urging the strike had fled, and twenty-four rather confused strikers surrendered themselves.

Transported under guard back to the city, the ragtag pack appeared before Judge Withers.[53] Withers expressed his sympathy with their di-

51. The Northeastern Railroad was approved in 1852, but by the time construction actually began in 1854, the cost of labor and materials had risen to the point that Charlestonians faced a $250,000 increase in the initial estimate of $1,240,337 (Phillips, *Transportation in the Eastern Cotton Belt*, 354–55; Charleston *Courier*, March 26, 1855).
52. Charleston *Courier*, March 12, 1855.
53. Although identified in the press only as "Judge Withers," this may be Thomas Jefferson Withers (1804–1865), intimate of James Henry Hammond and uncle of Mary Boykin Chesnutt. A Camden lawyer, he was elected a common-law judge in 1845 (Carol Bleser,

lemma and stated his unswerving agreement that white workers had the right to set their own price for their labor. But with "emphatic delivery and terseness of thought," he warned the aliens of the seriousness of their crime of using terror to achieve their goals on a soil that did not "nurture mobs, riots, or seditions." Believing he had made his point, Withers declined to "exercise severity" over unhappy and scared men he deemed victims: victims of a glib rabble-rouser who led them astray, victims of a contract labor system that an investigation by the court had shown placed them in miserable boardinghouses, victims of their poverty and deprivation ("said in no spirit of reproach") that had robbed them of proper intellectual and moral training. Since "the law has no vengeance," Withers felt justice would be served by a relatively light sentence of two months in prison and a five-dollar fine.[54]

But Withers had more to say. Revealing the heart of the city's fears, Withers warned the Irishmen that he detected a "proclivity to turbulence" among their people and "an inclination to make war upon the Negroes." He recollected the beginning of friction between the two groups when two Irishmen first began soliciting work as draymen, a job traditionally held by blacks. Competition heated up to such an extent that in a slugging free-for-all one of the immigrants knocked out the eye of a slave. That Irish rowdy received quick justice and a harsh sentence. Slaves, Withers explained to these newcomers, also had rights, not the natural rights touted by northern liberals but protections devolving from the property rights of their masters, which the law "must vindicate to the bitter end."[55] Justification of the southern system rested with its ability to insulate property owners from the conflict between labor and capital that tore at the underpinnings of free society.

Progressives searched in vain to carve out a middle way for the poor white in a society theoretically divided into master and slave. The proslavery apologists indulged in swollen overstatement and put forth three positions that robbed the southern urban society of the elasticity needed to accommodate the changes in its social and economic construction. The first contended unequivocally that the slave and the workingman could never coexist. "Free labor," William Henry Trescot warned, "hates slave labor."[56] The second argument that gained momentum among south-

---

ed., *Secret and Sacred: The Diaries of James Henry Hammond, a Southern Slaveholder* [New York, 1988], 328).

54. Charleston *Courier*, March 26, 1855.

55. *Ibid.*

56. William Henry Trescot, quoted in "The Free Schools of Charleston," *Southern Quarterly Review*, n.s., II (November, 1856), 149–50.

erners, especially as the depression of 1857 threw northern laborers into the depths of unprecedented suffering, touted slavery as the ultimate poor-law system.[57] Robert Southey, one of England's more mediocre poet laureates of the early nineteenth century, enjoyed renewed fame in the South for his tidy epigram "Slavery excludes poverty." The issue of poverty merged with that of slavery and occupied the interests of a wide-ranging group of Charlestonians. Sentiments such as those expressed in the Episcopal *Gospel Messenger* pushed the debate to the next logical conclusion: Slavery remained the only known solution to the "problem of labor," which was "how to secure the maintenance to all the poor, in return for the labor of all the able bodied among them."[58]

The third variant on this theme went a step too far: Workers who depended upon a daily wage for their living essentially *were* slaves. The southern propaganda machine eagerly scanned the reports of reformers in both the northern states and Great Britain investigating the plight of laborers. These stories of compromised farm girls enduring virtual bondage in the dark satanic mills of Lowell or tiny child laborers walking barefoot through the snow with their toenails sticking to the frozen pavement titillated southern readers. They responded with the same unseemly interest as their northern counterparts who thrilled to accounts of the brooding, evil South as an ungodly brothel where the idle slaveholders indulged their animal passions with chained black concubines. The *Southern Literary Messenger* finally reminded its eager subscribers that these tales of horror were not intended "to gratify the morbid appetite of sickly sentimentalists, but to furnish the basis of action for grave and wise statesmen and legislators." George Fitzhugh's reactionary quip that "labor has always entailed a kind of servitude" was echoed in archabolitionist Horace Greeley's hypothesis that whenever there was "power over subsistence, on one hand, and, of necessity, servility and degradation on the other—there is, in my view, Slavery."[59]

Two possibilities presented themselves: Devise a political and economic environment that would drive out free labor, or institute a pro-

57. In *The Cotton Kingdom,* Frederick Law Olmsted tries to discredit the materialist argument (see Chap. XV, "Slavery as a Poor Law System"), but the most successful parry is made in O. B. Frothingham's "Pauperism and Slavery." Frothingham moves away from the equitable consumption argument, which even the most energetic abolitionists sometimes had to concede, to a moral ground of guilt and sin.

58. *Gospel Messenger,* XXV (April, 1849), 22.

59. George Fitzhugh, *Sociology of the South, or, the Failure of Free Society* (Richmond, 1858), 38; Fitzhugh and Greeley, quoted in Marcus Cunliffe, *Chattel Slavery and Wage Slavery: The Anglo-American Context, 1830–1860* (Athens, Ga., 1979), 4, 24.

tected zone of employment closed to blacks. The most dramatic effort to restore the imagined former simplicity of southern social relations took the form of agitation to reopen the African slave trade closed by the Constitution in 1808. This proposal originated around 1839 in New Orleans, a town that also suffered from a fever-ridden climate and a large immigrant working class. After 1856, a movement gathered around South Carolina governor and Richland County planter James H. Adams, who speculated that with a renewed supply, the price of slaves would hit rock bottom and no matter how cheaply the Irish untouchables sold their labor, Africans would prove more profitable. After lengthy deliberation, special committees of both houses of the South Carolina legislature were swayed by the arguments of the fire-eating "Congo party," which voted to encourage the governor to take this plan to all the southern states for their united approbation. Adams and his supporters devised this proposal to answer northern resistance to the Fugitive Slave Law that had been strengthened by the Compromise of 1850.[60]

The actions of Adams and other agitators of the slave-trade question disgusted and repelled the majority of Charlestonians. Placing arbitrary restrictions upon free blacks also offended their sense of fairness, but the idea of eliminating the ambiguity of urban society had widespread appeal. A local fire-eater, Leonidas Spratt, went right to the heart of the matter. When a reopened slave trade flooded the labor market with newly imported inexpensive Africans, he argued, wages would plummet and starve the poor right out of Charleston.[61]

Spratt's proposition appealed only to the ideologue, but support did grow for the alternative suggestion that the state implement some sort of "split economy" (similar to that adopted by South Africa a half century later) that would reserve by law the more elevated positions for whites. Blacks (slave and free) would then perform only the lowliest forms of employment. Poor whites, however, could also compete for the menial jobs. This position won support among the urban "men on the make"— the small manufacturer, the artisan, the mechanic, the store keeper— who found that playing blacks and immigrants off against each other kept their labor costs low. They also sought protection from free blacks who were rising in increasing numbers to the ranks of skilled craftsmen and opening competing shops, and felt little of the same compunction

60. Ronald T. Takaki, *A Pro-Slavery Crusade: The Agitation to Reopen the African Slave Trade* (New York, 1971), 188–93; Wallace, *South Carolina: A Short History,* 522–23.

61. Charleston *Mercury,* February 13, 1861.

exhibited by the old town patriarchs to ease racial tensions in the city.

A recurring theme in southern labor relations since the colonial period, workingmen's complaints that slaves skewed the labor market had grown more urgent in all southern cities during the 1840s. In 1845, Georgia responded to petitions from its mechanics and limited the ability of blacks to make labor contracts. That same year, the Richmond *Enquirer* noted the misery of the "thousands" of the city's unemployed "who want to work but who cannot mix with black laborers" already working there. Tension continued unabated through the 1850s. In 1860, "A Master Mechanic," writing to the editor of the Charleston *Courier,* summed up the problem of labor as "Negro competition and Negro ascendancy." Unremedied, the writer feared, this situation endangered the future of skilled labor since "no man is disposed to place his son in a position that is in any way degrading." [62] The grand jury also wanted to purge from public view the common incongruous sight of blacks riding through the streets on omnibuses driven by whites. Laws requiring slave hiring their own time to purchase special "badges" were ordered more strictly enforced.

In 1860, Charleston foundry owner James Eason introduced in the South Carolina legislature a bill to ban blacks, slave and free, from competing equally with the skilled labor of the city. Noted for his regal bearing and self-possession, Eason, the "Duke of Hampstead," also possessed the common touch. After risking his life nursing the sick poor during the 1854 yellow fever epidemic, he enjoyed a reputation as the "mechanics' friend." As a member of the legislative committee on "colored populations," he introduced a petition signed by almost five hundred Charleston mechanics. They demanded a law "to prevent Free Negroes or persons of color from carrying on any Mechanical trade or calling, in their own name, or name of others" and thus achieving the status of master. Eason urged the state assembly to grant their wish so the "mechanical interests of our State" might enjoy "justice and equality in all the relations of life." "Already," Eason noted, "have many of our young and spirited men, been forced from the occupations of their choice on account of coming into competition with the free Negro, as master workmen, competing with them as Equals and having by the laws of our State, all the rights

62. Russel, *Economic Aspects,* 53; Charleston *Courier,* December 7, 1860; Takaki, *Pro-Slavery Crusade,* 44–56. Savannah workingmen felt much the same way as those in Charleston: "What respectable parent wishes to place his son at a trade (however profitable) working with or alongside an apprentice who is a slave?" (Savannah *Daily Morning News,* June 30, 1851, quoted in Richard Haunton, "Savannah During the 1850s" [Ph.D. dissertation, University of Georgia, 1963], 55).

and privileges which are attached and granted to a free white man." The committee further agreed that a man's occupation shaped all aspects of his life and that degradation in one's labor by the presence of black men in equal or even superior positions was reflected in his "moral well as social" relations.[63]

But what did this petition do for the common laborer? At the lowest levels of the economic chain, where Irishmen and blacks bloodied each other for the opportunity to drive heavy wagons around the city, competition remained unchanged. Eason's bill attacked the power of the master, not the institution of slavery. Supporters fully expected opposition from "those gentlemen" insulated from black competition and "denying the working man has any right to similar protection with themselves."[64] The artisans and mechanics who ran shops of their own used the sensitivity of the elite to any murmurings against slavery to win passage of a bill that allowed them the same monopolies enjoyed by "the Merchant, the Lawyer, the Doctor, the Wharfinger, the tradesman, or the shopkeeper." Eason's proposal locking blacks into permanent apprenticeships enabled mechanics to employ young slaves for pennies but blocked the owners of those slaves from demanding higher wages once the blacks had achieved a level of proficiency. Free blacks would thus fall into servitude to the artisans and mechanics of the city. Given the option, no enterprising artisan willingly trained his future competition. As a consequence, young white workers, especially, faced a decline in opportunities to learn a trade. Legislation to curb equality of opportunity only linked more hopelessly the status of the poorest whites and blacks.[65]

Charleston stood at a moment of crisis. The conservative reaction had attempted to stop the unraveling of the patriarchal republic by trimming away the power of the ragged edges, the free blacks and immigrants. Reformists, in contrast, tried to prepare the city for all contingencies. Even if slavery went down, white supremacy must be preserved. This meant elevating the white working class through education, improved health, and special legislation. The Charleston *Mercury* rationalized liberal reform as support for the old regime just before the new Model School opened in 1856:

---

63. Archer, *Reminiscences,* 7; James M. Eason, "Report of the Committee on the Colored Population," General Assembly Committee Reports, No. 90 (1861), in South Carolina Department of Archives and History, Columbia, S.C.

64. Charleston *Mercury,* November 30, 1860.

65. Savannah's master mechanics tried to have passed a city ordinance prohibiting "colored mechanics" from performing any work "however trifling" unless under their direction (Savannah *Georgian,* August 28, 1837).

The theory upon which Southern institutions rest is the equality of the ruling race. The maintenance of this idea is essential to our safety— essential to our civilization. How can it be better realized, than by equalizing the facilities of education, and inducing all classes of our citizens the rich as well as the poor, to partake of its benefits? . . . We have pronounced that every son and daughter of the superior and dominant race within our borders shall receive all the instructions necessary to prepare them for the responsibilities of their condition as themselves free, and the masters and mistresses of slaves. . . . The state cannot with justice or safety allow the white man to come into competition with the black simply as a laborer. . . . And the only way to preserve this distinction, is to give to every workman in the state the education of a responsible citizen.[66]

The safety of southern society clearly depended on providing jobs for poor whites that clearly set them apart from blacks. Seeing the conflict between the liberalism that animated Charleston's reformists and the die-hard refusal to acknowledge the value of free labor, however, William Henry Trescot feared that Charleston's efforts to educate all classes would have the unintended consequence of causing greater social unrest. If that "great throng" who "live and die working for no higher end than daily subsistence" are instilled with the "hopes and passions of a nobler life" at the same time that "the material interest and old organization of society refuse them admission into that sphere" that allows the use of their faculties, he predicted, "no power under heaven could prevent wild and ruinous social convulsion."[67]

In one of his moments of clarity, George Fitzhugh understood the greatest danger posed to the white man's democracy: "The poor can see things as well as the rich." Every time an able-bodied white worker put his family in the poorhouse or applied for rations to subsidize inadequate wages, the southern system faltered. Whenever a city commissioner agreed to buy passage back to New York City for an Irishman like Pat O'Brien, unable to find a decent job in Charleston, or arranged for the family of an ambitious newsboy to move to Alabama where they would enjoy "improved prospects," the confidence of the working class eroded.[68] Race meant nothing if it did not also guarantee a living wage.

Race did not even guarantee respect. In 1859, the commissioners of the poor received a report that a black butcher had insulted a white female pensioner when she applied for her weekly rations at the city mar-

66. Charleston *Mercury,* June 24, 1856.
67. William H. Trescot, "The State's Duties in Regard to Popular Education," *De Bow's Review,* XX (1856), 147.
68. George Fitzhugh, *Sociology for the South* (1854; rpr. New York, 1965), 227; Gilliland account book, November 22, November 15, 1860.

ket. The commissioners swung into action upon hearing this and drafted a formal complaint to the shop owner, who already had a reputation for handing out "indifferent and bad meat" to the poor. They got right to the point. If the butcher did not somehow remedy the woman's complaint "as regards the rudeness and impertinent language used by the Negro man serving beef . . . the Board will take measures to have the Negro arrested and punished." To prove their good faith, the commissioners sent a copy of the resolution to all those on outdoor relief.[69]

Despite the desperate rhetoric claiming that slavery was a guarantee of economic mobility for the poor, it was impossible to reconcile slavery with the liberal beliefs that actually powered Charleston's efforts on behalf of the poor. In the cities, especially, southerners had not been able to spread the blessings of their slave-based prosperity to those whites who worked for wages, nor had they been able to insulate their laboring classes from the same vagaries of the market that so afflicted northern workers. Especially after 1830, the number of slaveholders grew smaller, and in Charleston at least, the population more closely resembled those of northern cities—populations increasingly attracted during the 1850s to the aspects of the new Republican party that stressed social mobility and opportunity for workingmen.[70]

Those moved by the conservative impulse denied the changes in their city and desperately sought a single transcendent revelation to obliterate the threatening complexities of their age. Although on the face of it southerners supported slavery and all its corollary institutions, whether in the 1850s it truly held their minds and hearts with the same power that liberalism had seized northerners remained untested. Surely in Charleston, the self-proclaimed "Queen City of the South" and active candidate for capital of a southern Confederacy, consensus seemed endangered. Charleston radicals reacted against local agitation to limit slave labor. The desire to ban slaves from certain enterprises threw up red signals to Spratt that his beloved city was already deeply enmeshed in the "process of disintegration." New England abolitionists posed no more danger to the slave system, he warned, than the southern working classes armed with the destructive instruments of liberal democracy: "They will question the right of masters to employ their slaves in any works that they wish for, they will invoke the aid of legislations; they will use the elective franchise to that end, they may acquire the power to determine municipal

69. Minute book, March 23, 1859, in CPH.
70. Oakes, The Ruling Race, 228–30; William E. Gienapp, The Origins of the Republican Party, 1852–1856 (New York, 1987), 355–57.

elections; they will inexorably use it, and thus the town of Charleston, at the very heart of slavery, may become a fortress of democratic power against it." Spratt emerged as an early advocate of secession as a revolution to drive the forces of democracy beating on town gates.[71]

At the heart of the 1850s campaign against free labor and wage work, not only in Charleston but across the South, was "a fundemental rejection of liberalism." Where there had been an atmosphere of acceptance and accommodation toward the poor and laboring classes, who were seen as important components in the city's future, expressions of animosity were freely uttered. Daniel Hundley discoursed at length on the "poor white trash" of the South in his widely read *Social Relations in Our Southern States,* published in 1860. Hundley laughed at the concept of upward mobility among the lower orders: "Whoever yet knew a Godolphin that was sired by a miserable scrub." He mocked the Declaration of Independence, asserting that no law could grant equality among humans nor could freedom "put bread and meat into the mouths of beggars."[72]

As Charlestonians faced the critical year 1860, they realized that despite their many benevolent and generous qualities, there was truth in John Abbot's damning pronouncement: "The religion of the world, the literature of the world, the political economy of the world, the conscience of the world, is against the slaveholder."[73] The "spirit of the age" now meant free men, free labor, free soil. By staying in the Union, they faced inexorable external pressure to adopt the free institutions of a liberal society. If South Carolina seceded, the internal conflict between free labor and slave labor would remain. Whether Carolinians chose to confront the enemy without or the enemy within, the prospect for the continuation of slavery in its traditional form appeared uncertain.

When the warring Democratic party opened its convention in Charleston in 1860, it found a city that had no peace within itself. Rumblings of local ethnic, class, and racial unrest provided a backdrop to sectional tensions that fairly crackled. Conventioneers in that unusually hot April crowded into Hibernian Hall, an imposing Charleston landmark built by an Irish benevolent society, which opened in 1841. Yellow fever did not spare these newcomers to the city and hit unacclimated conventioneers with a fury. The meeting broke up in an angry prelude to the larger national cataclysm that was to come.

71. Charleston *Mercury,* February 13, 1861.
72. Daniel R. Hundley, *Social Relations in Our Southern States,* ed. William J. Cooper (1860; rpr. Baton Rouge, 1979), 251, 256.
73. John S. C. Abbott, *South and North* (1860; rpr. New York, 1960), 203.

When the war came, Charleston's public institutions and private charities invested their endowments in Confederate bonds and remained open for business as usual. The benevolent men and women of the city stayed very much in character. Unlike Richmond and most other southern cities, with no clear consensus whether care for the poor was a public or private responsibility, Charleston already had a relief system in place. Charleston women organized one of the South's first Soldiers' Relief Societies. The almshouse, situated in a location of safety, continued to operate on a very limited basis throughout the war. Businessmen, led by Henry D. Lesesne, longtime commissioner of the Charleston Orphan House, very quickly followed the New Orleans model of a "Free Market" to feed soldiers' families and others in need. In fact, a Savannah newspaper criticized the overly generous relief system in Charleston, where "the free market system has been sustained at immense expense by the wealthy citizens and their benefits confined to the poor alone," who are thus robbed of their "incentive for industry and economy."[74] Yet Charleston, already so alert to the potential for some sort of social upheaval, escaped the "Bread or Blood" riots staged late in the war by hungry women in Savannah and Richmond.

The commissioners of the orphan house promptly removed the children under their care to a farm near Orangeburg when the Federal shelling of the peninsula began in earnest in 1862. England-bound blockade runners darted out of the harbor avoiding Federal gunboats and often returned with shoes, books, or some other necessity for the children of the city. Christopher G. Memminger answered the call of the Confederate Congress to serve as secretary of the treasury, a position in which he did not enjoy the same success as in his more philanthropic ventures. The few members of the Ladies Benevolent Society who did not seek safety in the upper part of the state kept up its mission on a greatly reduced scale until February 9, 1865, just before the evacuation of the city. In its last issue before Charleston surrendered to Union forces in February, 1865, the *Daily Courier* (which held to the belief that speculation and southern corruption brought the Confederacy down) published its final "Text for the Times": "He that giveth unto the poor shall not lack; but he that hideth his eyes shall have many a curse."[75]

And when it was over, the charitable community of Charleston had experienced a notable reversal of personal fortunes. Henry Manigault,

74. Savannah *Morning News*, April 20, 1864.
75. Middleton, "Ladies Benevolent Society," 235; Charleston *Courier*, February 17, 1865.

descendant of the boundlessly rich Gabriel Manigault, lost his home and moved into the Charleston almshouse. A number of his old friends still dutifully sat as commissioners of the poor, and they named him superintendent of the institution in 1866. That same year, the Ladies Benevolent Society regrouped after being separated for four years by the war (any reference to which was deemed "quite out of place"). Its surviving members returned from their Upcountry exiles to find their treasury, like those of the other public and private associations, "wrecked." Still, they made plans to raise enough money from dues to begin their good works again, for the needs of the poor and the impulse to relieve them provided one of the elements of continuity in Charleston before and after the Civil War. Although the war stole away the material comforts most of these women had known, their experiences during the conflict also freed them from having to apologize for assuming a role in the rebuilding of the city. Rather than weep for the lost "patriarchal republic," the benevolent women of Charleston stiffened their spines, renewed their commitment to public service, and held in their minds "the scriptural injunction: 'Not to be weary in well doing.'"[76]

76. Middleton, "Ladies Benevolent Society," 233.

BIBLIOGRAPHY

PRIMARY SOURCES

PUBLISHED MATERIALS

"The Abiel Abbot Journals: A Yankee Preacher in Charleston Society, 1818–1827." Edited by John H. Moore. *South Carolina Historical Magazine,* LXVIII (April, July, October, 1967), 51–73, 115–39, 232–54.

Abbot, John S. C. *South and North.* 1860; rpr. New York, 1960.

"Address of the 55th Anniversary of the Orphan House." *Gospel Messenger,* XXI (January, 1845), 300.

Adger, John. *My Life and Times.* Richmond, 1899.

American Sunday School Union. *The Union Annual, 1837.* Philadelphia, 1837.

American Tract Society. *Report of Colportage in Virginia, North Carolina, and South Carolina for the Year ending March 1, 1855.* New York, 1855.

———. *Twentieth Annual Report.* New York, 1845.

Archer, Henry D. "The Public Schools of Charleston—Their Organization, Development, and Present Status." In *Year Book, City of Charleston, 1886.* Charleston, S.C., 1887.

Archer, Henry P. *Local Reminiscences, Delivered before the Mutual Aid Association, No. 1 of Charleston, S.C., June 6, 1889.* Charleston, S.C., 1893.

Bible Society of Georgia. *Annual Report.* Savannah, 1841.

"A Biographical Sketch of the Reverend W. B. Yates: The Seamen's Friend." In *Temperance Souvenir,* edited by Edwin Heriot. N.p., 1852.

Birney, Catherine. *The Grimké Sisters: Sarah and Angelina Grimké, the First American Women Advocates of Abolition and Woman's Rights.* 1885; rpr. Westport, Conn., 1977.

Bright, John M. *Charity: A Lecture Before the Robertson Association, Nashville, Tenn., October 14, 1858.* Nashville, 1858.

Bruce, Henry Clay. *The New Man: Twenty-nine Years a Slave, Twenty-nine Years a Free Man.* York, Pa., 1895.

Burke, Emily. *Reminiscences of Georgia.* New York, 1850.

Bylaws of the Orphan House of Charleston. Charleston, S.C., 1861.

Carey, Matthew. "Essays on the Public Charities of Philadelphia." In Carey, *Miscellaneous Essays.* Philadelphia, 1830.

Cassells, Rev. Samuel. "The Relation of Justice to Benevolence in the Conduct of Society." *Southern Presbyterian Review,* VII (July, 1853), 85–103.

"Celia Campbell." In *Yearbook of the City of Charleston, 1881.* Charleston, S.C., 1882.

"The Charities of the Church." *Gospel Messenger,* XXVII (November, 1850), 233.

Charleston Orphan House, *Anniversary Addresses, 1855.* Charleston, S.C., 1856.

"Christianity versus Philanthropy." *Southern Literary Messenger,* XXXIV (September–October, 1862), 574–76.

Church Home of the Diocese of South Carolina. *The Reports at the Eighth Anniversary Celebration of the Church Home, June 24, 1858.* Charleston, S.C., 1858.

————. *The Sermon and Reports at the Third Anniversary Celebration of the Church Home, June 11, 1853.* Charleston, S.C., 1853.

Claibourne, John Herbert. *Seventy Five Years in Old Virginia.* New York, 1904.

Colonial Records of the State of Georgia. Vol. V of 26 vols. Atlanta, 1732–52.

Colter, Calvin. *Protestant Jesuitism.* New York, 1836.

Constitution and Bylaws of the Female Humane Association of the City of Richmond, adopted 1833. Richmond, 1843.

Cooper, Thomas. *Lectures on the Elements of Political Economy.* Columbia, S.C., 1826.

Cooper, Thomas, and David J. McCord, eds. *The Statutes at Large of South Carolina.* Vol. II of 10 vols. Columbia, S.C., 1836–41.

Dalcho, Frederick. *An Historical Account of the Protestant Episcopal Church in South Carolina.* Charleston, 1820.

Dawson, J. L., and H. W. DeSaussure. *Census of the City of Charleston for the Year 1848.* Charleston, S.C., 1849.

"Diocesan Convention of South Carolina." *Gospel Messenger,* VI (February, 1830), 88.

"The Diurnal of the Right Reverend John England, First Bishop of Charleston, S.C., 1820–1823." In *Records of the American Catholic Historical Society,* Vol. VI of 32 vols. Philadelphia, 1895.

[Dupont, Rev. T. C.]. "Report of the Mission of St. Stephen's Church." *Gospel Messenger,* XXII (August, 1845).

Elliott, Stephen. *Journal of the Proceedings of the Twenty-Seventh Annual Convention of the Protestant Episcopal Church of Georgia.* Marietta, Ga., 1849.

England, John. *Letters of the Late Bishop England to the Honorable John Forsyth on the Subject of Domestic Slavery.* Baltimore, 1844.

Fitzhugh, George. *Sociology of the South, or the Failure of Free Society.* Richmond, 1858.

"The Free Schools of South Carolina." *Southern Quarterly Review,* n.s., II (November, 1856), 125–60.

Frothingham, O. B. "Pauperism and Slavery." *Liberty Bell,* XIII (1853), 163–72.

Gadsden, Christopher E. *An Essay on the Life of the Right Reverend Theodore Dehon, D.D.* Charleston, S.C., 1833.

Garden, Alexander. *Regeneration and the Testimony of the Spirit . . . Two Sermons Lately Preached in the Parish Church of St. Phillip, Charles Town, in South Carolina.* Charleston, S.C., 1740.

Gregg, William. *Essays on Domestic Industry: Or, an Enquiry into the Expediency of Establishing Cotton Manufactures in South Carolina.* Charleston, S.C., 1845.

[Grimké, Sarah, and Angelina Grimké]. "A Sketch of Mr. Grimké's Life." *Calumet,* II (January–February, 1835), 129–37.

Grimké, Thomas Smith. *Address at the Dedication of the . . . Depository for Bible Tracts.* Charleston, S.C., n.d.

———. *Address on the Patriotic Character of the Temperance Reformation.* Charleston, S.C., 1838.

Hall, Basil. *Travels in North America.* Vol. III of 3 vols. 1829; rpr. Graz, Austria, 1964.

Hammond, James H. "Progress of Southern Industry: Governor Hammond's Address Before the South Carolina Institute, 1850." *De Bow's Review,* VIII (June, 1850), 501–22.

Harden, William. *Recollections of a Long and Satisfying Life.* 1934; rpr. New York, 1968.

Helper, Hinton. *The Impending Crisis of the South: How to Meet It.* Edited by George M. Fredrickson. 1857; rpr. New York, 1969.

Hollinshead, Rev. William. *An Oration Delivered at the Orphan House of Charleston, October 18, 1797.* Charleston, 1798.

"The Honorable Thomas Smith Grimké." *Calumet,* II (January–February, 1835), 132.

Hundley, Daniel R. *Social Relations in Our Southern States.* Edited by William J. Cooper. 1860; rpr. Baton Rouge, 1979.

Hunt's Merchants Magazine, XXII (1851), 649.

Laurens, Henry. *The Papers of Henry Laurens.* Edited by George C. Rogers and David R. Chesnutt. Vol. 5 of 5 vols. Columbia, S.C., 1968–.

Lewis, Rev. George. *Impressions of America and the American Churches.* 1848; rpr. New York, 1968.

Lumpkin, J. H. "Industrial Regeneration of the South." *De Bow's Review,* X (January, 1852), 41–51.

McCord, Louisa Susannah. "Enfranchisement of Women." *Southern Quarterly Review,* n.s., V (April, 1852), 322–41.

McGruder, Rev. Thomas. *Report Presented to the Female Domestic Missionary Society of Charleston, South Carolina.* Charleston, S.C., 1837.

Miles, James Warley. "Address Before the Church Home." *Gospel Messenger,* XXIX (October, 1852), 193–201.

———. "First Annual Address Before the Church Home." *Gospel Messenger,* XXVII (July, 1851), 111–20.

Miles, William Porcher. *Report of the City of Charleston, 1857.* Charleston, S.C., 1858.

Mills, Robert. *Statistics of South Carolina.* 1826; rpr. Spartanburg, S.C., 1972.

"Modern Philanthropy and Negro Slavery." *De Bow's Review,* XVI (January, 1854), 263–76.

Moore, Caroline T., and Agatha Aimar Simmons. *Abstracts of the Wills of South Carolina.* Vol. I (1670–1740) of 3 vols. Columbia, S.C., 1960.

Oliphant, Mary C. Simms, *et al.,* eds. *The Letters of William Gilmore Simms.* Vol. III of 6 vols. Columbia, S.C., 1954.

Olmsted, Frederick Law. *The Cotton Kingdom: A Traveller's Observations on Cotton and Slavery in the American Slave States.* 1861; rpr. New York, 1953.

——. *A Journey in the Seaboard Slave States in the Years 1853–1854.* New York, 1856.

Parish, Elijah. *A Sermon Preached at Ipswich, September 29, 1815, at the Ordination of Rev. Daniel Smith and Cyrus Kingsbury, as Missionaries to the West.* Newburyport, Mass., 1815.

Parsons, Charles G. *An Inside View of Slavery.* Savannah, 1874.

Perry, Benjamin F. *Address Before the South Carolina Institute, November, 1856.* Charleston, 1857.

Phillips, Rev. Edward. "Discourse at the Opening of . . . Church of the Holy Communion, Cannonsborough, November 12, 1848." *Gospel Messenger,* XXV (January, 1849), 295–96.

Pinckney, Henry L. *An Oration Delivered in St. Finbar's Cathedral on the 17th of March 1832 before the St. Patrick's Benevolent Society and Irish Volunteers.* Charleston, S.C., 1832.

——. *A Report Relative to the Proceedings of the Relief of the Sick Poor.* Charleston, S.C., 1838.

——. *Review of the Preceding Year, 1838.* Charleston, S.C., 1839.

Pinckney, Thomas [Achates]. *Reflections Occasioned by the Late Disturbances in Charleston.* Charleston, S.C., 1822.

Pitt, Joseph. "Observations on the Country and Diseases near the Roanoke River . . . ." *Medical Repository,* V (February, March, April, 1808), 337–42.

"Plea for a Church Hospital." *Gospel Messenger,* XXVIII (March, 1851), 476.

Porter, Rev. A. Toomer. *Forty Years a Rector and Pastor.* Charleston, S.C., 1894.

——. *Led On! Step By Step.* 1896; rpr. New York, 1967.

Pringle, Robert. *Letterbook of Robert Pringle.* Edited by Walter B. Edgar. 2 vols. Columbia, S.C., 1972.

"The Public Schools of Charleston." *De Bow's Review,* n.s. (September, 1858), 366–70.

"Report from St. Stephen's Chapel, January 1–June 30, 1843." *Gospel Messenger,* XVIII (September, 1843), 168.

Report of the Board of Commissioners of Free Schools to the Citizens of Charleston. Charleston, S.C., 1857 and 1858.

Report of the Committee of the City Council of Charleston upon the Epidemic Yellow Fever of 1858. Charleston, S.C., 1859.

Report of the Executive Committee of the Bible Convention, November 25, 1841. Charleston, S.C., 1842.

"Savannah and Charleston." *De Bow's Review,* XIII (March, 1850), 243–45.

[Savannah] Union Society. *Minutes of the Union Society, 1790–1858.* Savannah, 1860.

"The Sisters of Charity of St. Michael's Church." *Southern Episcopalian,* VI (February, 1860), 586.

Smith, James H. *Eulogium on the Life and Character of Thomas S. Grimké. Delivered March 10, 1835, Before the Literary and Philosophical Society of South Carolina.* Charleston, 1835.

Smith, Josiah. "The Burning of Sodom with its Moral Causes, Improved in a Sermon in Charleston, November 1740." In Smith, *Sermons on Several Important Subjects.* Boston, 1757.

Smyth, Rev. Thomas. *Oration Delivered on the 48th Anniversary of the Orphan House in Charleston, South Carolina, October 18, 1837.* Charleston, 1837.

"South Carolina." *New England Magazine,* I (September–October, 1831). In Eugene Schwab, *Travels in the Old South.* 2 vols. Lexington, Ky., 1972.

South Carolina Branch of the American Tract Society. *Reports and Resolutions in Reference to the Action taken on Slavery.* Charleston, S.C., 1857.

"South Carolina Shoe Factory." *De Bow's Review,* X (January, 1851), 682–83.

"Speech of C. G. Memminger, esq., on the Occasion of Inaugurating the Common School System at Charleston, S.C., July 4, 1856." *American Journal of Education,* II (1855), 556.

Stirling, James. *Letters from the Slave States.* London, 1857.

"Sunday School for Children." *Southern Christian Advocate,* July 11, 1851.

Taylor, J. H. "Manufactures in South Carolina." *De Bow's Review,* VIII (January, 1850), 24–29.

Thornwell, James H. *Letter to His Excellency Governor Manning on Public Instruction in South Carolina.* Columbia, 1853.

Tocqueville, Alexis de. *Democracy in America.* 1832; rpr. New York, 1969.

Trapier, Paul. *Incidents in My Life: The Autobiography of the Reverend Paul Trapier, S.T.D.* Edited by George W. Williams. Charleston, S.C., 1954.

Trescot, William H. "The State's Duties in Regard to Popular Education." *De Bow's Review,* XX (February, 1856), 143–56.

Wallace, Cranmore. "Reports of Charleston City Missions." *Southern Episcopalian,* II (August, 1855), 490–91, III (August, 1856), 267–68.

"Wealth of the North and the South." *De Bow's Review,* XXIII (December, 1857), 587–96.

Weld, Theodore Dwight. *American Slavery as It Is: Testimony of a Thousand Witnesses.* 1839; rpr. New York, 1969.

Yates, William B. *An Historical Sketch of the Rise and Progress of Religious and Moral Improvement Among Seamen, in England and the United States, with a History of the Port Society of Charleston.* Charleston, S.C., 1851.

[Yeadon, Richard, George Buist, and Edward Elfe]. *Duties and Powers of the Board in Relation to the Free Colored Poor of the City.* Charleston, S.C., 1842.

"Young Men's Christian Association." *Southern Episcopalian,* IV (October, 1857), 364–66.

NEWSPAPERS

Charleston *Courier*, 1820–65.
Charleston *Evening News*, October 14, November 2, 1845.
Charleston *Mercury*, 1820–61.
Richmond *Daily Dispatch*, April 30, 1857, July 29, 1859.
Savannah *Evening Journal*, March 1, 1852.
Savannah *Georgian*, August 28, 1837.
Savannah *Morning News*, April 20, 1864.
South Carolina *Gazette*, February 2, 1765, November 11, 1740.
Southern Christian Advocate, June 20, 1851, September 30, 1853, April 2, 1857.
Southern Patriot, July 30, 1836, August 15, 1818.
United States Catholic Miscellany, April 18, 1857, December 1, 1849.

MANUSCRIPTS

Auditor of Public Accounts. "Report of the Poor, Lunenburg County, June 1, 1845." Virginia State Archives, Richmond.
Briggs, Willis Grandy. Papers. Southern Historical Collection. University of North Carolina, Chapel Hill.
Charleston City Council. Records. City of Charleston Archives. Charleston, S.C.
Charleston Orphan House. Records. City of Charleston Archives, Charleston, S.C.
Charleston Poor House. Records. City of Charleston Archives, Charleston, S.C.
Charleston Typographical Union, No. 43, Southern Typographical Union, No. 1. Minutes, 1859–62. South Caroliniana Library, University of South Carolina, Columbia, S.C.
Commissioners of the Free Schools. Papers. City of Charleston Archives, Charleston, S.C.
Commissioners of Free Schools of the Parishes of St. Phillip's and St. Michael's. Minutes. City of Charleston Archives, Charleston, S.C.
Duncan, William. Papers. Georgia Historical Society, Savannah.
Eason, James M. "Report of the Committee on the Colored Population." General Assembly Committee Reports, No. 90 (1861). South Carolina Department of Archives and History, Columbia, S.C.
Gilliland, William H. Account book. Perkins Library, Duke University.
Ladies Benevolent Society. Minutes. Typescript in South Caroliniana Library, University of South Carolina, Columbia, S.C.
Memminger, Christopher G. Papers. Southern Historical Collection. University of North Carolina, Chapel Hill.
Mitchell, Nelson. Papers. Mitchell-Pringle Collection. South Carolina Historical Society, Charleston, S.C.
Nashville City Council. Minute book. Davidson County Hall, Nashville, Tenn.
Protestant Episcopal Society. Minutes, 1838–62. Diocesan Library, Charleston, S.C.

Richmond Commissioners for Poor Relief. Record Book, 1875–85. Virginia State Archives, Richmond.

Richmond Overseers of the Poor. Annual returns, 1850. Virginia State Archives, Richmond.

Roper Hospital. Casebooks. Waring Medical Library. Medical University of South Carolina, Charleston, S.C.

St. Phillip's Episcopal Church. Vestry minutes. Typescript in South Caroliniana Library, University of South Carolina, Columbia, S.C.

Wills of Charleston County, South Carolina. Vol. LXII, 1862–68. WPA Typescript in Charleston Public Library, Charleston, S.C.

SECONDARY SOURCES

PUBLISHED MATERIALS

Abell, Aaron I. *American Catholicism and Social Action: A Search for Social Justice, 1865–1950.* New York, 1960.

Adams, James Luther. "The Voluntary Principle in the Forming of American Religion." In *Voluntary Associations: Socio-cultural Analyses and Theological Interpretation,* edited by Ronald Engle. Chicago, 1986.

Ahlstrom, Sidney E. *A Religious History of the American People.* New Haven, 1972.

Anderson, Michael. *Family Structure in Nineteenth Century Lancashire.* Cambridge, Eng., 1971.

Anderson, J. Perrin. "Public Education in Ante-Bellum South Carolina." South Carolina Historical Association *Proceedings* (1933), 3–11.

Banner, Lois W. "Religious Benevolence as Social Control: A Critique of an Interpretation." *Journal of American History,* XL (June, 1973), 23–41.

Berlin, Ira, and Herbert G. Gutman. "Natives and Immigrants, Free Men and Slaves: Urban Workingmen in the Antebellum American South." *American Historical Review,* LXXXVIII (December, 1983), 1175–1200.

Bertleson, David. *The Lazy South.* Westport, Conn., 1980.

Bolton, Charles S. *Southern Anglicanism: The Church of England in Colonial South Carolina.* Westport, Conn., 1982.

Boucher, Chauncey S. "The Antebellum Attitude of South Carolina Towards Manufacturing and Agriculture." *Washington University Studies,* III (1916), 243–70.

Boyer, Paul. *Urban Masses and Moral Order in America, 1820–1920.* Cambridge, Mass., 1978.

Bremner, Robert H. *American Philanthropy.* Chicago, 1988.

Brooks, Charles. *History of the Town of Medford, Middlesex County, Massachusetts.* Boston, 1886.

Brown, Richard Maxwell. *The South Carolina Regulators.* Cambridge, Mass., 1963.

Buckingham, James J. *The Slave States of America.* Vol. I of 2 vols. London, 1843.

Capers, Henry D. *The Life and Times of C. G. Memminger.* Richmond, 1893.

Carey, Patrick. "Voluntaryism: An Irish Catholic Tradition." *Church History,* XLVIII (March, 1979), 49–62.

Carr, Lois Green, and Russell R. Menard. "Immigration and Opportunity: The Freedman in Early Colonial Maryland." In *The Chesapeake in the Seventeenth Century: Essays on Anglo-American Society,* edited by Thad W. Tate and David L. Ammerman. Chapel Hill, 1979.

Carrigan, Jo Ann. "Privilege, Prejudice, and the Strangers' Disease." *Journal of Southern History,* XXXVI (November, 1970), 568–78.

Childs, St. Julien Ravenel. "Notes on the History of Public Health in South Carolina, 1670–1800." South Carolina Historical Association *Proceedings* (1932), 13–22.

Coclanis, Peter A. *The Shadow of a Dream: Economic Life and Death in the South Carolina Low Country, 1670–1920.* New York, 1989.

Conkin, Paul K. *Prophets of Prosperity: America's First Political Economists.* Bloomington, Ind., 1980.

Cooper, William J., Jr. *Liberty and Slavery: Southern Politics to 1860.* New York, 1983.

Cunliffe, Marcus. *Chattel Slavery and Wage Slavery: The Anglo-American Context, 1830–1860.* Athens, Ga., 1979.

Curti, Merle. "American Philanthropy and the National Character." *American Quarterly,* X (Winter, 1958), 420–37.

Dabney, Virginius. *Liberalism in the South.* Chapel Hill, N.C., 1932.

Davis, David Brion. *The Problem of Slavery in Western Culture.* New York, 1966.

Duffy, John. "Yellow Fever in Colonial Charleston." *South Carolina Historical and Genealogical Magazine,* LII (October, 1951), 189–97.

Easterby, J. H., ed. "Public Poor Relief in Colonial Charleston: A Report to the Commons House of Assembly About the Year 1767." *South Carolina Historical and Genealogical Magazine,* XLII (April, 1941), 83–86.

Elzas, Barnett A. *The Jews of South Carolina from the Earliest Times to the Present Day.* Philadelphia, 1905.

Ernst, Robert. *Immigrant Life in New York City, 1825–1865.* New York, 1965.

Flanders, Ralph. "The Free Negro in Antebellum Georgia." *North Carolina Historical Review,* IX (1932), 268.

Fort Sumter Memorial Association. *An Account of the Fort Sumter Memorial.* Charleston, S.C., 1933.

Freehling, William. *Prelude to Civil War: The Nullification Controversy in South Carolina, 1816–1836.* New York, 1965.

Furniss, Edgar. *The Position of the Laborer in a System of Nationalism: A Study of the Labor Theories of the Later Mercantilists.* New York, 1965.

Galenson, David W. *White Servitude in Colonial America: An Economic Analysis.* Cambridge, Mass., 1981.

Gienapp, William E. *The Origins of the Republican Party, 1852–1856*. New York, 1987.

Ginzberg, Lori D. *Women and the Work of Benevolence: Morality, Politics, and Class in the Nineteenth-Century United States*. New Haven, 1990.

Greene, Evarts B., and Virginia D. Harrington. *American Population Before the Federal Census of 1790*. Gloucester, Mass., 1966.

Greene, Jack. "Slavery or Independence: Some Reflections on the Relationship Among Liberty, Black Bondage, and Equality in Revolutionary South Carolina." *South Carolina Historical Magazine*, LXXX (July, 1979), 193–214.

Griffin, Clifford S. *Their Brothers' Keepers: Moral Stewardship in the United States, 1800–1865*. New Brunswick, N.J., 1960.

Griffin, Richard W. "Poor White Laborers in Southern Cotton Factories, 1789–1865." *South Carolina Historical Magazine*, LXI (January, 1960), 26–40.

Hannon, Joanne. "Poverty in the Antebellum Northeast: The View from New York State's Relief Rolls." *Journal of Economic History*, XLIV (December, 1984), 1007–34.

Hannon, Joan Underhill. "The Generosity of Antebellum Poor Relief." *Journal of Economic History*, XLIV (September, 1984), 810–21.

Haskell, Thomas. "Capitalism and the Origin of Humanitarian Sensibility." *American Historical Review*, XC (April, 1985), 339–61; (June, 1985), 547–66.

Higgins, W. Robert. "Charles Town Merchants and Factors Dealing in the External Negro Trade, 1735–1775." *South Carolina Historical Magzine*, LXV (October, 1964).

Hill, Christopher. *Society and Puritanism in Pre-Revolutionary England*. New York, 1964.

Hill, Samuel S. *The South and the North in American Religion*. Athens, Ga., 1980.

Himmelfarb, Gertrude. *The Idea of Poverty: England in the Early Industrial Age*. New York, 1984.

Holyfield, Brooks. *The Gentlemen Theologians: American Theology in Southern Culture, 1795–1860*. Durham, 1978.

Issac, Rhys. *The Transformation of Virginia, 1740–1790*. Chapel Hill, N.C., 1982.

Jaher, Frederic Cople. *The Urban Establishment: Upper Strata in Boston, New York, Charleston, Chicago, and Los Angeles*. Urbana, Ill., 1982.

Jenkins, William S. *Proslavery Thought in the Old South*. Chapel Hill, N.C., 1935.

Jernagan, Marcus W. *Laboring and Dependent Classes in Colonial America, 1607–1783*. New York, 1960.

Jervey, Theodore D. "The White Indentured Servants of South Carolina." *South Carolina Historical Magazine*, XII (October, 1911), 163–71.

Johnson, Michael P. "Planters and Patriarchy: Charleston, 1800–1860." *Journal of Southern History*, XLVI (February, 1980), 45–72.

———. "Wealth and Class in Charleston in 1860." In *From the Old South to the*

New: Essays on the Transitional South, edited by Walter J. Fraser, Jr., and Winfred B. Moore, Jr. Westport, Conn., 1981.

Johnson, Michael P., and James L. Roark. *Black Masters: A Free Family of Color in the Old South.* New York, 1984.

Jones, Howard. *Mutiny on the* Amistad: *The Saga of a Slave Revolt and Its Impact on American Abolition, Law, and Diplomacy.* New York, 1987.

Jordan, Wilbur K. "The English Background of Modern Philanthropy." *American Historical Review,* LXVI (January, 1961), 401–404.

———. *Philanthropy in England, 1480–1660.* New York, 1959.

Katz, Michael. *In the Shadow of the Poorhouse: A Social History of Welfare in America.* New York, 1986.

Katzman, David M. *Seven Days a Week: Women and Domestic Service in Industrializing America.* New York, 1978.

Kaufman, Allen. *Capitalism, Slavery, and Republican Values: Antebellum Political Economists, 1819–1848.* Austin, Tex., 1982.

Kennedy, W. B. *The Shaping of Protestant Education: An Interpretation of the Sunday School and the Development of Protestant Educational Strategy in the United States, 1789–1860.* New York, 1966.

King, Susan. *History and Records of the Charleston Orphan House.* Easley, S.C., 1984.

Kneece, Mattie Crouch. *The Contributions of C. G. Memminger to the Cause of Education.* Columbia, S.C., 1956.

Knight, Stephen J. "Discontent, Disunity, and Dissent in the Antebellum South: Virginia as a Test Case, 1844–1846." *Virginia Magazine of History and Biography,* LXXXI (October, 1973).

Koch, Adrienne. "Two Charlestonians in Pursuit of Truth: The Grimké Brothers." *South Carolina Historical Magazine,* LXIX (July, 1968), 159–70.

Kuyendal, John Wells. *Southern Enterprize: The Work of the National Evangelical Societies in the Antebellum South.* Westport, Conn., 1982.

"Ladies Benevolent Society." In *Yearbook of the City of Charleston, 1896.* Charleston, S.C., 1897.

Lander, Ernest. "The South Carolina Textile Industry Before 1845." South Carolina Historical Association *Proceedings* (1951), 19–28.

Lebsock, Susan. *The Free Women of Petersburg: Status and Culture in a Southern Town.* New York, 1984.

Lebergott, Stanley. *Wealth and Want.* Princeton, 1975.

Leiby, James. "Social Control and Historical Explanation: Historians View the Pliven and Cloward Thesis." In *Social Welfare or Social Control: Some Historical Reflections on "Regulating the Poor."* Edited by Walter I. Trattner. Knoxville, 1983.

Leiman, Melvin M. *Jacob N. Cardozo: Economic Thought in the Antebellum South.* New York, 1966.

Lerner, Gerda. *The Grimké Sisters of South Carolina: Rebels Against Slavery.* Boston, 1967.

Linden, Fabian. "Repercussions of Manufacturing in the Ante-bellum South." *North Carolina Historical Review,* XVII (1940), 313–25.

Lofton, John. *Denmark Vesey's Revolt: The Slave Plot That Lit a Fuse to Fort Sumter.* Kent, Ohio, 1983.

Lonn, Ella. *Foreigners in the Confederacy.* 1940; rpr. Gloucester, Mass., 1965.

Loveland, Anne. *Southern Evangelicals and the Social Order, 1800–1860.* Baton Rouge, 1980.

McCoy, Drew R. *The Elusive Republic: Political Economy in Jeffersonian America.* New York, 1980.

Maier, Pauline. "Popular Uprisings and Civil Authority in Eighteenth Century America." *William and Mary Quarterly,* 3rd series, XXVII (January, 1970), 3–35.

Martin, T. P., ed. "The Advent of William Gregg and the Graniteville Company." *Journal of Southern History,* XI (August, 1945).

May, Henry F. *The Enlightenment in America.* New York, 1976.

Meriwether, Robert L. *The Expansion of South Carolina, 1729–1765.* Kingsport, Tenn., 1940.

Merrens, Harry Roy, and George D. Terry. "Dying in Paradise: Malaria, Mortality, and the Perceptual Environment in Colonial South Carolina." *Journal of Southern History,* L (November, 1984), 533–50.

Middleton, Margaret S. "The Ladies Benevolent Society of Charleston, S.C." In *Yearbook of the City of Charleston, 1941.* Charleston, S.C., 1942.

Miller, Randall M. "The Enemy Within: Some Effects of Foreign Immigrants on Antebellum Southern Cities." *Southern Studies,* XXIV (Spring, 1985), 30–53.

Morgan, David J. "The Great Awakening in South Carolina, 1740–1775." *South Atlantic Quarterly,* LXX (Autumn, 1971), 595–606.

Morgan, Edmund. *American Slavery, American Freedom: The Ordeal of Colonial Virginia.* New York, 1975.

Morris, Richard. *Government and Labor in Early America.* New York, 1947.

Mullin, Bruce. *Episcopal Vision/American Reality: High Church Theology and Social Thought in Evangelical America.* New Haven, 1986.

Nash, Gary. *The Urban Crucible: Social Change, Political Consciousness, and the Origins of the American Revolution.* Cambridge, Mass., 1979.

Oakes, James. "From Republicanism to Liberalism: Ideological Change and the Crisis of the Old South." *American Quarterly,* XXXVII (Fall, 1985), 551–71.

——. *The Ruling Race: A History of American Slaveholders.* New York, 1982.

——. *Slavery and Freedom: An Interpretation of the Old South.* New York, 1990.

O'Connell, John J. *Catholicity in the Carolinas and Georgia.* 1878; rpr. Spartanburg, 1972.

Pease, William H., and Jane H. Pease. *The Web of Progress: Private Values and Public Styles in Boston and Charleston, 1828–1843.* New York, 1985.

Phillips, Ulrich B. *A History of Transportation in the Eastern Cotton Belt to 1860.* New York, 1913.

————. "The Slave Labor Problem in the Charleston District." In *Plantation, Town, and Country: Essays on the Local History of American Slave Society,* edited by Elinor Miller and Eugene D. Genovese. Urbana, Ill., 1974.

Pocock, J. G. A. *The Machiavellian Moment: Florentine Political Thought and the Atlantic Tradition.* Princeton, 1975.

Potter, David. *The South and the Sectional Conflict.* Baton Rouge, 1968.

Pyburn, Nita Katherine. "The Public School System of Charleston Before 1860." *South Carolina Historical Magazine,* LXI (April, 1960), 86–98.

Radford, John P. "Race, Residence and Ideology: Charleston, South Carolina, in the Mid-Nineteenth Century." *Journal of Historical Geography,* IV (1976), 347–60.

Ravenel, Mrs. St. Julien. *Charleston: The Place and the People.* New York, 1922.

Roberts, David. "Dealing with the Poor in Victorian England." In *Humanitarianism or Control? A Symposium on Aspects of Nineteenth-Century Social Reform in Britain and America,* edited by Martin J. Wiener. Rice University Studies, LXVII. Houston, 1981.

Rogers, George C., Jr. *Charleston in the Age of the Pinckneys.* Norman, Okla., 1969.

Rogers, Tommy. "The Great Population Exodus from South Carolina, 1850–1860." *South Carolina Historical Magazine,* LXVIII (January, 1967), 14–21.

Rosenberg, Charles. *In the Care of Strangers: The Rise of America's Hospital System.* New York, 1987.

————. "Social Class and Medical Care in 19th Century America: The Rise and Fall of the Dispensary." In *Sickness and Health in America: Readings in the History of Medicine and Public Health,* edited by Ronald L. Numbers and Judith W. Leavitt. Madison, Wis., 1978.

Rothman, David J. *The Discovery of the Asylum: Social Order and Disorder in the New Republic.* Boston, 1971.

————. "Social Control: The Uses and Abuses of the Concept in the History of Incarceration." In *Humanitarianism or Control? A Symposium on Aspects of Nineteenth-Century Social Reform in Britain and America,* edited by Martin J. Wiener. Rice University Studies, LXVII. Houston, 1981.

Russel, Robert R. *Economic Aspects of Southern Sectionalism, 1840–61.* New York, 1960.

Rutman, Darrett. *Winthrop's Boston: Portrait of a Puritan Town, 1630–1649.* Chapel Hill, N.C., 1965.

Schossman, Steven L. *Love and the American Delinquent: The Theory and Practice of "Progressive" Juvenile Justice, 1825–1920.* Chicago, 1977.

Schultz, Stanley K. *The Culture Factory: Boston Public Schools, 1789–1860.* New York, 1973.

Sennett, Richard. *The Hidden Injuries of Class.* New York, 1972.

Severens, Kenneth M. *Charleston: Antebellum Architecture and Civic Destiny.* Knoxville, 1988.

Shatzman, Aaron M. *Servants into Planters, The Origin of an American Image:*

Land Acquisition and Status Mobility in Seventeenth-Century South Carolina. New York, 1989.

Shryock, Richard H. "The Early Industrial Revolution in the Empire State." *Georgia Historical Quarterly,* I (June, 1927), 118–19.

Silver, Christopher. "A New Look at Old South Urbanization: The Irish Worker in Charleston, South Carolina, 1840–1860." *South Atlantic Urban Studies,* III (1979), 141–72.

Smith, Clarence M., Jr. "William Porcher Miles, Progressive Mayor of Charleston, 1855–1857." South Carolina Historical Association *Proceedings* (1942), 30–39.

Smith, Elwyn. "The Forming of a Modern American Denomination." *Church History,* XXXI (March, 1962), 74–89.

Snowden, Yates. *Notes on Labor Organizations in South Carolina, 1742–1861.* Columbia, S.C., 1914.

Soltow, Leo. *Men and Wealth in the United States.* New Haven, 1975.

Spangler, Joseph J. "Population Theory in the Antebellum South." *Journal of Southern History,* II (August, 1936), 360–89.

Stansell, Christine. *City of Women: Sex and Class in New York, 1789–1860.* New York, 1986.

Starobin, Robert. *Industrial Slavery in the Old South.* New York, 1970.

Stavisky, Leonard. "Industrialism in Antebellum Charleston." *Journal of Negro History,* XXXVI (July, 1951), 302–22.

Stowe, Steven M. *Intimacy and Power in the Old South.* Baltimore, 1987.

Takaki, Ronald T. *A Pro-Slavery Crusade: The Agitation to Reopen the African Slave Trade.* New York, 1971.

Thomas, Albert Sidney. *A Historical Account of the Protestant Episcopal Church in South Carolina, 1820–1957.* Columbia, S.C., 1957.

Thomas, John L. "Romantic Reform in America, 1815–1865." *American Quarterly,* XVII (Winter, 1965), 656–81.

Tobias, Thomas J. *The Hebrew Orphan Society of Charleston, S.C., Founded 1801: An Historical Sketch.* Charleston, S.C., 1957.

VerSteeg, Clarence L. *Origins of a Southern Mosaic: Studies of Early Carolina, and Georgia.* Athens, Ga., 1975.

Wakelyn, Jon L. "Antebellum College Life and the Relations Between Fathers and Sons." In *The Web of Southern Social Relations: Women, Family and Education.* Edited by Walter J. Fraser, Jr., R. Frank Saunders, Jr., and Jon L. Wakelyn. Athens, Ga., 1985.

Wallace, David D. *South Carolina: A Short History, 1520–1948.* Columbia, S.C., 1966.

Walsh, Robert. *Charleston's Sons of Liberty: A Study of the Artisans, 1763–1789.* Columbia, S.C., 1959.

Waring, Joseph Ioor. "St. Phillip's Hospital in Charlestown in Carolina." *Annals of Medical History,* IV (May, 1932), 283–88.

Way, William. *History of the New England Society of Charleston, South Carolina, for One Hundred Years, 1819–1919.* Charleston, S.C., 1920.

Weir, Robert M. *Colonial South Carolina: A History.* New York, 1983.

Welter, Rush. *Popular Education and Democratic Thought in America.* New York, 1964.

White, Laura. "The South in the 1850s as Seen by the British Consuls." *Journal of Southern History,* I (February, 1935), 29–48.

Williams, Francis Leigh. *A Founding Family: The Pinckneys of South Carolina.* New York, 1978.

Williams, Jack Kenny. *Vogues in Villainy: Crime and Retribution in Antebellum South Carolina.* Columbia, S.C., 1959.

Wood, Peter. *Black Majority: Negroes in Colonial South Carolina from 1670 Through the Stono Rebellion.* New York, 1974.

Woodward, Calvin. "Reality and Social Reform: The Transition from Laissez-Faire to the Welfare State." *Yale Law Journal,* LXXII (1962), 286–328.

Wyatt-Brown, Bertram. *Southern Honor: Ethics and Behavior in the Old South.* New York, 1982.

Zainaldin, Jamil S. "The Emergence of a Modern American Family Law: Child Custody, Adoption, and the Courts, 1796–1851." *Northwestern University Law Review,* LXXII (1979), 1054–61.

DISSERTATIONS AND THESES

Dann, John C. "Humanitarianism Reform and Organized Benevolence in the Southern United States, 1780–1830." Ph.D. dissertation, College of William and Mary, 1975.

Ellen, John Calhoun. "The Public Life of Richard Yeadon." M.A. thesis, University of South Carolina, 1953.

Hannum, Elizabeth Clarke. "The Parish in South Carolina, 1706–1868." M.A. thesis, University of South Carolina, 1970.

Haunton, Richard. "Savannah During the 1850s." Ph.D. dissertation. University of Georgia, 1963.

Lipscomb, Rev. Oscar Hugh. "The Administration of Michael Portier, Vicar Apostalic of Alabama and the Floridas, 1825–1829, and the first Bishop of Mobile, 1829–1859." Ph.D. dissertation, Catholic University of America, 1863.

Olsberg, Robert N. "A Government of Class and Race: William Henry Trescot and the South Carolina Chivalry, 1860–1865." Ph.D. dissertation, University of South Carolina, 1972.

Silver, Christopher. "Immigration and the Antebellum Southern City: Irish Working Class Mobility in Charleston, South Carolina, 1840–1860." M.A. thesis, University of North Carolina, 1975.

Waterhouse, Richard. "South Carolina's Colonial Elite: A Study in the Social Structure and Political Culture of a Southern Colony, 1670–1760." Ph.D. dissertation, Johns Hopkins University, 1973.

Index

Bethesda Orphanage: 156*n;* founded by
George Whitefield in Georgia, 11; as
model for Charleston Orphan House,
121
Bible societies, 21, 22, 31, 34–35, 116*n,*
167
Bingin, Eliza, 166
Birney, Catherine, 49
Blacks: population of, 11–14, 11*n,* 105–
107, 162; conflicts with immigrant labor, 15–16, 183–90; as craftsmen and
shopkeepers, 15, 188–89; colonization
in Africa by, 31; free blacks, 135–36,
177–81, 185–87; poor relief for, 177–
81; poverty of free blacks, 178–79. *See
also* Slaves and slavery
Boggs, Margaret, 94–95, 128–29
Boston: charity in, 8–9; poorhouse in, 15,
68; reform movement in early 19th cen-
tury, 22, 37; moral concerns in, 23; local
missionary work in, 32; wealth in, 44;
Bible societies in, 116*n;* education in,
131–32
Boston School Committee, 131–32
Bowen, Bishop Nathaniel, 41
Brookbanks, W., 89
Bruce, Henry, 108–109
Bubonic plague, 2
Buckheister, Frances, 131
Buckheister, John Andrew, 131
Buckheister, William Christian, 145
Buckingham, James, 160
Buist, George, 179
Bunch, Silas, 139–40
Burke, Emily, 86

Calhoun, John C., 149
Calvin, John, 8
Calvinism, 10
Campbell, Celia, 126
Canals, 76, 102
Cannon, Daniel, 17
Capitalism: and abolition, 24; and moral
reform, 25; and the changing concept of
poverty, 53–54
Cardozo, Jacob N., 92, 102–104, 103*n,*
106, 175
Carew and Hopkins' shoe factory, 92
Carey, Matthew, 91

Cathedral of St. John and St. Finbar, 108
Catholics: discrimination against, in poor
relief, 5, 28, 79; acceptance for, in
Charleston, 27, 107; concern over Protestant benevolent associations, 28–29,
37; and Bible societies, 35; charitable
fund raising activities of, 38–39; view of
poor, 75; as immigrants, 103; political
influence of, 107–108; poverty among,
107
Charitable associations. *See* Benevolent
associations
Charity: in England, 1, 3, 18; in 17th- and
18th-century Charleston, 3–20; as part
of Protestant religious practice, 3–4;
role of parish officers in, 6–8; in Boston,
8–9; and Great Awakening, 9–11;
George Whitefield's interpretation of,
11; in 19th-century Charleston, 22,
31–32, 32*n,* 45, 69, 121, 165–67,
191–92; Catholic activities, 38–39;
women's role in, 40–50, 166–69
Charleston, S.C.: Age of Benevolence in,
1–20; founding of, 1; during 17th and
18th centuries, 2–20; charity in 17th
and 18th centuries, 3–20; poor relief in
17th and 18th centuries, 3–20; immigrants in, 6, 13–15, 69, 103–107, 119,
162–63, 162*n;* leadership of, 6–8,
16–17, 19, 25; fires in, 10, 41, 110;
black-white population of, 11–14,
105–107, 162–63, 162*n;* poverty during 18th century, 13–15, 18; origins of
class structure in, 14; economy during
18th century, 14–16, 18–19; wealth in,
14, 19, 27, 44, 160–61; immigrant versus black labor in, 15–16, 181–90; patriarchal society of, 16, 19; at beginning
of 19th century, 19–20; incorporation
of, 19; religious benevolence during
early 19th century, 20–55; economy
during 19th century, 22, 27, 45, 67–68,
98, 101–103, 106, 110–12, 160, 176;
poor relief in 19th century, 22, 31–32,
32*n,* 69–97, 105, 121, 165–67, 191–
92; moral concerns in, 23; churches in,
25, 27–30, 38–43, 108, 119; missions
and missionary societies in, 25–26,
40–43; charity in 19th century, 22,

Pinckney's proposal for, 99–101; increased distance from white labor, 108–109; and consumption, 109–10; as positive good, 175–76; classical analogies for, 176–77; manumission of, 177; poor relief for, 177–78. *See also* Abolition
Smallpox, 82, 170
Smith, Adam, 103
Smith, Benjamin, 6
Smith, Thomas, 6
Smith, William Loughton, 7
Social control, 73–74
Social equality, 118
Social workers, 165
Soldiers' Relief Societies, 191
Sons of Liberty, 17
Sons of Temperance, 114
South: image of, 24–25, 184; ideal of freedom from work in, 69–70; paternalistic social order in, 69–70; internal improvements in, 102; economic independence of, 109–10
South Carolina: mortality rates in, 2n; parish system of government in, 3–4, 4n; poor laws of, 5; black-white population in 17th and 18th centuries, 11–14, 11n; slavery in, 11–12; indentured servants in, 12; moral concerns in, 23; American Tract Society in, 34; state legislature of, 142, 159n
South Carolina Assembly, 3, 12, 14
South Carolina College, 54, 54n, 95, 149, 153
South Carolina Homespun Company, 72
South Carolina Military Academy, 148
South Carolina Society, 16, 17, 44
South Carolina Temperance Society, 84
Southern Baptists, 35n
Southey, Robert, 184
Spanish: in Carolina, 3, 10
Spencer, Sarah, 89
Spratt, Leonidas, 185, 189–90
Springfield plantation, 162n
Stamp Act, 18
Stevens, Daniel, 124
Stiles, Ezra, 8
Stirling, James, 133

Stono Rebellion, 10n, 14, 98, 177
Stuart, Gilbert, 40
Suffrage movement, 119, 167
Sunday schools, 28, 31–35, 41, 127
Syphilis, 82

Tariff, 35, 67–68, 72
Taxation. *See* Poor tax
Taylor, John, 101
Taylor, Rev. Thomas H., 54–55
Temperance movement: 21, 34–35; and Thomas Smith Grimké, 31, 52; among the poor, 84–86; on the South, 114–15
Tesky, Louise, 89–90
Tesky, Robert, 89–90
Texas, 119
Textile industry, 72–73
Threshing machine, 23
Tocqueville, Alexis de, 1, 120
Toomer, Henry V., 83
Total Abstinence societies, 85
Transcendentalism, 25
Transient poor, 79
Transportation, 102, 161, 174, 182, 182n
Trapier, Paul: 108n; missionary to St. Stephen's Free Chapel, 42; rector of St. Michael's Episcopal Church, 42; observation on white labor, 107
Trapier, Sarah Dehon, 42, 43, 169n
Treadmill, 109
Trescot, William Henry: on the need for elevation of white poor, 106; advocate for sailor's relief, 117–18; on the antagonism between free labor and slave, 183; on public education, 188
Two-Bit Club, 16
Typhoid, 82

Unitarianism, 26
United States Naval Academy School, 143
Utopianism, 25

Vesey, Denmark, 98–99, 177
Virginia: poor relief in, 4, 4n, 44; slavery in, 12; moral concerns in, 23; spiritual decline in, 25; American Tract Society in, 34; manufacturing in, 111–12
Voluntarism, 30–31
Voluntary associations. *See* Benevolent associations